MW01069241

Rhino Tough

How a Small-town Entrepreneur
Tackled Wall Street and Came Away
with a $400 Million Deal

Stan Swofford

Primier LLC, Winston-Salem, North Carolina

ISBN 10: 0-9767829-1-X
ISBN 13: 978-0-9767829-1-9
Library of Congress Control Number: 2006935801
Printed in the United States of America

Book design by Beth Hennington
Jacket design by Tim Rickard

Published by Primier LLC, 101 N. Cherry St., Suite 700
Winston-Salem, NC 27101

In association with Down Home Press, PO Box 4126
Asheboro, NC 27204

Distributed by John F. Blair Publisher, 1406 Plaza Dr.
Winston-Salem, NC 27103

Dedication

For all the hardworking employees at Blue Rhino, whose names are listed in a special section at the back of this book. Their dedication and passion to succeed made Blue Rhino such a special company.
– Billy Prim

For Katy and Andrew, who believed in their dad; and especially for my wife, Kay, whose love and encouragement were a constant inspiration.
– Stan Swofford

Contents

Foreword
"The Happiest Day"

Billy Prim sucked in a big gulp of New York City air and laughed for the sheer pleasure of it. Nothing had ever tasted better. It was a glorious day. Times Square, bathed in spring sunshine, was beautiful. Life was beautiful. God had surely made this day, May 18, 1998, just for him.

This was the day that the forty-two-year-old would realize his dream—one he had nurtured since he visited Wall Street as a young man in his twenties. Billy dreamed of taking public a company he had built from the ground up, using the bedrock American business values and know-how embedded in him by his father and grandfather in Yadkin County, North Carolina.

They would have been proud of him today. It had taken him just four years to build Blue Rhino from what had started as a family sideline to the largest propane cylinder exchange business in the nation. The idea was wonderful in its simplicity. Billy had bet that the millions of members of the country's rapidly growing army of backyard gas grill barbecuers would pay for the convenience of exchanging their empty propane cylinders for full, refurbished, and ready-to-use cylinders that they knew were safe. He was right, but it had been far from easy to put that idea into practice.

Some, including powerful business leaders and money lenders, told him it couldn't be done—not nationwide, the way he intended to do it. The task was just too monumental, too costly, they said. His own company president had even tried to oust him.

But those naysayers didn't know the tenacity he had developed years earlier, when the deaths of his father and grandfather forced him to shoulder huge family and business responsibilities before he was twenty years old. By 1998, colorful Blue Rhino cylinders were already in thousands of stores across the country. The Blue Rhino logo, with its flaming, blue-tipped propane horn, was instantly recognizable to hundreds of thousands of backyard chefs. Soon, millions more would recognize it.

In a few minutes this May morning, Blue Rhino stock would be traded on NASDAQ for the first time. The initial public offering should generate millions of dollars, which would be used to establish more distributors throughout the country, who would service and replace Blue Rhino cylinders in thousands more stores.

But building distributorships and new store locations could start tomorrow. Today was a day to be savored, and Billy wanted to savor every second. He and his wife, Debbie, and his management team from Blue Rhino headquarters in Winston-Salem, all of them passionately proud of the job they had done, had flown up that morning for the IPO, set to begin at ten o'clock in the NASDAQ building. NASDAQ officials greeted them as they entered the trading room, dominated by its big electronic trading board. Billy and the team laughed appreciatively when they saw the board. NASDAQ had decorated it in their honor, with electronic blue rhinos with flaming horns.

Billy, whose work attire usually consisted of open-neck shirts and casual slacks, wore the Wall Street uniform of dark suit, white shirt, and blue necktie. With his thick, collar-length brown hair and slight moustache, he could have been mistaken for a modish New York City market trader, had it not been for his soft North Carolina drawl.

NASDAQ officials snapped their picture as they stood beside the big board. Then the market bell rang and the board came alive in a stream of bright logos, letters, and numbers signifying the trading of billions of dollars in stocks. But Blue Rhino was not among them. Five minutes passed. Ten. Then fifteen. Still no Blue Rhino stock trading. Billy struggled to appear calm.

"I had to," he would say. "I was the leader."

But, inside, he was agonizing. What could have gone wrong?

Then the first Blue Rhino logo appeared, and then another, and another and another, and they kept streaming across the board as the room erupted in cheers. "First it was thirteen," Billy says excitedly, as he returns to one of the happiest days of his life. "Then it was thirteen and an eighth, then thirteen and three-eighths, then thirteen and three-fourths, then fourteen. It was so exciting. What a wonderful time!"

Debbie screamed with happiness as Billy flashed her a thumbs-up sign. Everything after that remains in a fog because Billy was looking through tears of happiness. He remembers NASDAQ officials popping open the champagne and taking the Blue Rhino team to lunch at a Wall Street restaurant. He remembers his team being introduced in the restaurant as the newest member of NASDAQ, and recalls diners applauding and some asking him about Blue Rhino and its stock.

Most of all, he remembers how happily exhausted he was when he fell into bed that night and, just before going to sleep, talking with his father and grandfather. He thanked them for instilling in him when he was very young an appreciation for working and earning money; for putting him in charge of his own business when he was fifteen; and, most importantly, for instilling in him the importance of keeping his word.

He told them he knew they were proud and with him during his and Blue Rhino's special day. And then Billy fell into a deep, restful sleep, thinking how Blue Rhino was going to grow until it was in every backyard in America.

Billy had no way of knowing then, but before the year was out, he would need to summon every ounce of business strength, wisdom, and character that his father and grandfather had given him—just to keep Blue Rhino alive.

"I Love You, Billy Dean"

Nineteen-year-old Billy Prim dressed hurriedly in the pre-dawn darkness, not only because it was cold at four in the morning in December in Yadkin County, North Carolina, but because he didn't want to keep his grandfather waiting. Billy knew that his "Pa," as he called him, A. F. "Bill" Moxley, would have a breakfast of bacon, eggs, toast, and honey waiting for him, and would be anxious to talk about the coming workday.

That's how they had begun their days for almost three years, since February 12, 1975. That was the day Billy's father died, leaving Billy and Pa, with help from Billy's mother and grandmother, to run Moxley Store, their family farm supply business in North Oak Ridge, a crossroads community between the town of Boonville and the county seat of Yadkinville.

A stroke had slowed his grandfather to the extent that it was now largely up to Billy to make sure that the farmers around Boonville and Yadkinville had the supplies they needed, especially fertilizer for planting and kerosene, which they used to cure tobacco. Billy and his grandfather decided during those early morning breakfasts what supplies the store required for the day, and whether Billy needed to make a trip to Winston-Salem, Statesville, or Greensboro for fertilizer or kerosene.

Billy cherished this time with his grandfather, especially because of having to deal with the void left by his father's sudden death. But he was worried about Pa, whose movements had been slowed by a recent stroke, and his grief over the death of Billy's father, Dean Prim, Pa's son-in-law and longtime business partner.

Billy finished dressing quickly the morning of December 20, 1977, then made the short drive to the brick home that Pa shared with Billy's grandmother, Mae Moxley. The house was within a hundred yards of the farm supply and country grocery that Bill and Mae Moxley had operated since the 1950s, after Pa stepped down as sheriff of Yadkin County.

Billy ate and listened as his grandfather told him what he thought would be needed for the day. A trip to Statesville for fertilizer would, indeed, be necessary, he decided. Billy figured he could be back with a load before lunch. It was about five o'clock when Billy finished his breakfast and reached for his coat. That's when his grandfather stood up from the table and reached for Billy. "I love you, Billy Dean," he said, using Billy's middle name, as most family members did.

"I love you, too, Pa," Billy said, thinking his grandfather's sudden show of affection was a little strange.

Pa wasn't usually this demonstrative. He didn't have to be. Billy knew his grandfather loved him. They had enjoyed a close bond as long as he could remember. Pa had told him in countless ways that he loved him.

Billy tried to shrug off his vague misgivings as he walked back out into the cold December dawn, but his thoughts of Pa would stay with him through the morning.

Learning Life at Moxley Store

From the way people describe him, Bill Moxley had been a larger than life character long before Billy was born in 1956 and began looking up to him. He was a big man, more than six feet tall, outgoing and gregarious, quick with a joke, and ready to whip out his harmonica and play a tune. He was popular and well-known throughout the county. A Republican, he had served two four-year terms as Yadkin County sheriff, beginning in the late 1940s.

Billy's mother, Mayo, was Bill and Mae Moxley's only child. She remembers her father and his chief deputy and good friend, Loyd Prim, busting up stills and pouring out confiscated moonshine liquor from fruit jars.

Loyd Prim, his wife, Hazel, and their son, Dean, lived in the lower section of the building that housed the jail, and Hazel Prim cooked for the prisoners.

Dean and Mayo were almost the same age, although Dean was a grade ahead of Mayo at Yadkinville Elementary and High School because his birthday was in December and hers was in February. The two became sweethearts in elementary school and remained so throughout high school. They married just after Mayo graduated.

Meanwhile, a year or so before Mayo graduated, Bill Moxley left the sheriff's department after his second term, and he and his family returned to their home at North Oak Ridge. He took over the operation of Moxley Store, which his father had started in the 1930s and which his brother had managed while Bill Moxley was sheriff.

Loyd and Hazel Prim returned to their farm in the East Bend community in northeast Yadkin County, about 15 miles from North Oak Ridge. Dean Prim, as his father had done, went to work with Bill Moxley at Moxley Store. The two would become good friends despite their age difference, and Bill Moxley would make him an equal partner in the business.

Dean and Mayo moved into a four-room house near the store. Billy was born February 5, 1956. Mayo Prim was eighteen; Dean Prim was nineteen. Jeannie Prim was born a year later. When Luanne arrived, in 1962, they moved into a larger brick house a few hundred yards away, within walking distance of Moxley Store.

Life revolved around family and work, and life was good for the Prims and Moxleys of North Oak Ridge. It was a good place to raise a family and a good place to grow up.

"Everybody knew everybody, and everybody was always willing to help everybody else," said Mayor Harvey Smith, the longtime mayor of Boonville, a town of 1,103, about three miles from North Oak Ridge.

The country is rolling farmland, pleasing to the eye, especially in late summer when tips of the acres and acres of golden tobacco leaves appear to touch the blue sky.

Dean Prim and Bill Moxley were up before dawn every morning attending to the needs of Yadkin County farmers. Shortly after Dean went to work with Bill Moxley in 1954, the two initiated a major expansion of the farm supply store by purchasing a fuel truck and entering the fuel oil business.

Farmers had begun using kerosene to cure tobacco, which was, by far, the number-one cash crop in Yadkin County and all of North Carolina. Until then, the farm supply business was mainly the business of selling fertilizer, chemicals, seed, and feed. Now, there was a large and growing demand for fuel oil.

Mae Moxley took care of the grocery side of Moxley Store, where she sold items such as milk, bread, eggs, cheese, crackers, soft drinks, and so on. Later, Mayo and daughters Jeannie and Luanne helped in the store, including preparing and selling sandwiches and hot dogs. For the first few years of her marriage, however, Mayo tended to toddlers and children at home. She also cooked lunch and dinner for her parents and husband. It was a closely knit family in which every member was expected to work—including the children, as soon as they were old enough.

Billy was seven when he got his first job for thirty-five cents an hour, handing tobacco leaves almost as tall as he to a worker to be strung in a barn on his grandfather's farm. He drove the mules pulling sleds heaped with tobacco leaves through the fields, and later drove a tractor for seventy-five cents an hour. But the work he enjoyed most was with his father and grandfather at Moxley Store.

When he was fifteen, his father and grandfather gave him the grocery store to run after school. He was proud to be entrusted with it. "It was just a little bitty store," he said, thirty-five years later. "We didn't carry a huge selection—mainly milk, bread, drinks, and crackers that were mostly paid for on the honor system. I'd clean it up, restock the cooler, count the money and take it to the bank, pay the bills, order the stock and all that. It was their way of teaching me basic business principles."

Billy also learned much more at the store. He developed the foundation for his political and economic philosophy.

Moxley Store was the community gathering place. When people weren't at home, working in the fields or worshiping at North Oak Ridge Baptist Church, they probably were at Moxley Store.

If it was cold, folks would congregate around the store's pot-bellied stove. There was usually a game of Rook going on, and it was a sure bet that, after tobacco, the talk would turn to politics.

Most people in Yadkin County were Republican. Bill Moxley was one of the leaders of the Republican Party. Republican candidates for county, state, and national offices regularly made stops at the store. Among those who dropped by as Billy was growing up were U.S. Senators Jesse Helms and Jim Broyhill.

The store had a box people could drop their money in to pay for soft drinks. Senator Broyhill watched once as a customer got a Coke out of the cooler and dropped his money in the box. The senator turned to Billy's grandfather.

"Aren't you afraid someone might steal from you, Bill?" he asked.

"Senator," Moxley deadpanned, "there's not been a Democrat in this store in many a year."

Bill Moxley introduced his grandson to Ronald Reagan in the 1960s, long before Reagan became president.

"I was really brought up a Republican capitalist," Billy said, some forty years later. "I love the capitalistic society. I get a real kick out of understanding why this country developed the way we did and became the powerhouse of the world. It all goes back to our capitalistic society that allows us to fulfill our dreams without being born with a certain name or of a certain class. That's powerful in my mind."

Most teenagers, especially those who grow up in the country, can't wait until they are sixteen, the age they're allowed to get a driver's license in North Carolina. Billy was like his peers in that respect; but his dad and grandfather wanted him to get his license as much as he did. They needed him to drive trucks to Winston-Salem and Greensboro to pick up loads of fertilizer and kerosene, and later deliver it to farmers.

Billy had learned to drive when he was fifteen and was delivering supplies to farmers within a few miles of the store even before he got his license.

"Heck, all the lawmen in the county knew me," he recalled. "There was no problem driving without a license."

He actually drove trucks filled with kerosene and gasoline from Greensboro when he was fifteen, and a tractor-trailer loaded with fertilizer from Winston-Salem, although either his dad or Pa Moxley was with him on those trips.

After turning sixteen in 1972, Billy drove the tractor-trailer to Weaver Fertilizer near Winston-Salem late at night when spring planting began. He parked next to the loading dock and slept in the truck so he would be first in line at six in the morning.

"I'd be out of there by seven and on the way back home to dress and go to school," he said with a smile as he remembered those times. "I'd miss the first class, but the teachers knew what I was doing and didn't have a problem with it."

He'd make the trip again that evening as long as spring planting lasted. It was hard work, but Billy loved it. "It was something that nobody else got to do—drive a tractor-trailer. Besides, I liked work. I really did. I've always liked work."

The only thing he didn't like about it was that it didn't leave enough time to play baseball throughout his four years at Starmount High in Boonville, although he did play his senior year with the blessings of his dad and grand-father. Billy was a speedy centerfielder and a good hitter. He also played softball for Moxley's Store, which fielded a team in a tough recreational county league. The team played its games on a diamond carved out of one of the family's fields.

"It was up the road a mile or two from the store," Mayo Prim said. "Both Billy Dean and Jeannie liked to play, so we mowed it, smoothed it down some, brought in some dirt, and put down some bases. We even built bleachers and set them up. Pretty soon, everybody in the community would come there after church and choose sides and play. Then we started playing teams from other communities such as Jonesville and Elkin. That's when Moxley Store started sponsoring the team. Billy Dean was about twelve then and started out as the batboy."

Billy saw his childhood as a rural Yadkin County version of a "Leave it to Beaver." He loved riding a bike with his buddies, playing softball, and the delicious Sunday dinners at Grandma Prim's house. But the best part for him was working for his father and grandfather.

Pa and his dad taught him the basics of business early. Whenever a major decision was to be made—such as the purchase of a truck or trailer—they would include Billy. Pa or his father would look at the less expensive used ones before examining the newer models. Then they would always ask Billy what he thought they should do. Billy didn't fully realize it until years later, but his dad and Pa were preparing him then to take over the family business.

"Billy Dean, if you're smart enough to make money for someone else, you're smart enough to make money for yourself," Pa would say.

Billy learned from both.

His political and social skills, which would soon become invaluable to him, came from his grandfather. "I always thought I knew everybody and everybody knew me, and that it was all because of my grandfather."

His belief and insistence that people should do what they say came from his father. "My dad was a strict disciplinarian. If you told him you were going to do something, he held you to it. If you said you were going to make the honor roll, I don't care what it took; you were going to make it."

One of Dean Prim's proudest moments was when he and Billy, both members of the Boonville Jaycee chapter, were recognized as one of the first father-son Jaycee teams—and certainly one of the youngest—in North Carolina. His dad was only nineteen when Billy was born.

Billy graduated from Starmount High in 1974 as president of the senior class and an honor student. He was accepted at North Carolina State University in Raleigh that fall, although Billy would have preferred staying home and working full time with his father and grandfather.

He was a voracious reader and believed he could obtain the knowledge he needed on his own. His parents urged him to stay at State. His dad was a member of the Yadkin County Board of Education at that time, and his mother would later be elected to the board.

"They were big believers in education and civic duty," Billy said. He agreed to give State a try.

On February 11, 1975, he came home to celebrate Pa Moxley's sixty-second birthday with a big family dinner. Billy's dad had not been feeling well. He was overweight, smoked three to four packs of Pall Mall cigarettes a day, and according to Billy, "worked like a Trojan day and night."

He had recently suffered chest pains that his doctor diagnosed as indigestion. That night, however, he awakened Mayo to tell her that he was having severe heart pains. Mayo called out to her children that she was taking their father to the hospital in Yadkinville, about seven miles away.

He was unconscious when they arrived. He died before Billy, Jeannie, and Luanne could get there. Dean Prim was only thirty-eight. Billy was nineteen, the age Dean Prim became a father.

That time was so terrible for Mayo Prim that she blocked much of it from her memory. She remembers clearly, however, trying to persuade Billy to return to State. He returned, but only to get his things.

"I tried so hard," his mother said, still sounding exasperated with her son. "I said, 'Billy, don't you know that working for yourself is the hardest job in the world? You'll be working twenty-four hours a day, seven days a week.' I'll never forget what he said. He said, 'Don't you think I'm smart enough to be my own boss and make my own living?' I said, 'Well, yes, I do.' And he said, 'That's what I'm going to do. I want to be my own business person.'"

The closely knit family, stunned and numb with grief, struggled to move on. Billy became a kind of father to Luanne and a combination big brother and giver of fatherly advice to Jeannie.

"He always wanted to know where I was and where I was going," Luanne said.

When the boys started calling on Luanne, Billy made it a point to meet her dates when they came by. He would do the same with Jeannie's dates. Sometimes he would enlist them into helping him unload a trailer-full of fertilizer.

Both sisters say he was there for them when they needed him most. Jeannie, who enrolled at Wake Forest University in the fall after her father died, said she will never forget how Billy responded to her when she was distraught over failing a course.

"I was feeling so low," she said. "I thought I had let the family down because they were spending so much money for me to go college. And then Billy looked at me and said, 'What's the big deal? In the whole scheme of things, it's not going to matter. If you failed the course, you shouldn't beat yourself to death about it. You'll find a way to make it up. The family is proud of you and will continue to be proud of you.' I was so glad he said that. That was the kind of fatherly wisdom I really needed then."

Billy also needed wisdom and perspective then, and he got it from two sources, Mayo and Pa. Mayo did much of the company's bookkeeping, and Pa guided Billy every business day. But those days, 1975–1977, were becoming increasingly difficult for the country's economy, including Moxley's Store.

The Arab oil embargo of 1974 caused interest rates to skyrocket into the teens. The price of kerosene jumped from about fifteen cents a gallon to almost fifty cents. Fertilizer prices doubled and tripled between 1973 and 1975.

Farmers, so reliant on petroleum products and vulnerable to the politics of petroleum, struggled to pay their bills. Many couldn't. When farmers struggled, Moxley Store struggled with them. By the mid-1970s, the store's list of accounts receivable was growing into a troubling amount for the little farm supply business.

It was especially troubling for Pa. Although Bill Moxley was only sixty-two, he had not been well. His stroke had left him with limited movement on his left side. The stroke, plus the death of his son-in-law and the worsening business climate, had exacted a toll on his health. He yearned to help Billy, but he was often bedridden. Even so, he usually was able to rise early, cook breakfast for Billy, and then talk with his grandson about what the day was likely to bring, and how they wanted it to go. The morning of December 20, 1977, was no different until Pa hugged Billy as he was about to leave for Statesville and told him he loved him.

Billy, who had been driving tractor-trailers for almost six years, made it to Statesville and back for the fertilizer, a round-trip of about eighty miles, before noon. He was talking to a customer outside the store when his grandmother, Momma Mae Moxley, called to him in an anguished voice from her driveway. Billy ran toward her, fearful of what he was about to find and remembering the embrace from his grandfather just a few hours before. He followed his grandmother into the house. Pa was lying on the floor in a bathroom. He had shot himself.

Almost thirty years later, Billy's eyes redden and fill with tears as he struggles to talk about the deaths, less than three years apart, of his grandfather and father, and the impact they had on him—a young man in his late teens and early twenties thrust into a world that many seasoned businessmen would find hostile.

"Here we are—my mother, two younger sisters, my grandmother, and me. But Pa and my daddy sure had taught me the basics before everything caved in—how to run a business, banking relationships that are so important, and so on. It might have been small-time stuff, but the basic values of working hard, paying your bills, and doing what you say never change. I don't care if you're running CitiGroup or a little bitty country store."

Billy soon realized he would need every nugget of business wisdom his father and grandfather had taught him and a lot more they had not. He was forced to make numerous painful decisions that his father and grandfather never had to confront.

More and more farmers, including longtime friends, were unable to pay their bills. Meanwhile, Billy was facing thousands of dollars in bills due to banks and fertilizer companies. Suppliers began ratcheting up their credit terms.

"Interest rates were going through the roof," Billy said.

He decided he had to apply a basic business practice that, so far as he knew, had never been done in rural Yadkin County. He began charging interest on the money farmers owed Moxley Store, and he required them to pay in full by October 1, the date bills came due for agricultural supplies after farmers had harvested and sold their tobacco.

Barely in his twenties, Billy began looking farmers in the eye who were ten, twenty, even thirty or more years older, and telling them Moxley Store would no longer carry them on its books for free. He tried to explain that he didn't have a choice; that he had to pay the companies that sold him the fertilizer and fuel. Some farmers couldn't, or wouldn't, understand.

"There were tears, conflict, and heartache," said Billy.

It was especially painful when a farmer he had known since childhood told him, "Your daddy and granddaddy wouldn't do this to me."

"I learned a few things about people during that time," Billy remembered.

There were days when Billy—still grieving over the deaths of his father and grandfather while barbs of criticism were hurled at him—found it difficult to summon the energy and will to go to work. That was when he found that he had a sizeable number of people pulling for him to succeed, and they told him so.

Vanoide Fletcher, a tobacco farmer and former major league pitcher for the Detroit Tigers, came by the Prim house early and often, just to see how

Billy was doing. Billy is an avid baseball fan and eventually would become a principal owner of the minor league Winston-Salem Warthogs. He recalled that Fletcher, who was in his mid-fifties then, "knocked on the door at five o'clock in the morning to make sure I was up. He'd say, 'You can't let this get you down. Now, what are you going to do today?' He would push me to see people and get things done. He would speak up for me."

Businessman Don Angell, now the owner of Bermuda Run Golf and Country Club, also encouraged Billy—with pep talks and more.

"You've got to be the man of the family now, son," he told Billy.

Angell had been friends with Billy's father and grandfather, who loaned him $10,000 when the banks would not. He used the money to start a string of successful nursing homes. A candid, shrewd businessman, partial to outrageously loud shirts, Angell visited Billy shortly after Pa Moxley died. Although he was close to twenty years older than Billy, he felt a kinship with the young man struggling to keep the family going.

Like Billy, Angell had grown up in rural Yadkin County, the son of parents who operated a country grocery store. He sensed in Billy someone like he had been twenty years before—a young man, barely more than a boy, but fiercely independent and determined to succeed by being his own boss and doing it his way. During one of his visits, Angell told Billy that he had come to pay off the loan.

"Here's what I'm going to do," he said. "Your father and grandfather loaned me money when nobody else would, and it really turned out good for me. I'm going to pay you double what I owe you."

And that's what he did, Billy said. "It came at a crucial time."

Angell later would invest many thousands of dollars with Billy's business ventures, and Billy with his.

Don Angell's gift and the encouragement from him and others helped spur Billy on.

"I realized that if I was going to do it, it was going to have to be me, and nobody else," he said. "When you want something bad enough, when you absolutely have to do it, then you have to do it yourself. In the months after my grandfather died, I figured out it was going to take a certain amount of discipline to be successful. That hardened me. When those farmers said, 'You're not going to be successful,' or 'Your grandfather and father would never have done this,' well, that hurt to the core. I was not going to fail then. My mom and grandmother and two younger sisters depended on me, and I was not going to let anyone down. What doesn't kill you makes you stronger. You learn from it."

Discovering a Taste for Deals and Wall Street

After a few months, Billy's mother and sisters began to notice confidence growing in him. They already knew he enjoyed business and that he liked to lead, but this was something different—a willingness to change the status quo, to size up the situation and take risks. It was Billy's entrepreneurial spirit coming to the fore, a talent destined to define and distinguish him professionally.

The dictionary defines entrepreneur as "someone who organizes, operates, and assumes the risk for a business venture." The important word in that definition is "risk." Many people have organizational skills, and large companies are full of people with the abilities required to lead the day-to-day operations of a business. But people who have those organizational and operational talents, plus the inclination—some would say obsession—to assume the personal and financial risks of launching a new business venture, are few and far between.

Billy began showing signs of entrepreneurship in 1978 when he realized that the future for the farm supply business wasn't bright.

"That's what Billy is, an entrepreneur," says his sister Jeannie. "Fertilizer had been great for the business, but he saw that it was time to change, and he wasn't afraid to take the risk."

Billy didn't call it entrepreneurship then. It was just survival.

"You have to understand your business environment. I soon learned that I was in an area of business in which my customers didn't have much of a chance. Their expenses were going through the roof—fuel costs, fertilizer costs, interest rates, everything. I could see they were not going to make it. And I was going to be right there with them. You have to be able to recognize the situation for what it is."

Billy did, but, even so, he "struggled to stay with that fertilizer business until 1979 with farmers going broke and interest rates climbing." That was when he decided to go into the heating oil business. "People have to heat their homes," he said.

With the blessing of his mother, grandmother, and sisters, Billy sold the farm supply business to Royster-Clark, a large agribusiness company with offices nationwide. He also rented the store and warehouse buildings to Royster-Clark. He then bought a fuel oil distribution business with a service station from Bert Bennett of Winston-Salem, the owner of Quality Oil Co., and Herb Graham of Elkin.

Bennett was an old friend with whom Billy and his family had done business for years. He helped Billy put together the deal that allowed him to buy the service station and storage facilities from Bennett and the distribution business from Graham. Billy then changed the name of Moxley Store to Moxley Oil Co. and moved the family business office to Boonville.

Buying the heating oil business from Bennett was a good deal for Billy personally, as well as financially. It allowed him some time and freedom to learn more about something that had long intrigued him—Wall Street and the stock market. He wanted to meet people on Wall Street. Pa Moxley and his dad had first gotten him interested in the market. Although they weren't active traders or investors, they wanted Billy to understand it. Their attorney, Walter Zachary, put Billy in touch with Eric Wagoner, a young man from Yadkin County who worked with an investment banking firm on Wall Street. Wagoner was about five years older than Billy.

Under Wagoner's guidance, Billy began buying stocks, investing conservatively at first—in companies, funds, and securities that posed minimal risk. This eventually became boring for him. Wagoner recalls that Billy called him sometime in 1978 to say he needed "a little more action" with his investments.

Billy went to New York, and Wagoner introduced him to some of his Wall Street contacts. Billy loved it.

"I was like a sponge soaking up everything I could about what makes this country what it is—our ability to raise capital and fund entrepreneurship and ideas. To be at the financial hub of the world and seeing how the capitalistic system worked was fantastic."

Wagoner introduced him to Mike Long, a broker who traded in agricultural commodities such as pork bellies, cattle futures, and so on. Billy gave Long $5,000 to open a commodities account.

"Well, in just two or three months that five thousand had grown to thirty thousand," Billy said, grinning at the memory of his fledgling foray into the market. "I said, 'To heck with any heating oil business. I'm going to become rich trading commodities!'"

Long moved to another firm with higher stakes. It required a minimum investment of $100,000. "I told Mike I didn't have another sixty-five thousand. They let me in for fifty thousand."

In three months, Billy's $50,000 had grown to one $125,000.

"I was in the big money," Billy said, laughing at the memory of his naivete. "I got a telephone put in the car."

But Billy was on the biggest roller-coaster ride of his life. "It started going down, and did it ever go fast."

In five months, his account was down to $20,000. "It was great going up, but to go down like that almost breaks your heart."

It was Billy's first encounter with Wall Street, and it was "a huge learning experience"—one he would never forget—"about how things can be great and how they can go bad." He learned lessons and absorbed knowledge and ideas about raising and losing money that would be invaluable to him in a few years when he would play for much higher stakes.

Billy found himself gravitating toward friends often older than he by twenty years or more. He still had some softball buddies but none had an interest in business like Billy. The people he socialized with, such as Eric Wagoner or Don Angell, were likely to be business mentors as well as friends—"people I could learn something from as well as have a Budweiser with."

As he learned from them, Billy began to dream of building his own company, taking it public, and seeing its stock traded on Wall Street. No one from Yadkin County had ever done that.

Billy was about twenty-two when he met Dick Hardin and Ray Maynard, men who would help him enormously in realizing his dream. Hardin, twice Billy's age, was a senior executive with Unifi, Inc., a global textile manufacturing company, with headquarters in Greensboro. Maynard, twelve years older than Billy, was head of research and development for Unifi. He met Billy when Billy, in his own words, was "trying to peddle fuel and lubricants to them."

Maynard, an engineer from Great Britain who has worked throughout the world, was impressed and a little amused with the openness, ambition, and enthusiasm of the young man with the down-home Yadkin County accent. The two soon became friends.

Maynard remembers that Billy was constantly "planning and dreaming and asking questions and challenging. Sometimes he would look at me and say, 'You don't think I can do this, do you? You know, you might be working for me some day.' I'd laugh and say, 'Sure, Billy,' but, you know, that doesn't sound so far-fetched now."

Maynard introduced Billy to Hardin, who thought at first, "Here's just another country boy from Yadkin County." But that impression didn't last long.

Like Maynard, Hardin was impressed with the young man's ambition, drive, and intelligence. Hardin also saw a little of himself in Billy. Like Billy, he had been suddenly thrust at a young age—eighteen in his case— into the role of head of the family.

"I knew exactly what he was going through and how difficult it was," Hardin said. "I was impressed with his loyalty to his family and his willingness and ability to do what he had to do after his father and grandfather died." He and Billy formed a friendship that has lasted more than thirty years. "I used to call him my second son."

Billy believes that the friendships he developed with older, successful business people such as Angell, Hardin, and Maynard, helped him immeasurably.

"It got me started. I was able to achieve things that those a generation or two earlier were achieving. People would look at me and say, 'I expected someone much older.'" The friendships were real and have lasted decades, but they were also the product of a talent that every successful entrepreneur must have—the ability to network. "If there is a secret to success, that's it," he said. "All good entrepreneurs know how to network. You've got to ask questions, and you've got to know what questions to ask. 'Who does this? Who does that?' Pretty soon you can start connecting the dots."

Billy was visiting with Maynard and Hardin one evening when the talk turned to trucking. Unifi had a fleet of more than one hundred tractor-trailers, some of which it used to haul yarn on a regular run from Unifi plants in North Carolina to weavers in New York. Because they were private carriers, however, they had to make the return trip empty, and were losing considerable amounts of money.

Billy remembers that "Dick was disgusted, and then someone said I ought to start my own little trucking company and haul yarn to New York." Hardin agreed. The New York run was Billy's if he wanted it, Dick said. Billy, itching to start an enterprise of his own, in addition to Moxley Oil, jumped at the chance.

"I leased four or five tractor-trailers, hired some drivers, and went up to New York City, a southern boy looking for freight to haul back down South." Billy started networking, talking to people in the trucking, textile, and furniture industries, and people he had met through Wagoner, Maynard, and others. "I was going door-to-door. Then someone asked, 'Have you met Big Ruby?'"

Ruby, known as "Big Ruby" to legions of truckers up and down the East Coast, owned Jersey Truck Stop in Jersey City, N.J. He weighed about three hundred pounds and sat in his truck stop all day as he directed business with an ever-present cigar in his mouth or gesturing with it in his hand. Billy thought he looked old. "But everybody looked old to me then. I was just twenty-two. He was probably in his forties or fifties."

Big Ruby would have been an intimidating character to many, especially to any other twenty-two-year-old from rural Yadkin County, North Carolina. But not to Billy. Billy had done his homework. He knew that he had something Big Ruby needed—trucks and drivers. Big Ruby was a broker who arranged transportation for, among other things, shipments of parts and material—such as chemicals and glue—to furniture companies and other industries in North Carolina. Billy's trucks were going into the heart of furniture country. Big Ruby had plenty of work for him.

This was before trucking was deregulated. Billy's company, which he called BD Investments (BD for Billy Dean), took off from the beginning. Big Ruby had a load for him every day, then two a day when he got to know him better. Billy occasionally rode with his drivers, taking a turn at the wheel. He was making a thousand dollars a day in his trucking company, and the family business had become much more stable since he replaced fertilizer with heating oil.

"Things were going great. I was single with all kinds of money and having a big time."

Billy, Hardin, and sometimes Maynard and other friends made frequent golf and gambling trips to Nassau, Atlantic City, and Las Vegas. He and Hardin often booked seats on a Chalk's Ocean Airways seaplane to Paradise Island in the Bahamas that flew them to a seaplane terminal just outside Merv Griffin's resort hotel and casino.

"We were treated like royalty," he said.

Billy became an avid golfer and a friend of Kiti Maile, the late golf professional and Polynesian singer and dancer at Walt Disney World in Orlando. Maile, who died in 2003, introduced Billy to Jay Panzirer, the son of Leona Helmsley, the billionaire Manhattan hotelier and real estate magnate. Panzirer and Billy became friends, and Billy attended parties at Leona Helmsley's penthouse in New York. Jay Panzirer died of a heart attack in 1982, several years before his mother's highly publicized conviction and imprisonment for federal income tax evasion.

Those were years of learning for Billy, as well as fun. "I was getting exposed to many people and many things. It was like I didn't have any barriers. I had my eyes wide open, and I was taking it all in. I was traveling a lot and learning a lot. It was a lot of fun."

Billy wasn't blocked by any barrier, but his trucks hit one in the early 1980s that halted them like a head-on collision. It was called federal trucking deregulation, and its effects forced Billy to shut down BD Investments. Ironically for Billy, deregulation was implemented by one of his heroes, President Ronald Reagan.

"He was my idol, but he killed it. Prices fell so steeply that it wasn't profitable for BD Investments to continue. It had been a great run for all of us."

Billy's entrepreneurial instincts would soon lead him to another deal, one of the best he'd ever make. In 1981, at the suggestion of his Wall Street friend, Wagoner, he applied for admission to Wake Forest University's Babcock School of Business in Winston-Salem. The prestigious business school rarely accepted anyone without a college degree. It made an exception for Billy after the school's admissions committee interviewed him and after he scored in the ninety-eighth percentile on Babcock's entrance exam.

It was about thirty miles to Wake Forest University from Boonville, and the little town of East Bend marked about a third of the distance. East Bend was the home of Flynt Oil Co., one of Billy's main competitors in the heating oil business. Flynt Oil had most heating oil customers in the eastern half of the county. It was owned by Tyra Hobson, who was about sixty-five, and had operated the business for more than forty years.

Billy didn't know Hobson, but he was curious about his business. He had a little time to kill one Saturday morning so he pulled in and introduced himself. The two men clicked, despite their forty-year age difference. Hobson appreciated the young man's interest in his company and his knowledge of the business. Billy was reminded of Pa as he talked business with Hobson, who seemed to enjoy the role of mentoring the eager young man. Billy began leaving home earlier on Saturdays so he would have time to stop and chat with Hobson over a cup of coffee.

One morning Billy asked Hobson about his plans for his business. "What's your exit strategy?"

Hobson opened up to Billy. It just so happens, he said, that he'd been looking for someone who could take over the business and carry it on. Unfortunately, his children were not interested.

But Billy was, and he grew more and more so. "The more we talked the more I thought it would really add a lot to Moxley Oil."

Hobson said he'd sell his business for around $150,000.

But Billy had a problem. He didn't have the money to buy it. He had spent most of the money he made in the trucking business. Billy thought for a moment. "You don't want to be stuck having to pay a whole bunch of taxes. Why don't you finance it, and make me your retirement program?"

That sounded good to Hobson. He would finance it for 5 percent interest over ten years. But he had to be assured that Billy would take a personal interest in the business he had built over almost fifty years, and maintain a close relationship with his customers. In fact, Billy had to agree to let Hobson personally introduce them to him. Billy told Hobson that was how his grandfather and father taught him to run a business, and that he didn't know how to do it any other way.

It was a great deal for Billy that got even better. As they were preparing to close the deal, Hobson told Billy he had good news. His company had $50,000 in the bank, and it was Billy's to work with. "I had been negotiating under the assumption it would be an asset purchase," Billy said. "I had no idea I would get all the working capital. I wake up one morning, and I have $50,000 I hadn't realized I had before, and a business that's just doubled. And I didn't have to put any money in the deal. It was the best deal I ever made."

The deal also turned out to be a good one for Hobson. He died shortly after Billy gave him his last payment, knowing the company he had built was continuing to serve customers it had served for more than half a century.

The Hobson transaction taught Billy valuable lessons in the art of deal-making. "I learned about working capital—how you can leverage, use owner financing, and create something out of nothing. It opened my eyes to what you can do." He would find these lessons enormously helpful in a few years as he negotiated critical deals on a much larger scale.

The deal's only drawback was Billy's enrollment at the Babcock School of Business. He had to drop out of the program to operate the expanded business. But that was alright. As much as he wanted to continue in the Babcock program, it was a casualty he could accept.

In the five years since his father and grandfather had died, the business not only survived under Billy's leadership during severely adverse economic conditions, it had grown many times larger and was thriving.

Billy felt good about the business and good about himself. At a young age, he had overcome personal tragedies and business setbacks that would have defeated many older and more experienced people. His father and Pa, he thought, would have been proud.

One night in 1983, Billy and his pal, Dick Hardin, walked into Bennigan's restaurant in Winston-Salem and spotted a familiar and pretty face among the crowd. She was Debbie Westmoreland, a young woman with a warm and friendly smile. Dick knew her when she worked at his company, Unifi, several years before.

Billy had met her five years earlier and asked her out, but Debbie turned him down. She and her first husband had just divorced, and she was not quite ready then to start dating again, although, as she would later say, "There was definitely some chemistry. I remember thinking, 'Hey, I could have fun with this guy.'"

That spring night at Bennigan's, the chemistry clicked again. Billy, fit and tanned from softball and golf, asked her out again and she accepted. "I just had a good feeling about Billy. I could be myself around him. We had fun together, and we still do. We've been together ever since," she said, just before the two celebrated their twentieth wedding anniversary on January 16, 2006.

A quality Debbie sensed in Billy from the beginning, and one that she was especially attracted to, was the easy way he interacted with her two children. Sarcanda was twelve, and Anthony was fifteen when she and Billy married in 1986. Billy accepted them as his own, and they soon accepted him, responding to his gentle, yet firm and confident manner. The family lived in Tobaccoville, about fifteen miles from Winston-Salem, for a few months, and then bought a house in Boonville. The children enrolled at

Starmount, Billy's old school, where Sarcanda, known as "Sarci" to her family and friends, was a cheerleader and homecoming queen.

"We were all a little nervous at first, but he was so patient with us," she said. "Once we got used to each other, things were great, and they've been great ever since." Sarcanda and Anthony came to look upon Billy as a second dad.

Both Billy and Sarcanda's father, Ronnie Westmoreland, gave Sarcanda away when she married Joseph Bellissimo. "I think it's pretty special having two dads," she said. Billy dotes on her two-year-old, Alexander, or "Xander," as the family calls him, and her newest addition to the family, baby boy Jager, born in July 2005. "Billy's a wonderful grandfather," Sarcanda said.

Anthony said he and Billy got to know each other playing Billy's favorite game, golf. "Billy taught me how to play. He taught me many things."

One of Anthony's special memories is helping Billy deliver fuel oil on a snowy morning when Billy was short on drivers. Anthony was about seventeen or eighteen. "It was a big snow storm. I don't know whether some drivers couldn't get to work, or what, but Billy asked me to help make the deliveries. There were people, some of them elderly, who needed fuel. Billy knew every customer by name. I'm sure I didn't want to go, and I probably made that known, but I sure am glad now that I did."

Many of Anthony's and Sarcanda's memories, as well as those of the entire family, center around the many long, fun-filled summer days at the family's lake house at Lake Waccamaw in southeastern North Carolina, about forty miles west of Wilmington. "We were there almost every weekend," Anthony said. "Mayo would get me up about 6 a.m. and fix breakfast so we'd have the whole day on the lake."

Billy taught Anthony how to drive the family boat, as well as the car. "One of my proudest moments was when Billy tossed me the keys to the boat and let me take it out by myself. I thought I was on the way to becoming a man then. He taught me a lot."

When deregulation spoiled Billy's trucking business, he began searching for something to replace it. Finding another enterprise to supplement the income produced by the family's heating oil business became more important after he and Debbie decided to marry. Billy had been single and living alone. "It's a lot more expensive when you go from one to a family of four with two teenagers," Debbie said.

Billy thought convenience stores might be the way to go. The two businesses, fuel oil and convenience stores, were complementary. "Lots of folks in the petroleum business were going into the convenience store business. Look at what we're talking about here, gasoline and groceries, some-thing I'd been around all my life. It seemed like the natural thing to do."

It was also only natural that Billy, once he decided to risk going into the convenience store business, would try to learn everything he could about it. Attention to detail and a thirst for knowledge, especially about the task at hand, were traits he had inherited from his mother, Mayo Prim, as well as his father and grandfather.

Billy decided to seek advice from one of the most knowledgeable people in the world, when it came to convenience stores and fuel oil, and a man Billy admired a great deal—Leon Hess.

Hess was the founder and owner of Hess Oil Co. He also owned the New York Jets professional football team. The son of Russian immigrants, Hess entered the oil business during the Great Depression by selling "resid"—a thick, tar-like substance that refineries discarded—from a 1929 Dodge truck in New Jersey. Hess bought the resid and sold it to hotels, which would burn it instead of coal. He later bought a fleet of trucks, refineries, pipelines, and gas stations, and went into oil exploration. His company went public in 1962. When he died in 1998, *Forbes Magazine* estimated his personal wealth at more than $700 million.

Billy had never met Hess, but he did buy gasoline and lubricants from Hess Oil Co., and he thought that ought to at least be worth a letter asking advice from a man Billy considered one of the country's "great entrepreneurs." It was worth that, and more. Hess invited Billy to visit him in New York.

The meeting was in Hess' executive suite at the top of a skyscraper towering over the Avenue of the Americas. Hess, who was in his seventies at the time, put his young visitor at ease.

"I told him I was a customer and wanted to be just like him," Billy said. "I said I needed advice on how to get started and how to get there."

Hess reached behind his desk and pulled out a replica of the old truck in which he hauled residual fuel oil when he was twenty-two and struggling to make it on the grimy streets of Depression-era New York. Billy remembers the replica as "looking like a Model T with a wagon in the back."

Hess said he started with the truck and two five-gallon buckets. When he sold a truck load, he would go back to the dock and buy another.

Hess seemed to warm to Billy and told him that he "worked fourteen hours a day, six days a week, and eight on Sunday." Hess then paused for a moment and said, "And you know what? I've got a bunch of trucks now."

When Hess' secretary came in to tell him that his next appointment was waiting to see him, he told her to cancel the rest of his appointments for the day. "This young man wants to become somebody," he said. Hess and Billy talked for the rest of the afternoon.

Hess told Billy that the most important thing he could do was make certain that everything about his stores was first class. "He said it didn't matter whether I had one station or a hundred; they all had to be right. You can't miss a step. You have to find the right location. You have to hire the right manager. You have to have every one of them right. If you do one half-assed, it will affect all the others."

Billy felt honored to talk with Hess, who was notorious for shunning the limelight and almost never granting interviews. Later, when Billy told people in the oil and convenience store businesses that he visited with Hess, they were amazed.

The two men, one a great success with his career almost behind him, and the other, a young man eager to make his mark in the business world, established a rapport that afternoon.

"He was a self-made man," Billy said. "I knew that, and I liked that about him."

Billy believed he already had a pretty good location for his first convenience store. It was in downtown Boonville, and it was already an established service station. Best of all, it was already part of the family business. Billy had bought it from Bert Bennett when he switched from the farm supply business to heating oil.

Debbie quit her job as a receptionist for WXII-TV in Winston-Salem to help Billy convert the old two-bay station into a modern convenience store. It became the first of three Quick-Pik Food Marts. With an investment from his old friend Don Angell, Quick-Pik II, off I-77 near Elkin, and Quick-Pik III, in upscale Bermuda Run, soon followed.

Debbie took charge of the operation of the convenience stores and became an integral part of the family business. "It was a real tough job, one I wouldn't want to do again," she said. "You have to be open twenty-four hours a day. It's hard to get good people and hard to keep up with your money."

But she learned a lot about business and a lot about people. Billy learned to use her as a sounding board for major ideas and decisions, including important personnel moves, in all his business ventures. He would find that her business instincts were usually right.

Meanwhile, as Debbie directed the day-to-day operations of the convenience stores, and mother Mayo oversaw much of the heating oil part of the business, Billy continued to look for growth opportunities, ways to expand the family enterprise beyond the confines of piedmont North Carolina.

Although Billy kept it mostly to himself, his dream since Wagoner had introduced him to Wall Street remained the same—to build a company and take it public.

Billy believed he could do that. First, however, he needed a growth vehicle.

In 1987–88, he found one—propane. It might not get Moxley Oil to Wall Street, but it certainly could place it in a much better position for growth.

Although he had switched to heating oil in 1979, he kept the family in one niche of the farm supply business—kerosene for curing tobacco. In the almost ten years since, Billy had seen more and more farmers using propane instead of kerosene.

Propane is a clear, highly flammable and normally odorless gas derived from natural gas or crude petroleum. It first was identified in 1910. It is used to power some buses, forklifts, and some other machinery, as well as fuel for heating and cooking in recreational vehicles, campers, portable stoves, and, of course, barbecue grills.

In rural areas, such as Yadkin County, where natural gas lines are scarce, propane powers furnaces, water heaters, laundry dryers, and other appliances. In 1987–88, Billy saw Yadkin County farmers switching to propane because they considered it cleaner and more convenient to use than kerosene. He became convinced that propane offered the growth opportunity he wanted for Moxley Oil.

But if Moxley Oil were to grow as he wanted, Billy knew he would have to restructure the family business and change its name. Moxley Oil sounded exactly like what it was, a local, down-home business, and down-home businesses were not likely to attract much capital.

What the business needed was a name that would signify something bigger, at least an enterprise that was regional in scope—and that could grow even larger. Billy decided on American Oil and Gas.

About this time, and as if on cue, Billy met someone ideally able and willing to advise, assist and inspire him in guiding and growing his business. He and Billy would become like brothers. His name is Andrew J. "Flip" Filipowski.

No one would mistake Billy and Flip for brothers, although they are brothers-in-law—sort of. Flip is married to Debbie's sister, Veronica. The couple met in a restaurant in Myrtle Beach, South Carolina, in 1987. From all accounts, they were almost instantly smitten with each other, and it wasn't long before Veronica introduced him to the family. It's probably an understatement to say that Flip was unlike any other guy she had brought home to meet the folks.

When Veronica met Flip, he was already well known in Chicago among computer software entrepreneurs and venture capitalists. He had founded one software business, DBMS, Inc., which he built into a $25 million company before a hostile takeover forced him out at age thirty-six. That's the year he met Veronica, and the year he launched another software company, Platinum Technology, Inc., which he would sell twelve years later, in 1999, for almost $4 billion—at that time the largest amount ever paid for a software company.

That would be light years from where Flip grew up on Chicago's North Side, the only child of Polish immigrants who spoke no English. He wasn't joking when he would say, years later, that English was his second language. "Until elementary school," he said, "I didn't know English was the language of the United States."

Flip developed an excellent command of the English language, while retaining some of the salty speech, free spiritedness, and survival instincts that he honed on the streets of his neighborhood.

First-time visitors to his Winston-Salem, North Carolina, company, SilkRoad Technology Inc., often mistake the pony-tailed company president and CEO for a casual visitor. His usual attire, if the weather will allow it, is a loud short-sleeved shirt, shorts, and sandals, with his long, dark hair, speckled here and there with gray, tied neatly in a ponytail halfway down his back.

He once gave a keynote speech at a convention in Orlando wearing a suit coat and tie over shorts and sandals. John Cullinane, who gave Flip his first job in the software industry in 1979, said in *Software Magazine* that Flip "makes the rhinestone cowboy look conservative."

Billy may not always wear neckties, but he's considerably more conservative than the rhinestone cowboy. Nevertheless, he and Flip shared something that was far more binding than clothes, culture, or hairstyle. It was their spirit of entrepreneurship, something each recognized early on in the other, and it formed the foundation for a friendship as deep as that of any brotherly bond. It's deeper than that, Flip says.

"If you're lucky, you might have five or six people you can count on, no matter what. If you're arrested, you can call them, and they'll do whatever you need them to do—get you a lawyer, pay your bills, bail you out of jail. But a really great friend, a one-in-a-million friend, is going to be sitting on the bench with you, saying, 'Boy, did we ever fuck up!' Billy is that kind of friend."

Flip became that kind of friend to Billy, as well as a teacher. Billy watched as Flip built Platinum Technology into a billion-dollar business in a few years while building and operating a variety of other businesses—including software companies, a construction business, and a company that operated Boston Market restaurants in the Carolinas, Virginia, and Georgia. "Flip thinks big, and he taught me to think big," Billy said. "He said, 'Billy, if you've got the right idea, follow it, and the capital will follow you.' He's just a really smart guy who taught me a lot and inspired me."

Even more than capital, an entrepreneur needs friends and family, Flip said. There are too many steep hills and deep valleys to traverse alone. "You have to have somebody to help you over the hump. Billy and I have done that for each other. We've become like ham and eggs. Sometimes I'm way up. Sometimes he's way up. Sometimes I'm way down. Sometimes he's way down."

Entrepreneurs climb to lofty heights with beautiful vistas, and they should enjoy the view while they can. "But there's no such thing as a mile-high ride forever," says Flip. "Everything turns to shit sooner or later."

An Epiphany in Paris

When he met Flip Filipowski in 1987, Billy was still looking for something that would power him up that entrepreneurial mountain. Propane might not be it, but he believed it could take the family business to new heights, at least higher than kerosene had.

Moxley Propane was one of three entities under American Oil and Gas, Billy's new holding company formed under his restructuring of the family business. The other two entities were Moxley Heating Oil and Quick-Pik Food Marts, the convenience stores. The restructuring, in addition to giving the business a name implying largeness, provided investors with "more of a blended offering," Billy said.

"If just one of its parts took off, American Oil and Gas would make money for them."

Billy's friend, Tom Austin, invested $30,000 in the company, and Billy turned Don Angell's $250,000 investment in the convenience stores into equity in the overall structure. He then took his plan to Flip.

"I told Flip I was going to grow in the propane business and asked him if he would like to buy some equity in American Oil and Gas. Flip said, 'Sure,' and gave me a million dollars."

Billy knew that when his friends invested in American Oil and Gas they were not betting on convenience stores, heating oil, or even on propane, the new element in the mix.

"They were betting on me. That's the way it always is. You bet on the person. They were betting there was a jewel hidden somewhere in a niche of American Oil and Gas, and that I would be able to find it and mine it."

By 1989, Billy had opened American Oil and Gas offices in four North Carolina towns: Boonville, Elkin, Statesville, and Clemmons. He operated four convenience stores and supplied several others.

The propane division sold gas in bulk to farms, homes, and businesses. Billy, however, noticed almost immediately that there was a demand from backyard gas grill cooks to refill their empty propane cylinders. Usually the company sent them to Wolfe and Reece, a farm supply in Boonville that bought its propane from Moxley. But Wolfe and Reece closed at noon on Saturday for the weekend.

"Saturday and Sunday are the days people want to barbecue," Billy said, "but if you ran out of propane after twelve o' clock Saturday you could forget about barbecuing in Boonville."

Billy and Debbie knew this from their own experiences. "We used to cook out a lot," she said. "But Billy was always out of gas or running out of gas before he finished cooking. I think that got his wheels turning."

If the wheels in Billy's brain began turning in his backyard, they kicked into high gear in Paris in 1989. Billy and Debbie, who bought their gasoline and other petroleum products from Chevron, had been chosen Chevron "Jobber of the Year" and rewarded with a trip to Europe. They were touring Paris in a taxi when Billy saw something flash by the window that made him order the taxi driver to turn around and go back to a gasoline station.

What intrigued him was displayed under the brand name "Primagaz." In a cage outside the station were rows of filled propane cylinders. Customers brought their empty propane cylinders to the station and exchanged them for full ones. Billy had the taxi driver take him and Debbie to their hotel so he could get a camera, and he returned and took pictures. He then uttered to Debbie the understatement of his life: "You know, honey, this might be something we could do."

Billy and Debbie returned to Boonville and began to test in their stores whether people would pay for the convenience of simply dropping off their empty propane cylinders and exchanging them for those that had been painted and refilled with propane. Billy hired one of his fuel truck drivers to scrape rust off customers' cylinders, paint, and refill them. "We just had a few at first, maybe three or four a week," Debbie said. "Then it really took off, and it didn't take us long to know we were really on to something."

Billy said people liked the idea because it saved them time. "People have less time now. That's one thing I've seen change in my lifetime. People will pay to save time, and that's what I was giving them."

Billy's sister, Luanne, and her husband, Chris Holden, lived near Charlotte, where Holden worked as a sales representative for a paint and glass company. Billy had known Holden for years. He had played golf with him at the Yadkinville Country Club, where Holden had worked. In fact, it was through Billy that Luanne and Holden had met. The couple had no close ties to the Charlotte area. Billy sensed they would like to live closer to family, and that Holden might be interested in establishing a new division of American Oil and Gas—American Cylinder Exchange. He was right.

"Billy has a wonderful way of painting a picture, his vision, of how things are going to happen," Holden said. "He doesn't give any guarantees or absolutes, but he'll say, 'I've looked at this, and here's how I see it coming all together.' He has such confidence, and such passion, that you can see his vision. And that vision isn't just pie in the sky. It's grounded in careful study. Billy is a calculated risk taker. He studies the terrain. When Billy steps, he knows where he's going."

Where Billy intended to go with American Cylinder Exchange was into the larger towns and cities. The test he conducted in his own stores had shown that people in farming communities such as Boonville, Jonesville, and East Bend would pay five or six dollars extra for the convenience of exchanging their cylinders for cylinders they knew were "full, clean, and safe," Billy said. "I was getting nine to eleven dollars a cylinder. That was in Yadkin County, where people are pretty conservative. Man, I just knew that in cities like Raleigh and Charlotte, they would pay more."

Holden accepted Billy's offer to manage American Cylinder Exchange. His job was to get American Cylinder Exchange cages in front of as many stores as possible within a ninety-mile radius of Boonville. This was September of 1990. His immediate goal was to nail down at least seventy-five locations by February. At first, Holden would have to do it all. That meant convincing the store manager to go into the cylinder exchange business; putting up the display cage containing new cylinders; returning in a week to two weeks to pick up empty cylinders customers had left; and refurbishing those empties, including removing rust, painting, and refilling them. He also had to take care of financial matters and other concerns with the store managers.

Later, when Holden had American Cylinder Exchange up and profitable at stores across the state—as Billy thought would happen—Billy could use his truck drivers with American Oil and Gas to service the cages. That was the beauty of the idea. Heating oil demand began to drop sharply by the end of March, and drivers were idle from April through September. On the other hand, those are the peak months for outdoor grilling and should be high-demand months for full propane cylinders to heat the grills. American Cylinder Exchange should nicely, and profitably, fill the heating oil business's annual six-month financial void.

Billy and Holden converted the old Moxley Store fertilizer warehouse into a shop where the used cylinders could be refilled and refurbished to the point that they looked like new. Cylinders that needed rust removed and repainting went into an enclosed device called a shotblaster that literally blasted them with tiny round pieces of shot, stripping away rust and paint. This allowed Holden to give them a paint-job that made them look like new when he refilled them and replaced them in the cages.

Holden's first task was to convince store owners that they could make money by displaying the cylinder cages outside their businesses. All the store clerk had to do was exchange the cylinders. That meant unlocking the cage, handing a new or refurbished cylinder to the customer, and placing the empty cylinder in the appropriate place in the cage. The clerk also accepted the customer's money, $10.99. American Cylinder Exchange got $8 of that amount.

Billy had a network of friends in the convenience store business throughout the state. Many of them were in the fuel oil business and, like Billy, had gravitated into convenience stores. Billy called to tell them about his new venture and that Holden would be coming with his cages.

Holden's spiel, backed up by a brochure Billy wrote and had printed, emphasized the convenience of cylinder exchange. With his own empty propane cylinder mishaps fresh in his mind, Billy told Holden to focus on the Murphy's Law of backyard chefs. The law ensures that propane cylinders will become empty halfway through the cooking on a weekend when there is a houseful of guests. The law also makes it a certainty that the chef's wife will be thoroughly displeased. "So $10.99," Holden said, "is a small price to pay to maintain marital happiness."

Most convenience store owners didn't think much of the idea, at least at first, but since they knew and liked Billy, they listened to Holden and agreed to give it a try. Billy's old friend, Bob Sizemore, gave Holden his first location at Sizemore's Grocery in Winston-Salem, although Holden said he could tell that Sizemore "didn't think it was going to make any money. He was doing it for Billy."

Holden became accustomed to this reaction as he set up American Cylinder Exchange cages at convenience stores throughout the Piedmont Triad region of North Carolina, including stores owned by Billy's friends, Horace Bondurant, who owned Bondurant Oil in Mount Airy; Bert Bennett, owner of Quality Oil and the chain of Quality Mart stores; Tab Williams with Wilco; and John Taylor with Etna.

Holden transported his cylinders in a white Ford pickup hitched to a sixteen-foot trailer. He could carry about 125 at a time. At first, he could do it all—refurbish and refill the cylinders, deliver them to the stores, and pick up empties—all the while setting up new locations. He soon needed help, however, and Billy arranged for part-time help at first, and then full time, to help refurbish and refill the cylinders. Holden easily made his goal of seventy-five locations by February 1991. He had well over a hundred by summer. "There was a domino effect," he said. "When the stores saw it working, they all had to have it."

Bob Sizemore told Holden he was certain at first that American Cylinder Exchange would be short-lived at Sizemore's Grocery, "but you couldn't take it from me now."

By the summer of 1992, Holden had established more than two hundred locations. It was obvious that cylinder exchange, in general, and American Cylinder Exchange, in particular, had been accepted by backyard chefs throughout the Piedmont Triad region, which encompasses the cities of

Winston-Salem, Greensboro, and High Point. The program was also doing well in Statesville, Mocksville, and other smaller towns and cities.

Billy bought a truck with a trailer like the type beverage companies use to deliver bottled drinks. He shifted one of his drivers, Darrel Hutchens, to American Cylinder Exchange full time, and Frank Steelman gradually became full time as he took over the job of refurbishing and refilling the cylinders.

The new division was growing almost too fast for Billy to keep it supplied with cylinders. They were expensive. A new cylinder cost $13 or $14, although "blems" or seconds could be purchased for $11 or $12. Billy needed several thousand cylinders to keep up with the rapidly growing exchange program. But, as he told his buddy, Dr. Tom Austin, as they were on the way to the golf course one day, the new business was growing so fast that he didn't have the capital to sustain it.

"Hmmm. That's a business that sounds real interesting," Austin said. "What do you need?"

"I need a load of tanks," Billy said, "and about twenty grand to buy them."

"I'll call my banker," Austin said. "We'll pick up the check on the way."

Fifteen years later, Billy still laughed out loud when he thought about that morning ride to play golf at the Olde Town Country Club with Tom Austin, and their side trip to the First Union Bank in Yadkinville. "Can you believe it? On the way to play golf, he picks up a twenty thousand-dollar check to invest in my company. That's class. That's a friend."

"I thought it was a great idea," Austin said. "I believed in the concept, and I believed in Billy. If anybody could make it work, he could."

In 1993, the concept was working so well that it expanded to grocery stores, including Grandview Food Market's two stores in Winston-Salem and Byrd Food Stores in Burlington with dozens of locations in central and eastern North Carolina. "These were the first larger type stores we landed, and they were important," Holden said, "not just because of their size, but because they were grocery stores, and we could get the woman of the house involved. Why not do old Dad a favor and pick up a full cylinder for him, because if she doesn't, you know he's going to forget and run out Saturday night just when it's time to put on the steaks."

A bag boy could carry the cylinder to her car, just like a bag of ice. "It was a natural."

By 1993, American Cylinder Exchange had grown across the state line into convenience stores in South Carolina. It expanded into the southwestern Virginia towns of Galax, Stuart, and Hillsville when Holden and Billy persuaded Tom Cockerham, owner of Cockerham Oil, to set up display cages outside his Chevron convenience stores. By July 1993, American Cylinder Exchange was in more than three hundred convenience and grocery stores in the Carolinas and Virginia, and that month posted more than five thousand sales. That's when Holden began thinking, "Hey, Billy's really onto something here. How far is this thing going to go?"

Others wondered also, as they watched admiringly. Ralph Bolin knew where he wanted American Cylinder Exchange to go, and that was in his lawn and garden department at the Wal-Mart in Elkin, less than nine miles west of Boonville. Bolin, manager of the department, stopped by Billy's office one day. He said he was selling hundreds of gas grills, but no gas to go with them. American Cylinder Exchange ought to be there. Every time he sold a grill, he could sell a cylinder, too.

Billy was excited. If he could get American Cylinder Exchange in Wal-Mart, then other big stores—Home Depot, Kmart, Lowe's—would certainly want to follow suit. Bolin's regional manager liked the idea, too, but he couldn't give Billy the okay. That would have to come from Wal-Mart national headquarters in Bentonville, Arkansas. Billy flew to Bentonville. Wal-Mart selling gas grills without propane cylinders is like selling toys without batteries, Billy said. Gas grills are a major category for Wal-Mart.

"Sell a grill buyer a propane cylinder when he buys the grill, and he'll be back to exchange the cylinder for another and another, time after time after time. You'll have him at Wal-Mart on a regular basis. Chances are that he's going to buy something else just about every time. It's a no-brainer."

Wal-Mart's Bentonville brass liked the idea—a lot. They told Billy, however, that it had to be part of a national program before they could consider it. Put together a national program and we'll look at it, they said. We can't promise you anything, but we'll look at it.

Okay, Billy said to himself, but I'll be back, and sooner than you might think. Billy decided then and there that one day in the not-too-distant future his cylinders would be at Wal-Marts, Home Depots, Kmarts, Lowe's, and every other big box store worth mentioning, throughout the country.

Meanwhile, Billy had plenty to keep him busy during the early 1990s. He was heading American Oil and Gas with its four divisions: cylinder exchange, with more than three hundred locations in the Carolinas and Virginia; five convenience stores; heating oil; and propane. Billy also had a substantial investment in Platinum Rotisserie, the company Flip founded that operated Boston Market restaurants in a large part of the Southeast.

Platinum Rotisserie's offices were in several attractive dormitory-style brick buildings arranged in a pleasant, campus-like setting on Winston-Salem's west side.

Jim Fogleman was Platinum Rotisserie's chief financial officer. He had prepared figures for Billy for his presentation to Wal-Mart executives. Billy asked him and several other aspiring business executives—mainly people he had met in the Young Presidents Organization (YPO)—to help him put together more research, particularly research into the barbecue industry as it applied to "the big boys—Wal-Mart, Home Depot, Kmart, Lowe's, Sears, and everybody who sold grills."

Billy was meticulous, as usual. He and a YPO friend, Doug Mele, attended the convention of the National Barbecue Association and concluded that a vast market for gas grills was about to open. In fact, it was already taking off. He found that at that time, 1993, only 28 percent of barbecue enthusiasts used gas grills. "But I could see that was changing quickly. I could see how often they were refilling their tanks, and I could see how many new ones were being bought. I knew I had a winner."

Bagging a Rhino

By early 1994, Billy had all but decided that he was going to launch a major expansion of his cylinder exchange business, focusing on large retail firms with locations throughout the country. He would need to put together a management team, and he would need capital, millions of dollars, just to get started.

But first, he needed to come up with a name for this new and larger version of his cylinder exchange company. It would have to be something that would make his propane cylinders instantly recognizable anywhere.

Flip told Billy that it was "absolutely essential" to separate any new expanded cylinder exchange business from the "very uninteresting" oil and gas business.

"No venture capitalist would touch that," Flip said. "But the type of business Billy was articulating was a service and distribution business, and it sounded like it could be a good idea."

Flip had long maintained an ardent interest in wildlife conservation, especially efforts to save the rare and endangered black rhinoceros. He traveled to South Africa three or four times a year on conservation and business matters. In February 1994, Flip and Billy took Veronica and Debbie on a photo safari in South Africa. Flip also invited several friends and business associates from Chicago who had invested in his high-tech software firm, Platinum Technology.

Billy, still working on his business plan, took his data with him and calculated on the plane. The group flew into Johannesburg and took a small plane into the bush, deep in the Mala Mala Game Preserve.

It was breathtakingly beautiful, Debbie said. "We went out in the jeep during the day and took pictures, and gathered around the campfire at night."

They talked about the animals they had seen, and they discussed Billy's efforts to expand his cylinder exchange business. At some point, those two subjects came together. Billy said he wanted a brand like the Pink Panther, something that would be popular and instantly recognized. But it also would have to be an appropriate symbol.

"I'm going to be selling a premium cylinder," he said, "the best in the business."

Then it came to Billy. He and Debbie were in the jeep taking pictures, and Billy had zoomed in on a rhino. "It's a natural!" he told Debbie. "He's tough, sturdy, and looks like a tank." And the propane flame, he said, would make a perfect rhino horn.

Flip loved the idea, and agreed to ask another Chicago friend, Len Carlson, who was in the sign business, to come up with a rhino logo. Carlson was also a member of Platinum Venture Partners, a venture capital group in Chicago that Flip had organized. The group met periodically to hear business proposals from aspiring entrepreneurs who needed capital to turn their dreams into reality.

On one of the last nights of the safari as everyone gathered close and listened to the sounds of the wild just beyond the roaring campfire, Billy turned to Flip and said he truly believed that he was going to place his tough, attractive, rhinoceros-like cylinders in Wal-Mart, Kmart, Lowe's and other big stores, and that people were going to buy them.

"Do you think your venture capital group would invest in them?" he asked.

"I do," Flip said. "I think that's a great idea."

Billy returned home from the photography safari in late February 1994 and shifted into overdrive. Flip's venture capital group, Platinum Venture Partners, was scheduled to meet in Chicago in April. It was almost March, and there were crucial plans to prepare, decisions to make, and organizational chores to complete before he could hope to stand before this group of wealthy individuals, some of the most successful and knowledgeable business leaders and entrepreneurs in the Chicago area, and ask them to bet their money on him. First, he had to hire a management team, complete his business plan, and come up with a logo and brand name.

The search for a name and logo ended when Len Carlson sent Billy the first group of pictures of how a rhino logo might appear. Among them was a rhino that looked to be incredibly strong, sturdy, and tough—yet nice enough to play with the kids while Dad grilled the hamburgers. It had blue skin, for propane, and a flame for its horn.

"I think the blue softened it," said Flip, "so it wasn't just a hard-skinned, dumb-ass animal. It still looked tough but nice and playful, too."

Billy loved it. There was no doubt about the name for his new company. Billy incorporated it on March 24, 1994. It was officially Blue Rhino Corp.

Billy already had borrowed Jim Fogleman, Platinum Rotisserie's chief financial officer, to run some studies on the future of the barbecue market. Now, with Flip in agreement, Fogleman also became CFO of Blue Rhino. For the time being, at least, he also would remain CFO of Platinum Rotisserie. Billy asked Fogleman and Tim Stinson to put together a business plan to present to the venture capital group in Chicago.

Billy hired the remaining two initial members of his management team through contacts he had made in the Young Presidents' Organization, better known as YPO to its 9,500 members around the world who use its networking facilities. Jerry Callahan of Charleston, South Carolina, a young executive with Coopers & Lybrand accounting firm, became Blue Rhino's first president and chief operating officer.

A YPO member in Chicago told Billy that Craig Erbland of Atlanta might be the person he needed to head up the drive to sell Blue Rhino to major retailers like Kmart, Home Depot, and Sears. Erbland worked for The Scotts Company and had sold its agricultural and garden products to many of the large retailers. He became Billy's vice president of sales.

This was the team that Billy, Blue Rhino's founder and CEO, took with him to Chicago to try to convince a group of savvy and seasoned venture capitalists that they could make money by investing in Blue Rhino—that it was going to become a household name to backyard chefs across the country.

Platinum Venture Partners met quarterly to hear business proposals from young would-be entrepreneurs such as Billy. Although Flip had founded the organization and introduced Billy to its members, it was by no means a certainty that the group as a whole, or individual members, would invest in Blue Rhino. That depended entirely on what the venture capitalists thought of Billy's plan, and how well he presented it.

Billy told the group what his careful research had told him: that a huge wave of backyard cooks who still used charcoal—about 80 percent of all outdoor chefs—was about to crest and head straight for the gas grill sections of the big retail stores. Billy told the investment group members that he was going to be there when it broke, and that he wanted them to be with him. And then he told them how Blue Rhino worked in North Carolina, South Carolina, and Virginia, and how it would work and succeed throughout the country.

Most investment club members thought he did a great job. "Billy came across very well," recalled Craig Duchossois (pronounced deshy-swa), the CEO of Duchossois Industries. "He told us where he was going and how he was going to get there. There he was with a moustache, hair almost down to his shoulders, and that wonderful North Carolina accent. I don't know how he would have come across in San Francisco or New York, but our Chicago boys decided this guy's okay."

"I was impressed," said Steve Devick, a highly successful Chicago music producer. "He had it all mapped out. He knew where he was going and how he was going to get there. He was very convincing. Billy is a wonderful communicator."

Other members "jumped on the bandwagon," said Flip. "There was a lot of enthusiasm. I thought if Billy could get by the startup problems and get it launched he would have a damn good business. I just had an innate belief that it was a good idea."

But not every Platinum Venture Partner member thought so. Like Billy, Tom Gleitsman owned a petroleum distribution business and a chain of convenience stores. But unlike Billy, Gleitsman did not think a cylinder exchange business would succeed, at least not one of the scope Billy described. At best, a cylinder exchange business could succeed only as a "Mom and Pop" local or regional enterprise. It would be much too cost-prohibitive to take further, he said.

Gleitsman's skepticism did not sway the club from investing in Blue Rhino. Moments after Billy spoke, Jim Liautaud, a member of a well-known entrepreneurial Chicago-area family, shook Billy's hand. He said, "I've listened to high-tech deal after high-tech deal, and I want you to know that this is the first damned one I've understood. I want to give you a half-million bucks."

Billy's chest swelled with pride as other investment club members congratulated him and pledged to invest in Blue Rhino. Duchossois invested a million. Peter Huizenga, of the family that founded the giant Waste Management Corp. and Blockbuster, invested a million. Flip invested two million. Even Gleitsman, despite his outspoken skepticism, invested $200,000. All told, individual members of the club invested $6.2 million and the club as a whole invested a million dollars. "It made me feel good," Billy said, "because I've always tried to keep things simple so people can under-stand. This was a concept I could explain. People understood it. They either believed in it or they didn't."

Billy was probably even a better communicator than Devick, Duchossois, or any of the forty-five or fifty members of the investment club had thought. "The truth of the matter was that my management team still had their day jobs, but I would have never told this group that. The main thing I wanted them to hear was, 'Hey, here we are. If you want to get on board this train, you had better get on it now. Because we're in North Carolina today, but we're going national tomorrow, and if you don't hop on, you'll miss this train.' You just have to have that kind of confidence."

Raising $7.2 million bolstered Billy's confidence even more. He had hoped for five or six million, and had gotten more. It was good seed money to attract more to help finance the building of Blue Rhino's foundation and infrastructure. Billy calculated that his business plan would require $10 million. He would need to raise more money. Meanwhile, he also needed to appoint a board, hire more key people, and start building Blue Rhino's infrastructure, which meant more refurbishing and distribution centers in various parts of the country.

One of the investors with Platinum Venture Partners was also a member of Frontenac Company, one of the largest venture capital firms in the country, and he suggested that Billy make a presentation to Frontenac's consumer products division. Although Billy was called back for a second meeting, Frontenac turned him down. The investment firm's members were not nearly as entrepreneurial as the risk-takers at Platinum Venture Partners. Blue Rhino was still only a concept to the Frontenac members.

"It takes a special person to invest in a concept," Billy said. "Entrepreneurs can visualize what another entrepreneur is saying." Frontenac members were more analytical types. "An analyst is more of a show-me type person. Tell me what the answers are. They don't like the early stages. They want it there and proven, and then if you want to expand and you can show them you can do it, they'll invest in it."

Not to be deterred, Billy set up an appointment with someone he knew could envision a concept. He was one of the country's leading entrepreneurs—Kenneth Langone, financier and founder of Home Depot. Langone was on the board of directors of Unifi, the company through which Billy met his friends Dick Hardin and Ray Maynard. Billy told Langone about his plans for Blue Rhino, especially how well it would complement the sales of gas grills at Home Depot and similar stores.

Langone called a regional buyer of gas grills for Home Depot in Atlanta and asked him what he knew about the concept and whether Home Depot was interested in it. The buyer had heard about it but was uncertain whether it was something Home Depot would want. There were potential issues of safety and time involving store personnel that would have to be explored.

Langone told Billy that, although Blue Rhino had considerable potential, he thought it would be a conflict of interest for him to invest. He also said it would be a difficult challenge to build a Blue Rhino infrastructure to the point that it could service Home Depot.

And he was right, Billy said. Blue Rhino had to have a strong infrastructure. It was a tough challenge. "But when he declined to invest, it made me want to succeed even more."

Billy appointed several of his initial investors from Platinum Venture Partners to seats on Blue Rhino Corporation's board of directors, including Craig Duchossois, Steve Devick, Peter Huizenga, Jim Liautaud, and, of course, Flip, who was Blue Rhino's vice chairman.

These Platinum Venture members, and others in the club, had given Billy a lot of feedback about Blue Rhino's pros and cons as they saw them. Their main con had to do with safety and the company's liability. "They wanted to know what was going to happen if a truck should turn over and burn half the town down, or if people were to lose their house, and so on."

How much liability protection did Blue Rhino need?

Billy began researching liability lawsuits. He learned that a company had better be prepared for anything and everything; that even if it does nothing wrong, it can easily wind up on the losing side of a lawsuit—even a seemingly ridiculous lawsuit. One such case left Billy shaking his head in amazement, while underscoring the importance of plenty of liability protection. It was, perhaps appropriately, a case that grew out of a Texas barbecue. Billy sort of laughs and groans simultaneously while telling this story.

"This guy in Texas was apparently in love with his propane tank. One night about one o'clock in the morning he sees some grease on it. What does he do? He draws a bath, and he takes his tank, along with his scotch and water, with him into the tub. But he's got something else. It's a cigar, and he lights it. KA-BOOM! It burns him all over. And he's got the nerve to sue the tank company for not having lettering on the tank to warn him he shouldn't do that. Unfortunately, this guy won a settlement."

While the ridiculousness of the cases was Texas-sized, the settlements were not. In fact, Billy learned that there had never been an award larger than $1 million in a lawsuit connected with an injury associated with an accident involving a gas grill propane cylinder. He bought a $10 million policy, which he later increased to $30 million.

To prevent accidents and to ensure that Blue Rhino complied with the myriad state laws across the country regarding the sale, display, and distribution of propane cylinders, Billy hired the man who for years had inspected his propane business for violations of North Carolina safety standards. He was Jim Mizelle, head of the North Carolina state government division responsible for enforcing laws and regulations regarding propane.

"He was the guy who had been checking up on me all these years. He was respected throughout the industry as a leader for safety. I knew he was tough and that I could trust him."

Mizelle became Blue Rhino's vice president for safety and training. He immediately began writing a safety and training plan.

Meanwhile, Blue Rhino's president, Jerry Callahan, was busy putting together an operational plan. If Blue Rhino was to be a national company, there would have to be Blue Rhino distribution centers built at various locations throughout the country. Customers' propane cylinders, or tanks, would be transported to these centers where they would be refurbished—cleaned, painted, and refilled—and then distributed, like new, to stores throughout their respective areas. At that point, in mid-1994, there was still only one refurbishing and distribution center, the one that Billy and Chris Holden started in Boonville at what had been the old Moxley Store.

Billy and Callahan decided to build distribution centers in Zellwood, Florida; Livingston, Texas; and Los Angeles. Billy bought approximately four acres in Livingston, which is about seventy-three miles north of Houston and 214 miles south of Dallas. He leased the site in Zellwood, a few miles northeast of Orlando, and the property in Los Angeles.

Blue Rhino would need new tanks at the new locations, thousands of them, especially at first, in order to get cylinder exchange programs going. The largest tank manufacturer in the country at that time was Manchester Tank in Franklin, Tennessee, near Nashville. Manchester Tank was owned and operated by Darrel Reifschneider, whose father started the company in 1946. Billy flew to Nashville to meet him. Reifschneider took an instant liking to the younger man who had such big plans for his tanks. He gave Billy a million-dollar line of credit.

Billy also continued doing something he was very good at, something important to the success of any entrepreneurial venture, and that was networking and laying the foundation for future networking. He did this by securing an ideal position for himself among propane business leaders at the national level. Billy had Steve Devick, one of Blue Rhino's investors and board members from Chicago, introduce him to Daryl McClendon, president of the National Propane Gas Association. He had been in the propane business since 1968 and knew people throughout the industry.

They met at the Four Seasons Hotel in Chicago. Billy told McClendon that Blue Rhino was going to soon be the leading propane cylinder exchange business in the country. "I told him I wanted to be on the association board because I was about to become a national player. I told him how I was going to do it, and his eyes just kept getting bigger and bigger. I told him I had just raised the first seven million, and that I needed to meet people nationally. I said he had the authority to appoint me, and that I'd like for him to consider it." Billy invited McClendon to come to North Carolina to see for himself the venture that was about to go nationwide. McClendon accepted the invitation, and he was surprised at what he saw.

"I expected it to be just a little regional company, but it was much larger than I thought it would be," McClendon said. "I was impressed." McClendon told his board about Billy Prim and Blue Rhino, and asked its members if they would like to invite Billy to join them. They did, and Billy became a member of the board of directors of the National Propane Gas Association. Billy put McClendon on retainer to Blue Rhino as a consultant. It would be through McClendon that Billy would meet and hire some of the key people that would take Blue Rhino national, and McClendon himself would later play a crucial role in the development and growth of the company.

By late 1994, Billy was feeling good about Blue Rhino in many respects. In just ten months, he had organized the company; hired a management team and other key personnel; appointed a board of directors; established a million-dollar line of credit with Manchester Tank; gotten himself appointed to the National Propane Gas Association's board; built tank refurbishing and distribution centers in Florida, Texas, and Los Angeles; and raised $7.2 million.

But there was one just one thing missing—customers. Billy still had his local and regional customers, the convenience stores and small grocery chains, but no big national retail store—none of the big boys. And that's where Blue Rhino needed to be, because "our money," Billy said, "was going out the door." Billy wasn't panicked, not by any means. He had gone on sales calls with Craig Erbland, whom he hired to sell Blue Rhino to the big retailers, and Billy knew they were interested. But it was uncharted territory for them, and a potentially hazardous product. They were concerned about issues such as insurance and liability.

It seemed as if every time Blue Rhino cleared one hurdle, another sprang up, usually in the form of some type of risk management committee. None had said no, but no one had said yes, either.

Erbland had been courting Kmart, and it appeared that the senior vice president who could pave the way was about to say yes. There was just one thing. The executive was insisting that Erbland fly him in a private jet to Tampa, Florida, where he wanted to visit a strip club and eat at Bern's, a well-known steak house with a pricey menu that would never remind anyone of a blue-light special at Kmart. And then the next day—"if he feels like it," Erbland said—the executive might take care of business.

"Damn!" Billy exclaimed. "I thought Kmart was a pretty good company. Now I understand why they went bankrupt."

But Billy agreed to finance the Kmart vice president's trip to Tampa and a night on the town.

Happy with his evening, the executive approved entering into a business relationship with Blue Rhino, but it was the same old story. Kmart's risk management team would have to sign off on it, he said. The issue became mired in the big retail store's bureaucracy.

"They wanted to go over our insurance policy, and then they had to talk to so-and-so, and then another so-and-so. They dragged it out and dragged it out through the fall and Christmas—and we still didn't have a customer.

"And then good old Lowe's calls. They say, 'We like what you guys are doing. How about putting them in some of our stores?' Good old North Carolina boys. They're saying, 'How can we help you? Let's make this thing big. We think there are all sorts of possibilities.'"

Lowe's, second only to Home Depot as the world's largest home improvement retailer, began in North Wilkesboro, North Carolina, just forty-four miles west of Boonville, in 1946. At the time, Lowe's was a single hardware store owned by Carl Buchan and his brother-in-law, James Lowe.

Buchan, foreseeing the post-war building boom, bought out Lowe and began selling hardware, appliances, and building materials. The store was able to establish a reputation for low prices by eliminating wholesalers and dealing directly with manufacturers. Additional Lowe's stores sprang up in towns throughout North Carolina, and then in other states. By 2005, there were more than 1,200 Lowe's stores in forty-nine states, with sales totaling more than $36.5 billion.

Billy drove to North Wilkesboro and talked with Lowe's executives. It was fitting that Lowe's, a national company born and bred in North Carolina, would be the first big retailer to invite Blue Rhino, another local company with national aspirations, into its stores. Billy and the Lowe's executives had an excellent meeting. "I told them I wanted to start out in North Carolina and spread all over the country. That was just what they wanted. It was such a pleasure doing business with Lowe's."

Billy will never forget how proud he was when he first saw the colorful Blue Rhino cylinders, with the playful, but tough-looking little rhino with its flaming propane horn, on display at Lowe's in Winston-Salem.

"It was such a major turning point—our first big break. And they started selling like hotcakes."

Building a Passionate, Can-Do Culture

Throughout 1994, as he tried to persuade the big retailers to give Blue Rhino a try, Billy became keenly aware of the need for a top-notch professional to build and lead the company's sales department. He had Erbland, who was having limited success in attracting the big stores, but what Billy didn't have was someone with a background in sales analysis and marketing techniques—someone who already knew the barbecue industry and could put together a national sales and marketing campaign.

A member of a sales-rep group he was using temporarily told him he ought to get in touch with Rick Belmont, who was with Char-Broil in Atlanta.

Belmont, who was thirty-five then, had been with Char-Broil, one of the largest grill manufacturers in the country, for six years. As Char-Broil's product planning manager, he determined what products Char-Broil should build and how to market them. It was essential for him to understand retailers' needs. Soft-spoken and quietly self-assured, Belmont knew the industry well. He wasn't looking for work. He liked his job, but there was something vaguely dissatisfying about it. He was tired of the corporate system. It was too confining and a little boring.

So when Billy told him he was looking for someone who knew the industry and the market and would like to help build a company and take it nationwide, Belmont was all ears.

He liked what he was hearing, and he liked Billy. "There was something almost mystical about his manner," Belmont said. "He was incredibly relaxed. His style was self-confident and calm, not overbearing at all. He was sitting on a gold mine, and he knew it. I thought he was a great idea guy, an idea guy who could make ideas work. I saw a guy who said, 'We're going to do this,' and I believed him."

Belmont said that when he heard Billy say he was going to provide Blue Rhino consumers with a "precision-filled tank with gas that's clean and like new every time," he knew it would go. "I knew the market, and I knew that the consumer needed to get gas in a more efficient manner. I knew the safety concerns. Consumers needed this even if they didn't know they needed it."

Billy told Belmont that he wanted someone "who had an entrepreneurial spirit and was willing to take a risk." Belmont was willing.

"This was high-risk, yes. But every now and then you've got to climb up on a bridge and jump off. I had no idea how far it was to the water, or even if there was any." But Belmont was sure of one thing: the jump would not be boring. He accepted Billy's offer to become Blue Rhino's vice president of sales and marketing.

Success breeds success. A few weeks after Lowe's signed on, Kmart lifted its bureaucracy and invited Blue Rhino into its stores. And then Billy's attention turned to the retail giant Home Depot.

At that time Billy still had his bulk propane business, a division of American Oil and Gas Corp. Suburban Propane, headquartered in New Jersey, was the biggest propane company in the business. It even owned some cylinder exchange locations, including about seventy-five Home Depot stores in Texas and Kentucky.

Suburban told Billy that if he intended to go big time in the cylinder exchange business—as it appeared to them that he was—then perhaps he might want to sell his bulk propane division to Suburban. To sweeten the deal, Suburban told Billy it would be willing to throw in their cylinder exchange locations.

Billy sold his propane division to Suburban in a personal transaction for $3.5 million. He also bought the assets for all of Suburban's cylinder exchange locations—displays, customers, everything. And he got something else that might have been more important in the long run than all of the assets put together.

Suburban agreed in writing that it would not compete with Billy in the cylinder exchange business. That was huge. Billy had considered Suburban to be, potentially, his main competitor.

"It was a good deal. They were the major guys out there who I thought could compete with me. I got about a hundred Home Depot locations and some other outlets, a noncompeting agreement from Suburban, and some money in my pocket. It was a good day."

Once Billy got those Home Depot sites from Suburban, he and others, especially Belmont, his new vice president for sales, began to work on Home Depot executives to persuade them to put Blue Rhino into other Home Depot stores. Billy and Belmont flew back and forth, between Winston-Salem and Home Depot's corporate headquarters in Atlanta, pointing out to Home Depot's top executives how well the Home Depot locations with Blue Rhino were performing.

"We showed them the proof in the pudding from the Home Depot stores in the Suburban deal."

Home Depot allowed Billy to set up displays in several stores in Florida, Georgia, and North Carolina. "And they sold like gangbusters," Billy said.

They were almost too successful. Home Depot executives turned 180 degrees when they saw how Blue Rhino was ringing up sales. They wanted Blue Rhino in all their stores right away, and Blue Rhino wasn't ready.

The little company was scrambling to set up in Lowe's stores, and to identify and solve the many problems associated with such a move. In addition, Craig Erbland had recently signed on Scotty's, a chain of about forty home improvement stores in Florida and Georgia.

"We had little infrastructure," Belmont said. "There was an operation in Boonville out of the family feed and seed where we were filling some bottles. There was another in Livingston, Texas. And one in Orlando was starting up. There was one in Fort Wayne that hadn't started up, and there was one planned for Atlanta. That was it."

But Home Depot "loved us," Billy said. "They were ready to go full gangbusters whether we were ready or not."

A store in Key West was having its grand opening and Home Depot wanted Blue Rhino to be a part of it. "We would lose $10 a tank, and we'd have to jump through hoops to do it. I said, 'Can't you give us a little time?' They said, 'Guys, we're going to do this nationwide, and if you don't do it, we're going to get someone else.'"

Billy was not going to allow that to happen. Blue Rhino serviced the store from its Boonville plant, painting the tanks, loading them on rental trucks, and hauling them almost one thousand miles to Key West. It's a drive of about twenty hours, but if that was what it would take to get and keep Home Depot as a nationwide Blue Rhino customer, Billy would have filled and painted the propane tanks and hauled them down there himself.

A Blue Rhino cage filled with Blue Rhino tanks ready for exchange was part of Home Depot's grand opening in Key West in 1995. "We did what we had to," Belmont said. "If servicing Key West from a thousand miles away was what it would take, that's what we were going to do."

A little more than a year after Blue Rhino was born, the company had contracts with two of the nation's largest retailers, Home Depot and Kmart, and one that was about to become one of the largest, Lowe's. Billy and Belmont were working hard on Wal-Mart, Sears, and others.

"My job was to sell a vision—and convince them that they wouldn't be placing bombs in front of their store," Belmont said. "I told them the risk was minimal. I sold the opportunity. I told them this was the wave of the future for getting gas to customers, which it was." He and Billy emphasized the necessity of selling gas with a new grill.

"We told them their customers will appreciate it. It's an introduction to future revenue because it's reoccurring. You'll sell it twice a year, at least, to the same customer."

Belmont told his potential customers that Blue Rhino was a "credible, well-financed company with a knowledgeable and talented board of directors." They were not just wealthy business owners, although some of them were quite wealthy. They were risk-takers, people who understood people who took risks.

"You couldn't have built this company with rich executives alone," Belmont said. Blue Rhino was a different kind of company, and it needed unusual types on its board of directors—such as that represented by Flip Filipowski, for instance.

"Flip was this weird guru that no one knew but Billy," Belmont said. "Flip turned switches on and off that nobody but Flip knew about."

Go with Blue Rhino, Belmont told the big retailers, and "we'll meet your needs. We'll put the mechanism and infrastructure in place and have it ready to go when you're ready."

Years later, he smiles at what he said was his naiveté during those early days. The company was signing on retail customers so fast that it soon became difficult to build that infrastructure and provide that support.

If Belmont was naive, so was everyone else at Blue Rhino. But they were sincere in their naiveté and passionate about Blue Rhino.

This was a hectic, heady, adrenaline-filled time for Billy, Belmont, and everybody else in the fledgling company. Every one of the fifty or so people working there when Belmont joined the company in early 1995—from office assistants to vice presidents and Billy—had a sense of mission and feeling that they were building something that had never been built before, and they were.

Figuratively, and in some cases literally, they were writing the how-to manuals for their jobs as they learned from day to day what worked and what didn't. Always, there was a sense of urgency; that this was their time, Blue Rhino's time, and it was up to them to make the most of it.

Susie Simpson had the distinction of being the first person hired at Blue Rhino. She went to work as a data clerk on the Friday before Memorial Day, 1994. "It was fast and furious from the beginning, and it stayed that way," she said.

People were passionate about what they were doing, and that came from Billy. His passion for Blue Rhino was infectious.

"Billy's passion had a way of rubbing off on everybody," said Abbye Caudle, his longtime executive assistant.

That passion, plus Billy's management style, which allowed people considerable latitude to accomplish their work the way they wanted, attracted talented, creative people with an entrepreneurial spirit similar to Billy's.

When Dave Slone heard that his job as training manager would require him to define, learn, and teach all the Blue Rhino jobs, he offered to work for a subsistence salary for the first six months if Billy would hire him. A retired combat systems officer for a U.S. Navy nuclear submarine, Slone got the job for considerably more than subsistence pay. He became a key employee.

Dick Arthur, another key employee hired during Blue Rhino's salad days, said the opportunity to create his job, "to make it up as we go, was extremely compelling." Arthur, also a retired military officer, worked with Slone to train Blue Rhino distributors.

A tone was set during those first few months as Blue Rhino blinked and took its first tentative steps. It was a tone of urgency, but also patience, grounded in the confidence that Blue Rhino people—the "herd" as they began to call themselves—had what it took to succeed. That tone, that culture, emanated from Billy, said Belmont.

"We had no idea what was going to jump out from behind the next tree. Billy created and fostered a culture that said it was okay to make mistakes. Just learn from them and move on. In fact, if you aren't making mistakes, you probably aren't driving fast enough. Well, that culture created a wonderful camaraderie. People were not at each other's throats. It was a close group."

Blue Rhino would soon need all the close-knit cohesiveness, camaraderie, and goodwill that Billy's style and culture could summon. The company was only a little more than a year old in mid-summer of 1995, but already there were powerful forces at work—some generated by chance, accident, and economics, and some by design, that threatened to halt Blue Rhino, and Billy, before they could muster a charge.

The telephone's urgent ring jarred Billy and Debbie Prim awake the morning of July 21, 1995. Billy glanced at the clock. It was 4:30 in the morning. He steeled himself as he picked up the phone. This was not likely to be good news. It wasn't.

The caller was Ricky Trivette, a friend and member of the Boonville Fire Department. Trivette was at a fire that very moment, one that was furiously burning Blue Rhino's cylinder refurbishing and distribution center in Boonville, the company's flagship center at that time. There had been an explosion that blew out the sides of the building, and firefighters were hearing other blasts. Trivette said the fire was too dangerous for firefighters to get close.

"It was scary to hear that," Billy said.

The explosion and fire, which rocked Boonville, but injured no one and damaged nothing but the plant, were triggered by a series of unexpected events and mistakes.

One of the twenty-pound cylinders fell from its hook as it was moving by conveyer through the paint-drying department. The fall apparently damaged the tank's valve, causing gas to escape. The night crew went on break, shutting the system down until their return. Meanwhile, the propane from the cylinder continued leaking.

When the men returned, they turned on the vent, which sucked up the propane and deposited it into the heaters drying the paint. The propane exploded, blowing off the building's roof and sides.

Officials later concluded that the tanks themselves did not explode. The only explosion was from the gas that escaped from the cylinder that fell from the paint line. The only injury was a minor laceration sustained by one of the night crew members as he fled the burning building.

All in all, Billy felt lucky. It could have been much worse. His crew could have been injured or killed; townspeople could have been injured or killed, and lost their homes as well.

But it was bad enough. From a public relations standpoint, damage to the company's image alone had the potential to be disastrous. Blue Rhino's recent successes in courting big retailers such as Lowe's, Home Depot, Kmart, and Wal-mart were endangered, and could be eliminated altogether unless Billy acted quickly and decisively.

"Those big stores are not going to want to become involved with a company that is controversial or whose safety record is being questioned," he said.

Billy put Belmont in charge of public relations and dealing with the media regarding the explosion. His and Billy's policy was to be as accessible and open as possible. The story did not make the national press, although local papers, particularly the *Elkin Tribune*, played it as a major story. Belmont visited Lowe's to assure the retailer that safety was a top priority at Blue Rhino. As if to underscore that assurance, Billy placed Safety and Training Director Dave Slone in charge of the Boonville plant as it was being repaired. He also issued a press release the day after the explosion announcing plans to replace the plant's heating system.

Slone installed a redesigned heating room that included a soft floor beneath the cylinder drying area and a new heat system that prevented the possibility of gas getting into the heater and causing another explosion. Slone also initiated measures emphasizing cleanliness and organization, including verification measures making it unlikely that a dangerous situation, such as the one that led to the gas leak that caused the explosion, would happen again. Blue Rhino lost no customers because of bad publicity from the explosion and fire.

Production problems caused by the fire were far more serious. Slone believes they could have paralyzed Blue Rhino had it not been for the excellent relationship Billy had with Darrel Reifschneider and Manchester Tank Co. The fire destroyed the plant's ability to refurbish cylinders, and most cylinders coming into the plant from customers needed at least some sandblasting and painting. The fire did not, however, affect the plant's ability to refill and ship the tanks.

"We had a strong demand from customers for filled tanks, but few tanks were coming to us suitable for filling," said Slone.

The solution? New tanks, thousands of them.

If Blue Rhino couldn't refurbish customers' tanks, it would supply them with brand new ones. Slone said Reifschneider called Billy shortly after the explosion to say that Manchester "stood ready to help" in any way Blue Rhino needed.

The first of more than twenty tractor-trailer loads, at two thousand tanks per load, arrived from Manchester Tank Co. in Franklin, Tennessee, within days of the explosion.

"In my opinion," said Slone, "it was this strong relationship between Billy and Darrel that got us through the weeks following the explosion."

A Sweetheart Deal Leads to a Feadship Flare-up

The new tanks, probably fifty thousand or more, allowed Blue Rhino to meet customers' growing demands during the weeks required to get the Boonville plant fully operational again. But that was only a stopgap measure. Billy would need many more if he hoped to satisfy a rapidly rising number of calls from big retailers who wanted Blue Rhino in their stores. The requests began in earnest when Home Depot signed on and insisted that Blue Rhino go nationwide.

Blue Rhino was in danger of being swallowed up by its own success. By early autumn of 1995, Billy was close to deciding that Blue Rhino would have to make a basic structural change before it could succeed in growing into a nationwide company.

It would be impossible, he believed, to raise sales revenue fast enough to build all the distribution centers, complete with equipment, trucks, and personnel, while offsetting losses. It would cost almost a half-billion dollars. "I didn't think I could ramp up sales to that point to offset the losses."

But there was another way. The company could reach agreements with independent distributors at strategic locations throughout the country. It could service the distributors and provide them with training and expertise, but let them take the risk and pay for materials and start-up costs. Eventually, Blue Rhino would buy them out.

Blockbuster began this way, decentralized, and grew into a $5 billion company.

The more Billy looked at the distributor model, the more he was convinced that Blue Rhino needed to adopt it. However, his president, Jerry Callahan, disagreed. The matter became contentious between them.

Callahan wanted Blue Rhino to own and control it all, Billy said. "He wanted us to build all the distribution centers, hire all the drivers, route every truck in the country, and control everything from Winston-Salem."

There was a basic difference in the way the two men preferred to deal with people. Billy would rather "trust someone to be a good entrepreneur working in Seattle for himself so I didn't have to control him." But Callahan had "zero trust. He'd say, 'Billy, he'll steal from you.' I said, 'Jerry, I just don't agree with that.'"

Regardless of how Blue Rhino was to be structured, it needed an infusion of cash—and fast. The $7.2 million Billy raised from Platinum Venture Partners and its individual members disappeared quickly as bills poured in asking for payment for the construction of the new refurbishing centers and their start-up costs. Meanwhile, Home Depot and the other big retailers continued to push for Blue Rhino in their stores across the country.

By summer's end their requests, at least to Billy's ears, sounded like a crescendo.

"So here we are in September, and we've got all this demand. We're growing like a weed, but we're out of money. What are we going to do?"

Or, more to the point, where is he going to get it? Once again, Billy looked toward Chicago.

Billy met John Muehlstein, a Chicago attorney, when he joined Flip in the Boston Market venture. Muehlstein is a managing partner in Pederson & Houpt, a law firm that represents entrepreneurs and venture capitalists. He is a nephew of Peer Pederson, founder of the law firm and a man with a reputation for possessing an astute nose for business and a well-honed enjoyment of Chicago's nightlife.

Pederson had numerous contacts in the world of venture capitalists. He was the attorney and longtime friend of H. Wayne Huizenga, one of the founders of the giant Waste Management Corp., who acquired Blockbuster Video. Muehlstein and Billy became friends. Billy, who appreciated Muehlstein's unflappable nature, called him "cool-hand Luke," and later appointed him to a seat on the Blue Rhino board.

Billy was curious about where the financial backing had originated for some of the Boston Market investors, and Muehlstein told him that it came from Pederson, or that Pederson had arranged it. Billy thought, "Man, I've got to meet this guy."

He calculated that he needed about $13 million to build the distribution centers, equip them, and hire the people Blue Rhino needed to put the company in position to execute its next phase.

He asked Muehlstein to help him arrange a meeting, and Muehlstein readily agreed. He liked Billy's style. "People wanted to work for him. They believed in him. I told Peer we ought to listen to him." Pederson invited Billy to Chicago to talk.

Billy met Muehlstein and Pederson at the Four Seasons Hotel for breakfast. Pederson, who was in his seventies then, looked the way that many would picture the founder and head of a successful Chicago venture capital law firm. He was about six feet-two, with graying hair, dressed stylishly, though conservatively, in suit and tie. His manner was friendly, if a little crusty. His speech was to the point and enlivened with occasional four-letter words.

Billy knew that the success or failure of Blue Rhino might well be determined by the outcome of this meeting. More than ten years later, he remembered the exact table where the three were sitting in the Four Seasons.

"I tell him the story. I tell him all about me. And I tell him about Blue Rhino and what I know it can be. I tell him what I need to do, build five more centers, and so on."

Pederson looked at him for a moment. "I like this deal. I like you. How much do you need, and when?"

"Thirteen million," Billy said, barely able to believe his ears. "Yesterday."

"Can you give me until Friday?" Pederson deadpanned.

"I said, 'Yeah, I think I might be able to do that.' I was expecting him to say it would take him at least ninety to a hundred and twenty days to conduct due diligence. He said Friday. This was Tuesday!"

As it turned out, Billy didn't get his money by Friday, but it did take less than thirty days. Pederson called thirteen people who had invested in Waste Management or Blockbuster, people he knew were looking for new investment opportunities.

This was an exceptionally good deal for Billy. In addition to allowing him to get the capital he needed and getting it quickly, the terms of the subordinated debt deal did not have the diluting effect on his or others' ownership that a straight equity deal would have had. He raised capital in the form of subordinated debt with warrants attached. Raising it this way allowed shareholders to suffer much less dilution than they would have by raising straight equity.

"This was a sweetheart deal that closed in nothing flat. Peer put together a list of investors who took the $13 million of subordinated debt. Very little due diligence. If it had been a bank, it would have taken forever. But Peer looked me in the eye and said, 'I like you. This is a good kid. Let's finance him.' He talked to people who knew me, and he liked what they had to say."

During their meeting, Billy mentioned that Peter Huizenga, who inherited Waste Management stock worth well over a half-billion dollars when his father died, was an investor in Blue Rhino and a member of its board of directors. "What?" Pederson said. "You've got Peter on your board?"

"Why, yes," Billy replied, surprised at Pederson's reaction. "Isn't that a good thing?"

Pederson smiled slightly. "Have you dealt with Peter before?"

The shrewd Pederson knew what he was talking about. A few days after Billy returned to Winston-Salem, he received a call from Peter Huizenga, who said he had heard that Billy was raising money from Pederson and his group.

Blue Rhino should not be raising large amounts of money just to be able to go with large companies such as Home Depot, he said. Instead, Billy needed to stick with the smaller stores, the Mom's and Pop's, the convenience stores, and so on, and grow slowly.

Huizenga noted that Tom Gleitsman, a Platinum Venture Partners investor who had expressed skepticism in Billy's business model, agreed with him. Gleitsman owned convenience stores and was in the petroleum distribution business. He had told Billy that Blue Rhino should remain a regional business and not attempt to go national. Do it that way, Huizenga said, and he would give Blue Rhino all the money it needed. Huizenga had invested a million dollars in Blue Rhino; Gleitsman had invested $200,000.

Billy told Huizenga that he would talk with other board members. Then he called Flip and Craig Duchossois.

Billy and Duchossois, or "Craig D" as some called him, had become friends. Duchossois admired Billy's ambition and leadership skills. Billy admired Duchossois's business smarts as well, and trusted his advice. He also liked his personality and style. Like Billy, Duchossis shared a passion for golf. They, along with Pederson, participated in hotly contested outings on the golf course—matches made more interesting by some hefty wagering. Duchossois was a man of impeccable dress and manners.

"He wants to be a friend to everybody," Billy said. "He's the kind of guy who will call during difficult times just to say, 'How are you, buddy? Don't worry. I'm on your side.'"

Duchossois, who stands about five feet, four inches, is chairman of Duchossois Industries, a billion-dollar holding company that, among many other entities, includes Churchill Downs and the Chamberlain Group. His friends say he is quite tall when he stands on his wallet.

Duchossois arranged a meeting on his father's yacht, a luxurious Feadship (pronounced "fedship"), docked just off Navy Pier on the lakefront near downtown Chicago. Present were Billy, Flip, Duchossois, Pederson, Muehlstein, and Peter Huizenga.

"It was a dramatic scene," Billy said. "We're on this beautiful yacht, one of the largest in the world. Peter's there and he's dressed to the hilt."

Huizenga proceeded to tell the group that they were "out of their minds" if they thought they could take Blue Rhino nationwide. "The big stores will just spread you out," he told Billy. "You can't handle all the propane tanks all over the country."

Billy was diplomatic. "I hear what you're saying. But our strategy all along was to take this to the big box stores. Yes, there are early losses, but it will all come together when we get enough critical mass."

Huizenga said Billy had no idea how much Blue Rhino could lose.

Flip had heard enough. Flip told Huizenga that he was not going to allow someone who had never begun or operated a business to tell Billy how to run his. "We don't need you trying to tell people how to run their business. You don't belong in this deal."

Flip told Huizenga to keep quiet, or he would throw him off the boat.

"I was overwhelmed," Billy said. "Peter jumps up and leaves. Peer laughs and says, 'I told you.' But Craig is the ultimate gentleman. He said we don't need this bad blood and controversy. He said to call Peter up and make a deal to give him his money back. I said, 'Okay, Craig, but I don't have a million dollars.'"

Billy went to Huizenga's office the next morning and offered to return Huizenga's million-dollar investment. Huizenga accepted and resigned his seat on Blue Rhino's board of directors. A few days later Tom Gleitsman called Billy to say he also wanted out. Billy paid the total $1.2 million out of the $13 million he raised from Peer Pederson's group of investors. It was money that Blue Rhino needed badly, but Billy believed it was better to return it.

"I was afraid Peter was going to mess up the whole deal. Then I would have been broke and forced to come to him for money."

The Huizenga incident, though painful and costly, may have helped Blue Rhino survive. Although Billy had already decided that the company would have to change its business model to one based on a system of independent distributorships, Huizenga's departure probably underscored the necessity of making that change and perhaps accelerated it.

"Peter, in his own awkward way, helped save the company," Duchossois said. "He told us we were, I think the quote is, 'fucking nuts,' if we didn't leverage the expenses by putting some of it on the distributors; that trying to wrap your arms around everything would knock you out before you got your foot in the door. I think Peter caused us to look at things differently."

A footnote: Five years after the Feadship meeting Billy was conducting a presentation for potential Blue Rhino investors at the Union League Club in Chicago when Huizenga walked into the room. Billy, not sure whether Huizenga might try to discourage people from investing in Blue Rhino, continued his talk as Huizenga made his way to a seat in the front. When Billy finished, Huizenga stood and said, "Folks, I was one of the earliest investors in this young man's company, and I made a mistake and pulled myself out. I lost faith in him. I thought he was going down the tubes. But I learned that Billy is a fighter. He'll fight for your investment. He made the changes he had to, and he stopped the bleeding and turned it around. I want you to know that I'm a buyer today."

Huizenga's words to that conference of investors meant a great deal to Billy, then and through the years. "I really appreciate that compliment from Peter."

Billy returned to Winston-Salem more certain than ever that Blue Rhino would have to change its business structure to an independent distributor model. His studies of large, fast-growth companies, such as Coca-Cola and Budweiser, convinced him that Blue Rhino could not go it alone. He told his management team that he had determined it would cost the company $400 million to expand nationwide on its own. "Guys, we can't do this by ourselves," he said, mainly to Callahan, who remained wedded to the concept of central ownership.

Billy told his team that he knew people all over the country in the propane business who would become independent distributors for Blue Rhino. Becoming a distributor would provide a propane dealer with much needed business between May and September, when it was on the seasonal downside. For most dealers, the start-up costs would be minimal, Billy said. Most already had a lot of the necessary infrastructure and equipment, including the trucks needed to transport cylinders. They had to buy equipment to refurbish the cylinders, including a shotblaster, painting booth, and perhaps an air compressor. The distributor would have to absorb those and other start-up costs. Blue Rhino would pay the distributor on a per-cylinder basis.

"This way, we will not have to support all the capital expenditures," Billy told his team. "It will allow us to grow all over the country."

Callahan remained unconvinced. But he agreed to go along.

Billy read everything he could find on independent distributorships, such as those associated with Budweiser and Coca-Cola. He had been a distributor himself for Shell and Chevron, and was familiar with Boston Market's franchise program. He wanted to take the best aspects of each of those programs and apply them to a distributorship model for Blue Rhino.

Billy wanted a system that would allow Blue Rhino to control its brand marketing, displays, information system, and sales force, while distributors owned the equipment to refurbish and deliver the cylinders. Such an arrangement would allow Blue Rhino to use its capital to promote the Blue Rhino brand and grow through internal expansion and acquisitions.

Coca-Cola's system looked as if it would fit Blue Rhino best. "Coca-Cola doesn't own all of the filling plants, or all of the bottles, or all of the delivery trucks," he said. "But it does own the brand name and trademark, and focuses on expanding sales through consumer and retailer brand trust and loyalty."

Billy, with the help of attorneys John Muehlstein and Mike Black, from Pederson & Houpt law firm, wrote a distributor agreement modeled after Coca-Cola's system. Basically, the responsibilities of the independent distributors were to refurbish the cylinders, fill them with propane, and distribute them to the stores, while following the specifications, marketing, and safety standards required by Blue Rhino. In addition to being paid by Blue Rhino, the distributors also would receive Blue Rhino's training and expertise in marketing and sales, and the benefits of its state-of-the-art computer system.

On December 21, 1995, the board of directors of Blue Rhino Corp. met in the tenth floor boardroom of Flip's company, Platinum Technology, Inc., in Oakbrook Terrace, Illinois, just outside Chicago. The main item of business, in addition to dealing with the resignation of Peter Huizenga, was a briefing from Billy and a discussion of the new independent distribution plan. Callahan, a member of the board as well as president of the company, had flown to Chicago with Billy, as had CFO Jim Fogleman. Rick Belmont, who gave a sales report to the board, was at the meeting, as was Joe Culp, whom Billy had recently hired to be vice president of distributor development. The meeting was about to end when Callahan stood and asked to address the board. Belmont and Culp were asked to leave the room.

Billy listened, dumbfounded, as Callahan read a prepared statement.

Callahan told the board that Billy's economic and business philosophies were wrong for Blue Rhino and that he was leading the company down a path to ruin. Callahan said he was ready to replace Billy as CEO if the board agreed with him. Otherwise, he was going to resign from the presidency of Blue Rhino and from his seat on the board.

"I was shocked," Billy said. "This came out of nowhere. I had no idea."

Most of the board members appeared shocked, too. Some looked at each other in disbelief.

"It was the most unusual boardroom scene I have ever witnessed," said Steve Devick. "It was an ambush. It came right out of the blue. It was a mini-coup attempt."

Callahan, now a consultant who "fixes troubled companies," denied he was trying to persuade the board to oust Billy and appoint him to lead the company. "I didn't want Billy's job," Callahan said. "I just wanted the board to rein him in. He was making promises he couldn't keep, and I had lost confidence in him."

Callahan said he told the board he would stay if it was their wish, but that he was "ready to resign."

There was no support for Callahan on the board. "I guess we have a resignation before us," Devick said. The board voted unanimously to accept Callahan's resignation.

Flip said Callahan had attempted to lobby him before the board meeting. "He told me we had to get rid of Billy. I walked into that board meeting knowing Callahan was going to lose his job."

Billy and Callahan flew back on the same plane. Not a word was spoken between them until they were midway through the flight. Finally, Billy looked at him and said, "Why did you do that? Why did you surprise and attack me that way? I knew we had a difference of opinions, but why that way?"

Callahan said he thought it was the right thing to do.

The incident shook Billy. He called Debbie before he got home. "I could tell by his voice that something was wrong," she said. "He was not only shocked; he was hurt."

Billy replayed it in his mind, analyzing it and reanalyzing it. "It's the sort of thing that returns to you."

He and Jerry Callahan were looking at Blue Rhino and seeing two totally different companies.

"Callahan saw a vertical structure, centralized, owning and controlling everything from the beginning. I saw a company rapidly expanding across the country with a brand name everybody recognized because it had built a system of independent distributors and was unencumbered by all that equipment and debt it would have under a vertical structure. The company I saw had a bright future with lots of sunlight shining through the clouds. I could see a lot of demand, and I could see the new model working. But I know that it takes a certain type of person to buy into this philosophy and vision."

Not everyone, he said, can look at dark clouds and see sunlight.

Sunlight is hard to see when you're alone, far from shore, and in the middle of a fierce storm. To some at Blue Rhino who knew the gravity of the company's financial situation, that's where Billy seemed to be when he took on the duties of the company presidency.

"Blue Rhino has given me some incredible highs and incredible lows," said Rick Belmont.

The last part of 1995 and the first few months of 1996 were so low it was "gut-wrenching," said Belmont. "It looked like we were going to have to shut down."

But you wouldn't know that from talking with Billy who, typically, found a lot of sunshine peeking through the storm clouds. At the frequent all-hands meetings, in which all Blue Rhino employees participated, Billy never hid the fact that Blue Rhino had a problem. But it was a good problem, he said, one brought on by the demand for Blue Rhino cylinders and service. Dick Arthur was amazed at the cool and calm demeanor Billy projected during this time.

"He exuded confidence and control. He never broke a sweat, even though I knew he had to be like a duck way out in the middle of the lake, paddling hard and furiously. I watched in awe and admiration. He really showed his mettle."

Looking for Sparks in Their Eyes

Billy took the role of president of Blue Rhino after Jerry Callahan's departure. In his mind, Billy wasn't working just to save Blue Rhino; he was preparing for a nationwide charge. And he didn't have a lot of time.

Billy knew that it was only a matter of time before another entrepreneurial-minded person—probably a propane dealer with a local cylinder exchange business—recognized the national potential that he saw for the business.

Several immediate crucial actions needed to be taken, he realized, all related, and all leading toward his long-term goal of building his company and taking it public. First and foremost was to begin building a Blue Rhino independent distributorship system. Second, and crucial to the success of the independent distributors, was to build a state-of-the-art information technology and communications system. Third was to hire a chief financial officer, who would be at his side as Billy took Blue Rhino to Wall Street.

Jim Fogleman, who was also a member of Blue Rhino's board of directors, had been the original CFO, but Billy had shared him from the beginning with Platinum Rotisserie, the umbrella company for the Boston Market franchises that Billy invested in with Flip and others.

In early 1996, as Blue Rhino prepared to build a national presence that Billy hoped would culminate in an initial public offering, the company needed a full-time CFO. Fogleman, while keeping his seat on the board for several more months, returned to Platinum Rotisserie full time. Billy hired Larry Brumfield, a member of Blue Rhino's auditing firm, Coopers & Lybrand, to become CFO. Brumfield brought controller Kurt Gehsmann with him, a move that greatly improved the accounting department.

Blue Rhino also had been sharing Platinum Rotisserie's information system's expert, Bob Travatello. Billy knew that the success or failure of the independent distributor system he had planned for Blue Rhino would depend largely on the speed and quality of the company's communications and information systems. Blue Rhino would have to know, and know immediately, about the thousands of transactions occurring daily at independent distributor sites throughout the country.

This would require a state-of-the-art system simple enough to allow drivers delivering the cylinders to punch information into devices small enough to hold in their hands. It also would have to be sophisticated enough to synthesize information into data that would provide corporate headquarters with instant and accurate numerical snapshots.

Billy gave Travatello a choice: he could work for Blue Rhino full time to develop a company information technology system, or he could work full time with Platinum Rotisserie. Travatello sensed that something big and exciting was about to occur. He opted to go with the herd.

Billy knew it was crucial for him to get a system of independent distributors under contract, trained, and operating as soon as possible. If that didn't happen quickly, the opportunity to build an instantly recognizable brand using the Blue Rhino logo would be lost.

One of his first actions was to hire Joe Culp, who had been in charge of Suburban Propane's northeast regional operations, and make him Blue Rhino's vice president of distributor development. Daryl McClendon, the National Propane Gas Association director who became a consultant for Billy, found Culp and recommended him to Billy. Culp's job was to build a national network of independent distributorships. These would be run by people, usually in the propane business already, who would refurbish, refill, and distribute Blue Rhino cylinders to retail stores that Rick Belmont and his team of salespeople seemed to be signing up by the dozens daily. A few months later, Chris Holden became Culp's assistant.

Billy had given Holden a choice in 1994 of either joining Blue Rhino as a director of operations or helping manage American Oil and Gas, the family business in Boonville. Because Blue Rhino would require a lot of traveling and he and Luanne were beginning their family, Holden decided to stay with American Oil and Gas. In 1996, with the family started, Holden was ready to go with Blue Rhino when Billy again presented him with the choice.

Holden brought valuable experience with him. He had helped to manage a traditional propane business, like those operated by the people he and Culp hoped to recruit as independent distributors for Blue Rhino.

Just as important, or more so, Holden knew intimately the problems and challenges of setting up a cylinder exchange business. He had done just that, largely on his own, with American Cylinder Exchange. He had refurbished and refilled the cylinders, hauled them to the stores, and placed them in the display cages, which he had put in place after dealing with the store managers. Holden had done it all.

Culp and Holden knew the ups and downs of the propane business. They knew business was slow from May to September, the most popular months for grilling, and that propane business owners would most likely be interested in a business opportunity that would utilize their equipment, trucks, and drivers during the spring and summer. Culp and Holden talked their language and understood their problems, and Holden could tell them in detail about the cylinder exchange business.

Holden and Culp hit the road together for the first time over the Fourth of July, 1996, the peak holiday for grilling and the beginning of the slowest month of the year for the heating oil business. Culp had already signed up several distributors, beginning with Dixie Gas in Bolivar, Tennessee, and they hoped to add to the list as steaks, hamburgers, and hot dogs sizzled on grills across the country—or didn't when backyard chefs ran out of gas.

They started in the Northeast with a call on Tri-State Gas in Delaware, and then headed west to the center of the country with stops in St. Louis at Bolton Oil and Gas, and in Sikeston, Missouri, home of Reliable Propane. They explained to business owners what they would have to invest—trucks, refurbishing and painting equipment, and so on; and what Blue Rhino would supply, which included training, a brand name that would become nationally recognized, and a national sales force.

"I'd explain what I did with American Cylinder Exchange and how good it had been for us," Holden said. "All of a sudden, I'd see a spark in their eye, and they'd say, 'Hey, I can do that!'"

Holden's first solo call was on Dave Goss with Goss Gas in Reno, Pennsylvania, a picturesque community of about five hundred, ninety miles north of Pittsburgh on the banks of the Allegheny River. When Goss signed up, Holden and Culp notified the Blue Rhino retail store sales force that there was a distributor who could call on and service stores in the area.

Culp and Holden recruited independent distributors from North Carolina to California and from Florida to New England. When they signed them, they turned them over to either Dave Slone or Dick Arthur for training. The training took at least a week, and they were on call if distributors had problems.

"Flight attendants knew us by our first names," Arthur said. "There was one in Pittsburgh who always had a cinnamon roll especially for me."

They logged an incredible number of miles on the ground, as well, sometimes to places so isolated that their presence was a topic of conversation. Arthur knew he was a news item in a tiny town in the center of Missouri when he stopped to ask for directions. It looked like a town out of the old West, he remembered, with four or five buildings and a grain elevator. The town was so small it wasn't even on Arthur's rental car map.

Arthur was wearing a coat and tie, which set him apart from everyone else. When he walked into the post office, one of the locals looked him up and down and said, "Why, you must be the man here to see Dennis from that Blue Hippo place."

It was important that any glitches or problems with new distributors be solved quickly before they spread to other sections or caused permanent damage. Often when a flaw or recurring error was spotted at the corporate level, Slone, Arthur, or one of the other field workers would be asked to help solve it. Arthur was once asked to perform a special favor as he prepared for a training mission to Goss Gas in Reno, Pennsylvania.

Bob Travatello, who was in charge of Blue Rhino's information technology systems at the time, told Arthur that a driver had been sending data to company headquarters that didn't make sense. Drivers were required to send information to company headquarters when they delivered cylinders to retail locations. Some rudimentary knowledge of math was required.

This fellow was doing something wrong, and it had to be fixed. He was skewing the figures for Reno. Arthur was the perfect person to solve the problem. He had once taught seventh grade science and math. As coincidence would have it, he had taught in the Reno area.

"You're the man, Arthur," said Travatello. "Straighten this guy out. Teach him what his teacher didn't."

Arthur was excited as he waited in the room where he was going to tutor the man. "I was going to straighten out this guy who had really been messing up bad. Well, in he walks, and he stops short. 'Why, Mr. Arthur! Hello!' I'd been the guy's seventh-grade math teacher."

Arthur made sure his student got it right the second time around.

By the fall of 1996, Billy was feeling good about Blue Rhino. The tension over the way the company should be structured evaporated when Jerry Callahan left. Culp and Holden were on the road signing up one new independent distributor after another—so fast that Slone and Arthur, who trained them, had long backlogs. A nice problem, Billy would say.

Rick Belmont and his sales crew were burning up the roads, too, and chalking up some impressive numbers. By November, Blue Rhino cylinders were on display and available for exchange at more than three thousand locations in twenty-one states—a thousand more sites than in November of 1995. Those sites accounted for more than $500,000 in sales in November 1996, almost $300,000 more than the previous November.

"We're starting to grow like a weed," Billy said. "Sales are really improving. With this new model, the economics are so much better. I can visualize. I know what my overhead is and how many cylinders I need to deliver in a month to break even."

Billy and each of Blue Rhino's approximately one hundred employees were still basking in the flattering light of invaluable publicity the company received in August when the nationwide newspaper *USA Today* published a story that described Blue Rhino as trying to establish itself as "a national brand leader."

The article, which was picked up by other newspapers, quoted Billy describing how he came up with the Blue Rhino image and logo as he was taking a picture of a rhino when he was on the safari in South Africa:

"Then I imagined a bright blue rhino with a bright gas flame. I figured it could do the same job for us that the Pink Panther does for Owens-Corning."

The *USA Today* story noted that some 33 million gas grill owners in 1996 were using about 1.4 cylinders of gas per year. The average refill cost was $12.99. That meant the market was worth about $700 million, and it was growing by 20 percent a year. Billy's ebullience was evident.

"If I could just capture the growth market, that's $140 million a year."

There was a major problem preventing Blue Rhino from capturing that market, however. The company couldn't build distributorships fast enough. It didn't have the capital. A lot of its money was already tied up in equipment—trucks, cylinders, display cages, and so on—at the distribution locations built before going to the independent distributorship model.

Billy needed to expand as quickly as possible before the big propane companies, such as AmeriGas and Ferrellgas, which had already taken notice of brash and bold Blue Rhino, decided to cut him off. And Billy knew they could, and probably would, do just that.

One way to obtain the capital to grow would be to take Blue Rhino public—and realize his dream. But Billy could see a potential roadblock to Wall Street. He knew that investors would not be interested in a small distribution company with high capital needs. He believed strongly, however, that investors would be attracted to a company that concentrated on marketing, branding, and transactions, while its independent distributors managed the capital-intensive business of purchasing trucks, trailers, cylinders, and other necessary equipment.

It was in late fall 1996, when Daryl McClendon, still living in Chicago and working as a consultant to the propane industry, received a call from Billy. He wanted to take Blue Rhino to "another level," McClendon recalls Billy telling him. Would McClendon meet with him and CFO Larry Brumfield to talk about getting there?

Intrigued, McClendon said, of course. They met for lunch at McClendon's golf club.

Billy told McClendon that he wanted to build another company, called Platinum Propane, which would be a distributor for Blue Rhino in important areas such as the Carolinas, Georgia, and Florida, where Blue Rhino had invested heavily in refurbishing centers and equipment. Other potentially lucrative areas, such as New York and Chicago, would also be part of Platinum Propane. The new company would get all the assets Blue Rhino had invested in these locations, such as refurbishing plants in Boonville, Georgia, and Florida; tanks; trucks; and other equipment. But it would also get Blue Rhino's debt. This would allow Blue Rhino to focus its time and money on growing locations, a crucial factor in getting the company to the size and scale that would support a nationwide enterprise and ensure a successful initial public offering.

Billy told McClendon that Platinum Propane would focus on the high-growth areas. It would be a cylinder exchange company, and nothing else. It, of course, would benefit from the Blue Rhino name and logo, and the services of the Blue Rhino sales, marketing, and technical professionals.

Platinum Propane would be entirely separate from Blue Rhino, although it would have some of the same investors. McClendon would also be welcomed as an investor—especially if he would agree to be Platinum Propane's president and CEO.

"Daryl, I need somebody to run this company," said Billy, "and I can't think of anyone more capable than you. Are you interested?"

McClendon was interested. "Billy's a great optimist, and he could sell ice cubes to Eskimos. But even so, I saw a great opportunity here."

McClendon wrapped up his consulting business and went to work as president of Platinum Propane. The first item on his agenda was to help Billy, who was board chairman, to raise money for the new company.

Initial major investors included some of the original investors in Blue Rhino—Billy and Flip, Dick Hardin, and Craig Duchossois. Billy and McClendon also made presentations to investment groups in the Chicago area. David Doerge, a former Goldman Sachs investment banker who started his own firm, Doerge Capital, headed a group that invested about $3.5 million. McClendon invested $500,000, and later, as Platinum Propane continued to expand into new markets, he invested another $400,000.

Within a year, McClendon had nine distributorships working hard and growing under the Platinum Propane banner, including a company called Ark Holding that Platinum Propane managed. Ark Holding had locations in several mid-Atlantic and northeastern states and parts of Colorado and Utah. Although Platinum Propane managed Ark, it remained a separate entity under a separate group of investors.

Platinum Propane also included distributorships that covered the Carolinas, Georgia, Florida, Chicago, New York, Los Angeles, Arizona, and Seattle. Platinum Propane leased property from Blue Rhino in Florida and Los Angeles and built a plant in Chicago.

Braxton "Bud" Kiger, who had been with Blue Rhino almost from its beginning, and was director of the crucial core Carolinas distributorship before it became part of Platinum, remained in charge of the Carolinas. McClendon staffed other centers with Blue Rhino people, who easily made the transition, or with people he knew through his many years in the industry.

As its distribution centers came on line in major urban areas such as Chicago, Phoenix, and Los Angeles, Platinum Propane, focusing only on cylinder exchange, secured larger and larger chunks of those lucrative markets. By late 1997, there were more than fifty distribution centers in the

Blue Rhino system. Platinum Propane represented nine of those.

It wasn't long before Platinum Propane became a major growth engine for Blue Rhino—exactly what Billy had intended it to be. It allowed Blue Rhino to shed debt and other costs and freed it to concentrate only on expanding and servicing its retail customers and its growing system of independent distributors. It also allowed Blue Rhino to become profitable quickly.

Craig Duchossois admired the move for its boldness and imagination. Billy, who had only recently abandoned the vertical or centralized ownership business model in order to survive, decided that he needed to integrate that model in certain key areas. He did it a different way, however, using another company to establish a presence and control in those areas.

"It made a lot of sense," said Duchossois. "Sometimes you have to tweak your strategy, and Billy was willing to do that."

Later, outside forces, some of them seemingly bent on destroying Blue Rhino would question the propriety and ethics of the relationship between Blue Rhino and Platinum Propane. But in 1996-97, as more and more backyard barbecue aficionados were becoming acquainted with, and liking, Blue Rhino, it soon became apparent that Platinum Propane would supply much of the fuel as the Blue Rhino flame spread across the country.

When distributors finished their initial training under Arthur or Slone, they were turned over to a Blue Rhino business development director for long-term nurturing. The business development directors, or BDDs—Jeff Dean, Mark Zimora, Terry Gadberry, and Tom Richens—acted as permanent liaisons between independent distributors and Blue Rhino.

Ultimately, it was the distributors—people such as Bill Tipton in Lubbock, Texas; Steve Huffstetler in Sikeston, Missouri; Janice Williams in Bolivar, Tennessee; and dozens of others across the country—in whom Blue Rhino staked its reputation. If they didn't do their jobs, Blue Rhino would suffer.

It was very much to Blue Rhino's benefit for its independent distributors to succeed. If they needed financial or business advice, a BDD would see to it that they got it. If they needed more training in Blue Rhino computer technology, they got it. Or if they needed some heavy lifting and long-distance driving for twenty hours straight, or more, to install displays across Texas or Minnesota, well, a BDD would be available for that, too.

Jeff Dean was on the road for four years, cheering, cajoling, and working side-by-side with Blue Rhino independent distributors. Billy had hired Dean in 1994 to be general manager of American Oil and Gas. He and Chris Holden, who was in charge of distribution there, became friends. Holden came to Blue Rhino about nine months after Billy sold American Oil and Gas to Suburban. Dean followed a few months later when Holden told him about an opportunity to join the team of business development directors.

After training from Dave Slone, Dean was ready to hit the road. His territory extended from North Carolina to New Mexico, although he was often called into Texas, and as far south as Puerto Rico, where Blue Rhino served customers through an independent distributor in San Juan.

Dean loved his job, despite the travel and long hours. He liked the independent distributors who made up the network Holden and Culp were rapidly building. Most were competent, hardworking people who welcomed the chance to make money and avoid laying off workers during the slow time of the year for their home heating businesses. And they liked Jeff.

Soft-spoken and patient, their tall, easy-going teacher was eager to improve their businesses. All he asked was that they be willing to work with him as long as it took to do the job. Sometimes that was asking a lot—especially if they were working in say, New Mexico or Texas, where Blue Rhino locations were far apart on desert highways that stretched forever before disappearing into shimmering waves of heat.

Sometimes, especially when just beginning with Blue Rhino, distributors were strapped for cash and unable to hire the drivers needed to service their Blue Rhino cylinder locations. "Or they might have taken on additional stores when they didn't have the money to expand," Dean said.

That was apparently the case with Bill Tipton, who operated a Blue Rhino independent distributorship in Lubbock, Texas. Some of Tipton's locations, which were scattered over three hndred miles or more of central and west Texas, hadn't been serviced for weeks. His retail customers were getting more than a little antsy when Dean called to offer a suggestion.

"I said, 'Bill, you rent a truck, and I'll go with you and we'll set 'em up. We'll stay as long as it takes.'"

Tipton rented a truck and trailer, and the two men loaded them with cylinders, colorful Blue Rhino signs, decals, and other items. They left Lubbock at six in the morning and began setting up displays and filling cages with cylinders. Fortunately, they packed plenty of signs and decals because a trailer door latch slipped open and littered miles and miles of a Texas highway before Dean and Tipton noticed the Blue Rhinos swirling in their wake.

They set up nineteen locations before sitting down wearily to eat a late-night dinner at a greasy spoon in Iraan (pronounced Ira-ann), a Pecos County town of about 1,200.

Then Tipton pointed the truck toward Lubbock, about 250 miles north. A couple of hours later, Jeff, sleeping fitfully and probably dreaming of flying Texas-size rhinos, was jolted violently awake. The truck and trailer were careening through the Texas badlands. Tipton had fallen asleep and run off the road.

"Hey, Bill!" Dean yelled over the bouncing, bumping truck and trailer.

"Pull over and let me drive a little bit."

When Dean pulled into Lubbock, it was four o'clock in the morning, twenty-two hours after they had begun the day.

Problems seemed more numerous in Texas, or maybe it was because it took so long to get from one problem to the next. It helped if you had some company, especially when something went wrong. Like the time Tom Richens picked up Slone and Dean at the Dallas-Ft. Worth Airport in a rental car. Tom took a wrong turn on a side road and tried to correct things by driving over the highway median. He tore out the whole underside of the car.

Dean was part of another larger-scale aid mission when he and BDD team members Terry Gadberry and Mark Zimora, along with Holden, flew to Minnesota to assist a distributor who had about a hundred display locations that needed setting up. They rented trucks, went to work, and had them operational in five days.

As Holden, Culp, and the BDDs scurried around the country recruiting and nurturing independent distributors, Rick Belmont was collecting, compiling, and studying data that would tell them which area of the country to concentrate on next. When the distributors came on board, Belmont supplied them with lists of retailers in their areas who were potential Blue Rhino customers. Belmont traveled as much or more than the BDDs, as he searched for the best retail sites in every region of the country. Then he supplied his sales team with the results of his market studies.

Belmont worked with everybody—Culp, Holden, and the other operations people; his sales force; the independent distributors; and the retailers. He also talked with consumers exchanging their cylinders as he examined Blue Rhino displays in his and Billy's ongoing quest to build brand awareness.

As Blue Rhino's growth increased from a wobbly walk to a clumsy, lumbering trot, and on to a full-fledged charge, a natural friction developed between operations—those who recruited the independent distributors, helped set them up, and nurtured them—and the salespeople, who recruited retailers to buy the cylinders and allow distributors to set up Blue Rhino exchange cages. Both groups worked in teams as Blue Rhino built its network of independent distributors and retail customers across the country. Culp and Belmont conducted weekly phone conferences with the teams.

"We could hear the bickering in the background," Belmont said. "Operations would say, 'He's not selling the account.' Then, from sales, 'I can't sell because you won't deliver.' Sometimes it got a little hot."

But people were too busy building Blue Rhino to stay angry. "You can't hold a grudge when you love what you're doing," Belmont said. "And everybody loved what they were doing." So much so that people readily volunteered to work during big outdoor grilling holidays, such as Memorial Day and the Fourth of July.

"If someone was needed in Texas, you can bet that a clerk here at corporate would volunteer."

Belmont often rode the display routes himself with independent distributors.

"We were a family. We might bicker sometimes, but we were growing and pulling together."

That kind of side-by-side, in-the-trenches work led to some long-lasting relationships, personal as well as professional, between Blue Rhino employees and independent distributors. Each distributor was special, said Holden, who estimated that he recruited between twenty and twenty-five of the approximately fifty-three independent distributors Blue Rhino had contracted with by late 1997. He enjoyed working with all of them, some because he just liked the people and others because he respected their business operations. "They were all different, with their own personalities."

But Holden, Dean, and others who recruited and trained independent distributors during Blue Rhino's formative years agreed that the most unusual personality probably belonged to Dixie Gas of Bolivar, Tennessee, Blue Rhino's first independent distributor, also known as "The Dixi Chix."

Dixie Gas Co. is owned by Janice and Ben Williams, who have operated it in Bolivar—a town of about 5,800, approximately seventy miles east of Memphis—since the early 1970s. Ben's father started the company in 1957.

The couple, especially Ben, loved animals—exotic birds, chickens, ducks, cats, and other creatures that flew, walked, or crawled, including a pot-bellied pig spray-painted blue who answered to the name, "Rhino."

Customers often would see these creatures flying, walking or crawling in, out, and around Dixie Gas.

Ben is a collector who "just can't say no," Janice said. When he bought ducks or guineas or whatever, "the salesperson would tell him to buy some extra because some will die, but they never died."

In January 1996, Janice Williams was filling in for her husband's secretary, who had resigned, when an ad in the trade magazine *LP Gas* grabbed her attention. It was a Blue Rhino ad calling for independent contractors to operate propane cylinder exchange businesses.

"I thought cylinder exchange was a great idea. I could see as a female that it was all about being a convenience for women. And we were looking for something to get us through the summer."

She answered the ad, and in a few days, Culp and Dean arrived in Bolivar to iron out an agreement.

Blue Rhino's first independent distributorship was its most colorful for certain. Parrots and macaws chattered with customers. Some said one could say "Blue Rhino," but Williams said she wasn't sure. Chickens occasionally walked in if a door was left open. A sign on the counter read, "Eggs for sale."

Ben had a pet python that Holden said was kept locked in a room away from the chickens and other birds.

"I never saw it," Holden said. "I never wanted to see it."

Rhino, the pot-bellied pig, was a favorite. Williams said her husband accepted the pig as payment from a couple who didn't have the money to pay their gas bill.

"Like I said, Ben never could say no."

The chickens and other fowl apparently did not give rise to the "Dixi Chix" sobriquet, although they might have had some influence. The nickname referred to Janice and her bookkeeper, Mary Gomez, a no-nonsense woman described by her bosses as someone who "spoke her mind whether you liked it or not."

The women spelled their moniker differently from that of the popular singing group because they didn't think the "real Dixie Chicks would like it very much."

If Dixie Gas and the "Dixi Chix" stood out as the most colorful among Blue Rhino's expanding independent distributorship system, it soon became apparent to Blue Rhino business development managers that Reliable Propane in Sikeston, Missouri, and American Propane in Oklahoma City were two excellent examples of well-run business operations.

When Joe Culp visited Reliable Propane in 1996, Steve Huffstetler, general manager and one of the owners of the company, didn't have to listen long to realize that Reliable and Blue Rhino would make a good fit. Reliable already had a small cylinder exchange business going in Sikeston, a city of a little less than seventeen thousand about 146 miles south of St. Louis.

"We had a hundred accounts, maybe a few more," Huffstetler said. "It was time to get bigger or get out."

Huffstetler could see that Blue Rhino had, or was about to get, what Reliable needed to get bigger, but could not get on its own—a national sales force, technical expertise, and, perhaps most important, a brand image.

Huffstetler's instincts were correct. Using what he called Blue Rhino's "cutting edge" knowledge to reduce distribution and production costs while "emphasizing and excelling at safety," Reliable's cylinder exchange customer base grew to almost 1,500 in a few years, branching out from Sikeston to include most of rural Missouri and parts of adjacent states.

Huffstetler watched, fascinated, as Billy did what he said he was going to do—build Blue Rhino into an image recognized across the country.

"That's what he set out to do, and he did it. Now I hear people say, 'It's time to get another Blue Rhino.'"

Huffstetler said much of Blue Rhino's success occurred because Billy "put the right people in the right seat on the bus. And he expected them to make mistakes. When they did, he would say, 'Okay, now that you know where the hole is you can go around it.' Yes, the Blue Rhino mix was good from the beginning."

It also was good for Jim Grigsby and his partner, Herb Hampton, at American Propane in Oklahoma City, which also had a cylinder exchange business

"We started one when we saw people were willing to pay if they could just hand us their old tank, get a full one right away, and head off down the road," said Grigsby.

But American's customers were limited to those in and around Oklahoma City, and mainly in their own small convenience stores and service stations. Grigsby said he and Hampton realized immediately that Blue Rhino was offering "a chance to get on a train that we didn't want to miss." They knew there was no way that American Propane could, on its own, marshal a sales force that could rein in all the big box stores that Blue Rhino could get.

"We knew that if we didn't get on the train, somebody else would, and we didn't want that to happen."

The ride across Oklahoma was a little slow at first. "Everything was so labor intensive, more so here because we're so rural," Grigsby said. It could easily be a two hundred-mile trip to service one display cage. "There was a lot of windshield time." But with Blue Rhino's administrative and techno-logical support, especially in the areas of computer and communications tech-nology, the American and Blue Rhino Express rounded a curve after about three years, and took off. It's been making money ever since, Grigsby said.

Beyond the profits, however, the relationship with Blue Rhino has been fun. Grigsby said he'll never forget a Blue Rhino distributor convention in Las Vegas when the former Chicago Bears football great Mike Ditka was the motivational speaker. Grigsby remembers Ditka coming across as extraordinarily enthusiastic. That probably was because Ditka spoke to the group shortly after he and Billy soundly defeated Peer Pederson and his partner on the golf course. Ditka, in addition to his speaker's fee, won a sizeable bet. "We waxed them," Billy said.

Ditka, who was staying in a VIP suite at the luxurious Bellaggio Hotel and Casino, had to leave Las Vegas immediately after his speech. Billy and Debbie, who were also staying at the Bellaggio, had heard Hampton say how much he would like to stay at the Bellaggio some day. Debbie offered the suite to Hampton and Grigsby.

"I'd never seen anything like it, and I haven't since," Grigsby said. "They asked us if we needed anything, and I said a beer might be nice. In a few minutes, a waiter brought the best beers from all over the world. I picked one and he opened it, and said he'd be back in about ten minutes to open another one for me. And that's the way it was, anything we wanted when we wanted it. I hadn't known you could live like that."

His and Hampton's relationship with Billy and Blue Rhino was eye-opening from the beginning. Grigsby marvels at how Billy can spot an opportunity and seize the right moment to turn it into reality. "Billy's philosophy is, 'If you can think it, you can do it.' And he's always thinking."

A Path to Profitability

Billy knew that the best distributors in the world still need detailed information from points of sale at the retail locations in order to route trucks and make certain they arrive before customers are out of stock. He also knew that would require an extremely sophisticated information system capable of recording and analyzing the detail from transactions at every one of those locations.

The system had to be smart enough and fast enough to take figures supplied by drivers from thousands of locations in the field and transcribe them instantly into information to be used to accurately bill customers such as Wal-Mart, Sears, Lowe's and Home Depot. Some of those major retail giants were getting so they wouldn't consider doing business with any company that didn't have a system that could provide this rapid and accurate information.

Billy knew he couldn't hope to expand nationwide without such a system. And, needless to say, there was no point in even dreaming about going to Wall Street without a world-class information system firmly in place. That would be something deep-pocket investors would insist on. Once in place, it would be a major selling point when the time came to urge those investors to reach into their pockets. Blue Rhino operations and salespeople had already been promising a high-tech information system as they recruited distributors and retail store customers.

In late 1995, Billy asked Bob Travatello to develop a hand-held computer system for drivers. Travatello accomplished that task, which included teaching the system to Dave Slone, Dick Arthur, and others who trained the distributors. Travatello had that system up and going by late spring of 1996, and it worked well—certainly far better than the system Blue Rhino had been using, which consisted mainly of pencil and paper and the telephone.

But by May 1996, Blue Rhino was in three thousand stores in twenty-one states, a fraction of the number of locations Billy envisioned. Billy wanted a system—and Wall Street investors would expect such a system—that could accommodate many times that number, a system that could just as quickly and smoothly work for three hundred thousand locations as it could for three thousand.

"I had been preaching all along about how we were going to use cutting-edge technology to keep track of things out in the field and to bill customers," said Billy. "The trouble was, it was going to cost about a zillion dollars."

Billy needed to find a company that already had such a system in place and would be willing to assist Blue Rhino in establishing one, or at least share the knowledge of how to do it.

As luck would have it, there was a company right next door, and Billy was on good terms with its key people, including its chief technology officer. It was the R.J. Reynolds Tobacco Company, the second largest cigarette manufacturer in the country, and its chief technology officer was Marvin Martin. Billy talked with Martin and learned that R.J. Reynolds had a system that allowed it to manage cigarette displays for major retailers throughout the country. Billy knew that if the system worked for R.J. Reynolds and its cigarette displays, it could be customized to work for Blue Rhino and its propane cylinders.

"I said, 'Marvin, this sounds exactly like the kind of system Blue Rhino needs. I'd like to buy the rights to it.'"

"Let me run it up the flagpole," Martin said.

The flag went up without a hitch. R.J. Reynolds would do more than sell Blue Rhino the rights to its information technology system. The tobacco giant was inviting Billy to use its newly established consulting arm, Information Management System Services, to which he could outsource vital tasks such as building and writing a database and code for the new system.

And there was more, Martin said. Billy was welcome to hire, as a permanent key employee, the young woman who helped develop and put in place much of the system at R.J. Reynolds. She understands it as well as or better than anyone, Martin said. Her name was Kay Word.

She and Martin were dating and planned to marry soon. Word had worked for R.J. Reynolds for ten years. She was secure in her job as director of sales force communications, for which she was paid a six-figure salary. But R.J. Reynolds had hundreds of executives at the director level. She had often wondered what it would be like to help build a company—to know that her work and decisions really mattered and to be able to see their impact.

"That's something that everyone who works in business management dreams about," she said.

Her dream sharpened into focus when she talked with Billy. "I loved his idea. I loved the concept. I knew I could build the system he needed and make it work."

Billy liked Word's can-do enthusiastic attitude. "She was smart. I could see right away that she really understood our needs and how to build the system we needed." Billy offered her the new position of vice president of information systems at Blue Rhino. She accepted, and a few months later, in 1997, she and Martin married.

Kay Martin was struck by how laid-back and casual Blue Rhino was, compared to the conservative corporate atmosphere at R.J. Reynolds, yet how passionate employees were about building Blue Rhino into a national company. She knew that Blue Rhino's atmosphere and passion emanated from Billy.

"I thought he was charismatic," she said. "His vision appealed to me. People wanted to work for him. I wanted to work for him."

There was a moment that defined Billy's personality to her that Kay Martin will always remember. It occurred just before an important meeting of Blue Rhino executives and bankers. Everyone except Billy was seated around a conference table in the board room.

"We were all set to begin," she said. "The bank associates were there, and we were ready to answer their questions. It was all very serious. Then I heard—we all heard—this whistling just as the elevator doors opened. The whistling continued all the way down the hall to the conference room, and then in walked Billy still whistling a tune. It was marvelous. No matter what, he was always relaxed and casual. His demeanor was laid-back. Without a doubt, he was the most unusual person I have ever worked for."

Martin especially liked Billy's managerial style. Her experience at R.J. Reynolds had taught her that ranking executives expected written plans, position papers, and so on, after they gave orders. Not Billy.

"If I told him that I'd put something together on paper and get back to him, he would say, 'No, Kay. Just get it done. Come back to me if you need something.' That was refreshing and appealing to me, and so different from what I had been used to. I came from an environment with so much red tape that it could take years to get something done."

But Billy didn't have years to get a world-class information technology system in place, one that would attract the institutional investors he needed to take Blue Rhino to Wall Street. He figured he had maybe a year or less before the big traditional propane companies would realize the financial potential of what he was doing and try to wrest it from him.

In January 1997, Blue Rhino hosted its first independent distributor conference in Clemmons, a bedroom community about ten miles west of Winston-Salem, North Carolina. The theme of the conference was ideas and how idea-sharing would bring success to everyone associated with Blue Rhino. Billy told the distributors that they and Blue Rhino were building partnerships that would develop into full-time businesses for many of them. Blue Rhino was committed to helping them succeed, he said, and a major element in realizing that success would be the world-class information technology system that Blue Rhino had already begun to build.

Kay Martin was Blue Rhino's first female executive. "It was just Billy and the boys and me," she said, laughing. "Everyone was wonderful to me from the beginning, and that's the way it stayed." Though attractive and friendly, it was Martin's obvious competence and knowledge of her job that impressed her new colleagues and employees. As vice president of information systems, she was Bob Travatello's boss, and the two clicked immediately. "We hit it off right away," Travatello said. "She's very genuine. We worked side by side and always had great rapport."

When Martin joined the company, Blue Rhino and its independent distributors were using the system Travatello developed. The hand-held computers he introduced, though seemingly almost revolutionary at first, had become "big, bulky, and archaic," Martin said. They were also unreliable. Every night two people in Martin's department downloaded the day's information from those hand-helds, or tried to. "They would sit there for hours at a time, and there were always constant problems and issues."

Martin knew that it would take much more than new hand-held computers to fix Blue Rhino's problems, although people were telling her that's all she would need.

"Most people said just buy new hand-helds and everything will work. I knew that wasn't so, and I had to do a lot of convincing. People didn't understand that new hand-helds, no matter how good they were, couldn't do the job we needed done now and in the future, especially in the future, unless we built a database first."

That meant gathering information, writing codes and programs, devising a new accounting system, and developing software for an information technology system that would serve seven thousand customers right away, but with the capability of serving hundreds of thousands in a few years.

Martin didn't have to convince two key people of the importance of building a completely new information base. Billy had anticipated that necessity. That's why he hired Martin. And Flip Filipowski, vice chairman of Blue Rhino's board, certainly knew that a complete makeover would have to be accomplished.

Martin was aware of Flip's almost legendary reputation in the software industry. He had started Platinum Technology just ten years earlier, in 1987. Now, it was a billion-dollar company and the eighth-largest software company in the world. Sometimes Flip would sit down and ask her questions about how the work toward a new system was going.

"Now, that could be a little intimidating," she said.

Martin and Travatello called the new information system they were building "OASIS," for Online Accounting Sales Information System, and they worked toward it as eagerly as thirsty travelers heading for an oasis in the desert. They contracted with outside vendors, including R.J. Reynolds' consulting arm, Information Management System Services, to write the database code, prepare the new accounting system, and distribute the new hand-held computers. They were ready for Billy to unveil OASIS at the distributor conference in Orlando, Florida, in January 1998. Billy also announced that, as part of the new system, Blue Rhino was giving each distributor a computer. "We'll train you on this new system, and it's free," Billy said. "This is what you get when you go with Blue Rhino."

Kay Martin planned and supervised the building of a state-of-the art information system that—when Billy sensed the time was right—would allow Blue Rhino to capture the attention of Wall Street and the investing public. Martin stayed with Blue Rhino only two more years. She left in late 1999 or early 2000 to care for her husband who had become ill with cancer. Marvin Martin died in 2002. Kay Martin said her years with Blue Rhino were some of the most challenging and enjoyable in her life.

Billy sensed in the summer of 1997 that the time was almost right for Blue Rhino's debut on Wall Street. "I could smell it," he said.

Wine lovers are proud of their ability to identify the aroma of fine wine. The best journalists can sense a story, a talent some describe as "a nose for news." The best entrepreneurs have a nose for Wall Street.

Wall Street was getting hot in the summer of 1997, and the rising temperature had nothing to do with the weather. It was all about money. "The public market was getting hot, and I could feel it," he said.

Billy didn't have to go to Wall Street to detect the rising financial temperature. It was considerably hotter that summer—as in millions of dollars hotter—in Blue Rhino country than it was a year earlier. Blue Rhino sales topped $6 million in that summer quarter, twice the amount for the summer quarter of 1996. Blue Rhino tanks were in five thousand stores, two thousand more than midsummer, 1996. Billy's instincts told him the time was getting right to invite the public to share in Blue Rhino.

First, however, Billy needed a CFO to help him lead the company to Wall Street. Larry Brumfield left Blue Rhino in 1997, and Billy began searching for a new CFO in the summer. Daryl McClendon told Billy he knew the perfect person. He was a young man who had worked for McClendon at Skelgas in Chicago. His name was Mark Castaneda.

Anyone who met Mark Castaneda in the 1990s knew he was headed in one direction—up. Those who knew him or had worked with him, including McClendon and Joe Culp, sang his praises. He would be an excellent choice for Blue Rhino's CFO, they said— smart and especially knowledgeable about the public markets and the financial side of business, with just the right mix of ambition and a strong work ethic. Castaneda wanted to take a company public almost as much as Billy wanted it.

There was something else, too, something not quite tangible but it was present, nevertheless, and it would be a desirable quality, indeed, in the company's chief financial officer. Castaneda gave the appearance of being a person of high character and trustworthiness. People who met him could not imagine him taking the company on a financial track unless it was strictly straight and narrow.

At the same time, he was fun-loving and outgoing.

"He was just a great guy," said Abbye Caudle, Billy's executive assistant. "Mark was always pumped up and excited. He could take a negative situation and make it a positive."

If there was anything at all that might make someone think twice about making Castaneda a chief financial officer, it would be the initial impression he gave. Some, before they talked with him, might think he was too young to guide a company through the wilds of Wall Street. He was only thirty-two in 1997, but his boyish face made him look younger, and his exercise regimen—he was a long-distance runner—kept him trim.

Castaneda was CFO of All Star Gas in Lebanon, Missouri, when Billy called. He wasn't interested. What he knew about Blue Rhino told him it wouldn't be successful. His company was selling bulk propane, four hundred gallons at a time.

"Joe Culp told me they were handling four gallons at a time. I thought all that handling would cost too much money, and that you would have to charge too much."

Also, he was absorbed in the task of taking his own company public. There were problems, not of his making, and he didn't want to leave at such a crucial time.

But Billy, the consummate salesman, was persistent. He called again in July, when it was obvious it was going to be impossible for Castaneda's company to go public at that time. Billy told him he wanted to go public, too, and that he thought Castaneda was the CFO to get him there. Castaneda agreed to meet with Billy in Kansas City, about a three-hour drive from Lebanon.

His first impression of Billy was that he had a "pretty thick accent."

"My second: 'This is a very sharp guy.' He understood a lot more about the financial aspects than I expected. He struck me as being a positive person, even visionary. I didn't think he would be a micromanager."

Castaneda also liked the fact that Billy wore his hair long at the time. "Well, relatively long. For a businessperson, I thought that was kind of cool. I liked him."

But Castaneda turned Billy down. "I still had reservations. Blue Rhino was still a pretty small company, and it had never made a profit. I wasn't sure it would ever make a profit. I just didn't think it would work. It was too risky for me. I told Billy that it wasn't right for me at that time."

Billy wasn't about to give up. So far as he was concerned, he had met his CFO, and he sensed that Castaneda, with a little nudge in the form of numbers, would climb on board on his own. After another series of phone calls, Castaneda agreed to meet with Billy again in September, this time in North Carolina. Castaneda never really had a chance.

"I'm more of an analytical person," he said. "I needed to hear the numbers, and Billy was able to give them to me."

Billy gave them to him at a beautiful setting, Billy's and Debbie's lake house on the shore of Lake Norman, not far from Charlotte. Billy walked him through the long-term plan for Blue Rhino.

"It was absolutely compelling," Castaneda said. "What was really compelling was the trend, and Billy had the data."

Castaneda watched and listened, almost mesmerized, as Billy pointed to a chart showing Blue Rhino locations and expected locations. Billy gave him the numbers on how many gas grills were already out there and needing their propane cylinders serviced regularly, and how many were being sold each year. Already, there were more gas grills sold than charcoal, and there was no doubt that the trend would continue. The numbers proved it.

"He's telling me that people are going to pay for the convenience of exchanging cylinders, and he's already lining up the stores all over the country. He says it's a no-brainer for the retailers, and he makes me see that. It's hassle-free; the tanks sit outside the store and don't take up shelf space. They don't have to order them. We do it for them. It's great for the consumer and great for the retailer."

Billy told Castaneda that each time a Blue Rhino consumer visited the store to exchange his cylinder he bought a "market basket" of goods totaling about $45. "And he comes back time after time."

Billy's knowledge and command of his data and passion for Blue Rhino impressed Castaneda. "Billy had his numbers, and I started to believe pretty quickly that Blue Rhino was going to work. He impressed and converted me, and I agreed to come on board."

Castaneda came on board running; in fact, he was running before he came on board. In September, shortly after he agreed to become Blue Rhino's chief financial officer, he met Billy's board of directors in Chicago and heard Billy deliver a venture capital presentation. The presentation solidified Castaneda's belief that he made the right decision to join Blue Rhino and that the company would make money.

"Billy made a lot of sense. Everybody was going to make money."

The key, which quickly became apparent to Castaneda, was Billy's decision to change Blue Rhino's business model to one in which the company leveraged off its independent distributors. "Instead of building infrastructure, Billy said why not use the infrastructure our distributors already have, and, for that matter, why not use the cylinders a lot of them already have?" Changing the business model saved Blue Rhino, Castaneda said. "Otherwise, the company would have run out of money."

Castaneda's first official day with Blue Rhino was October 17, 1997. It was also the date of Blue Rhino's first meeting on the road toward its initial public offering, or IPO—the first step in Billy's quest to take the company public. When Castaneda walked into the room, he saw three dozen or more people seated around a big conference table. They included accountants, investment bankers, market analysts, securities specialists, and at least two sets of attorneys. Some were associated with three investment banking firms Billy had chosen to take Blue Rhino public: Hambrecht & Quist of San Francisco and New York; NationsBanc Montgomery Securities, also head-quartered in San Francisco; and Dain Rauscher Wessels out of Minneapolis, but with offices on the West Coast.

Billy's intuition told him that growth capital would be more obtainable on the West Coast, home to Silicon Valley and many emerging small-cap, growth-oriented companies. Billy had put out feelers to investment bankers on the East Coast, but they thought Blue Rhino was too small.

"And we were small," Billy said. "Our trailing year we had just $14 million in sales, and we lost money." The East Coast bankers wanted to see what they called a "path to profitability."

The West Coast investment bankers Billy selected also wanted to see that path, but for them it could be somewhat narrower so long as it showed a strong likelihood of growth. It would be their job to sell Blue Rhino to all the major institutional investors in the country. First, however, they would perform "due diligence," the process of scrutinizing a company from top to bottom to ferret out any potentially embarrassing or damaging problems, including liability issues, that would preclude or prevent the IPO. Hambrecht & Quist, headed by Dan Case, would lead the IPO, assisted by Montgomery Securities and Dain Rauscher Wessels.

Due diligence revealed a potential problem, one that could deter investors. The company had been coming up short in its revenue projections. "For example, if our forecast for the quarter was $6 million, we would actually realize only $4 million," Castaneda said. "We were consistently short in our forecasts. This is a cause for concern. You can't have that when you go public."

The investment bankers delayed the process for a quarter. That meant it would probably be spring before Blue Rhino could even hope to charge down Wall Street. That was a setback, but it allowed Blue Rhino's controller, Kurt Gehsmann, to make some adjustments in revenue forecasting.

Billy also used this time to make Blue Rhino more attractive to investors by acquiring Bison Propane, a cylinder exchange business in Wichita, Kansas, owned by C.J. Lett, a wildcat oil driller Billy came to know and admire. The stock transaction netted Blue Rhino more than a thousand new display locations, and Billy purchased about five hundred more locations in Tennessee and Alabama. On January 1, 1998, four Blue Rhino directors—Flip, Craig Duchossois, Len Carlson, and Jim Liautaud—loaned Blue Rhino $3.25 million to purchase these new locations.

A few weeks later, Blue Rhino took a major competitive step by investing in a small Illinois company called Bison Valve, owned by Michael Waters, who had developed a safety valve that would prevent the overfilling of propane tanks. The federal government had placed the industry on notice that by April 2002, all cylinders would have to be equipped with an OPD, or overfill prevention device.

Blue Rhino loaned Bison Valve, which was not affiliated with Bison Propane, $635,000. It was the first step toward acquiring the company and placing Blue Rhino in a position that would allow it to manufacture its own OPDs, and produce and sell them to the entire industry. It was a selling point potential investors could appreciate.

Early in 1998, the investment banker team took another look at Blue Rhino, and liked what they saw. Gehsmann's adjustments improved the accuracy of the company's quarterly forecasts, and the foundation was there for excellent numbers to back up those forecasts. Castaneda filed Blue Rhino's prospectus with the U.S. Securities and Exchange Commission in February.

He followed that up in March with a press release announcing that Blue Rhino had filed a registration statement with the SEC regarding the company's plans for an initial public offering of 2.7 million shares of common stock, with an offering price expected to be about $13 a share.

The public announcement, more than anything else, underlined and emphasized Blue Rhino's intention to go public. The press release stated that net proceeds from the offering would be used mainly to pay off outstanding indebtedness, and as working capital. It said some proceeds might also be used to pay for new acquisitions. Castaneda advised in the release that copies of Blue Rhino's prospectus could be obtained by writing to Hambrecht & Quist LLC, NationsBanc Montgomery Securities, Inc., or Dain Rauscher, Inc.

The prospectus is a required legal document that includes facts and details about a company that are immensely important to investors. The prospectus describes a company's potential; it also provides investors with some idea of the risks of buying a company's stock. It must clear the SEC before a company is allowed to proceed with its public stock offering.

The SEC examined Blue Rhino's prospectus for a month and responded in mid-April with a list of more than fifty questions and additional requirements. Finally, by May, the SEC was satisfied, and Billy and Castaneda prepared to embark on an exhausting, two-week sales presentation that would take them to investment houses in cities throughout the country. It was time for the "road show," the last leg of a long journey toward a dream Billy had begun many years before in Yadkin County. In two weeks, if all went well, that dream would become reality when the road show closed on Wall Street.

Blue Rhino headquarters at 104 Cambridge Road in Winston-Salem is in the heart of the Atlantic Coast Conference—arguably the most exciting college basketball conference in the nation. Tournament time in March and April brings an excitement that people who haven't experienced can't quite understand, as fans focus their attention and support toward one of the four major college teams in the area—Wake Forest Demon Deacons, University of North Carolina Tar Heels, Duke Blue Devils, or N.C. State Wolfpack. The intensity and passion can build to a level that, by opening tip-off, is almost palpable.

That was the kind of excitement building at Blue Rhino as it became apparent that sometime in the spring Billy and Castaneda were going to take the company public. By May 1, as they were about to start the road show, the atmosphere at Blue Rhino was as electric as the air in Winston-Salem's Lawrence Joel Coliseum before a Wake Forest-Carolina basketball game. It was a fantastic time, said Chris Holden.

"It was like working to get to that championship game, a time of great excitement. Everybody is working and pulling together, and we're almost there. Most of us had been in the workforce before. But I don't think anyone had experienced this feeling."

The excitement intensified as May 4, the date for the beginning of the road show neared. Billy and Castaneda spent their days like athletes in training for a final championship run. Billy wanted to leave as little as possible to chance. He wanted to know who he would be talking to at each of the sites in the dozen or more cities he and Castaneda were about to visit.

Did they represent a hedge fund? Mutual fund? What were their likes and dislikes, and what about Blue Rhino might they particularly like or not like? Would tactics and strategy employed in Dallas work in Los Angeles and Boston?

Billy even hired a public speaking coach. He and Castaneda practiced before the coach and before each other. When Billy went home, he practiced before Debbie.

Meanwhile, Abbye Caudle worked with Hambrecht & Quist, preparing schedules and itineraries that would take Billy and Castaneda across the country and back with dozens of breakfast meetings, lunches, and dinners along the way.

She was also busy searching for and buying Tender Tails—Tender Tails Rhinos, that is. To be precise, they are called Precious Moments Tender Tails

Yadkin County Sheriff Bill Moxley and Chief Deputy Loyd Prim empty jars of illegal moonshine in 1948.

Billy at 20 months with his father, Dean Prim.

Billy's grandmother, Mae Moxley, with her daughter, Mayo Prim, Billy's mother.

Billy at 15 with his father, Dean Prim, sisters Jeannie and Luanne, and mother, Mayo Prim.

Eric Wagoner and wife, Sharon.

Billy and Don Angell toast the opening of Quick-Pik II.

Boonville cylinder refurbishing plant; Moxley home is at left

Chris Holden

Chris Holden hauled cylinders in this trailer for American Cylinder Exchange, forerunner of Blue Rhino.

American Cylinder Exchange display

Chris and Luanne Holden

Former N.C. Gov. Jim Martin with Billy at the Bing Crosby Celebrity Golf Tournament near Winston-Salem, N.C.

Billy and Tom Austin team up for the Bermuda Run Classic.

Dick Hardin, Ray Maynard, and Billy

Andrew "Flip" Filipowski, wife Veronica, and daughter Alex

Billy and Flip

Rick Belmont

Craig Duchossois

John Muehlstein

Peer Pederson

Bob Travatello and son, Connor

Billy and his management team at NASDAQ on IPO day. L to R, Billy, Tom Ferrell, Rick Belmont, Joe Culp, Mark Castaneda, Kay Martin, and Jerry Shadley.

NASDAQ celebrates Blue Rhino on its IPO.

Mike Moe of Montgomery Securities, later of Merrill Lynch, congratulates
Billy on IPO day.

Billy and Debbie with Daryl and Irene McClendon, left, and Darrel Reifschneider at the
World LP Gas Forum in Rome, October, 1998.

Abbye Caudle

Susie Simpson and former Vice President Dan Quayle
at the Dean Prim Classic in 1998.

Malcolm "Mac" McQuilkin, Dick Hardin, and Don Angell.

Luanne and Chris Holden with Kiti Maile, the late golf pro and Polynesian entertainer at Walt Disney World in Orlando.

Jack and Patty Denman, Blue Rhino distributors from Dallas, at distributors conference in Orlando, 1998.

Bud Kiger and Mark Castaneda at distributors conference in Orlando, 1998.

State-of-the-art R-4 Technical Center cylinder refurbishing plant in Yadkin County, N.C.

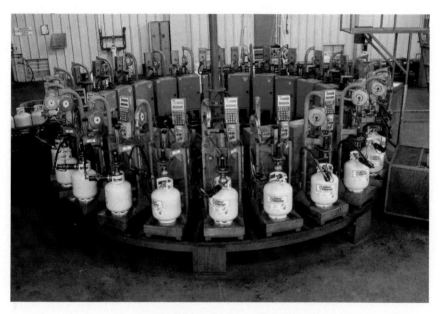

R-4 Technical Center refilling carousel

More than 3 million cylinders a year are refurbished at the R-4 tech center.

Dave Slone is General Patton and the theme is "United We Stand" at the
2002 distributors conference in Greensboro, N.C.

Billy, Debbie and the family at daughter Sarcanda's wedding in May 2002.

NASDAQ invited Billy to open trading on July 3, 2002, because
Blue Rhino was one of its best performing stocks.

Billy and Richard Brenner

Dana Reason, Miss North Carolina 2003, presents Billy with the Ernst & Young Entrepreneur of the Year Award.

Debbie and Billy with Xander Bellissimo, their first grandchild, born in 2004.

Jim Ferrell

Blue Rhino's Board of Directors on Feb. 9, 2004, when it merged with Ferrellgas. L to R; Mark Castaneda, Richard Brenner, Billy Prim, John Muehlstein, Andrew "Flip" Filipowski, David Warnock, and Steve Devick.

Rhinos. They are little stuffed rhinos, perfect for a baby's bed—white with blue horn, blue feet, and a blue tail. A Blue Rhino employee brought one to work one morning, and a light bulb went on in Caudle's head.

They would be perfect to give investors on the road show—"precious little mementos of Blue Rhino to keep on their desks." She scoured Hallmark shops, which carried the baby rhinos, in cities across North Carolina and Myrtle Beach, South Carolina, and bought every one she could find, hundreds of them. Then she packaged them and had them shipped to the road show sites so they would be there for Castaneda and Billy to distribute to their audiences.

Those first audiences were in Houston and Dallas—big cities in a state renowned for Big Oil, Big Barbecue, and, Billy and Castaneda hoped, Big Money. "Starting in Texas was by design," Castaneda said. "It's a big grilling state. We wanted to start in a place where we could grab some momentum."

And grab momentum is what they did, Castaneda said—although it probably wouldn't have mattered where they began the road show because Billy gave a great performance no matter what city they were playing. That was extraordinary, Castaneda said, because the road show was a grueling, numbing cross-country task.

Beginning May 4, when the two traveled to San Francisco for meetings with Hambrecht & Quist and NationsBanc Montgomery Securities, Billy and Castaneda conducted forty-seven meetings in fourteen cities in eleven days. They were accompanied by Abby Adlerman, managing director for corporate finance at Hambrecht & Quist's San Francisco office. Their days usually began at 8 a.m., or earlier, with a breakfast presentation, and ended late at night, often in another city, sometimes in another time zone.

Castaneda provided Blue Rhino's financial history and outlook. "I gave them the historical financial numbers, and then what our balance sheet would look like after the IPO. And then I showed them our target numbers. I talked about five minutes and answered any questions they might have, and then Billy told the Blue Rhino story."

Billy had two main props—a rusty and battered propane cylinder which looked unsafe to refill and re-use, and a shiny, clean, safe- and sturdy-looking Blue Rhino cylinder.

"It was a simple story, and he used that to our advantage," Castaneda said. "He presented it as a problem that had a solution, and Blue Rhino was the solution. It was a compelling story, and Billy, who is a great storyteller, made it even more compelling." Not only that, but Billy was able to tailor the Blue Rhino tale to individual audiences.

"He matched the presentation to the people at the meeting," Castaneda said. "In Los Angeles, for example, there was a person who had been talking about NASCAR, apparently a racing fan, so Billy used NASCAR terms during his presentation. It was fun to watch."

Castaneda watched again in Salt Lake City as Billy told the Blue Rhino story at a breakfast meeting of officials of the Church of Jesus Christ of Latter Day Saints. Near the end of his talk, Billy commented on the extraordinary beauty of the famous temple at Salt Lake City's Temple Square.

"Would you like a tour of the chapel?" one of the officials asked.

A tour would be wonderful, Billy said.

At the end of the tour, the official pulled Adlerman aside. It was her job to take orders for the IPO from investors. Billy and Castaneda watched as she recorded the church's sizeable investment order.

"Well, Mark, I'm going to take that to be a good sign," Billy said. "The Lord must be on our side."

Once again, Billy had tailored his talk and connected, Castaneda said. "They thought, 'Hey, this is a great guy. Let's show him our church.' I saw him do this day after day, and he seemed to have just as much charisma and energy at the last meeting as he had at the first."

A few days later in New York, Castaneda watched in awe and amusement as Billy, still fresh after a marathon series of presentations to Wall Street investors, tried to sell the Blue Rhino idea to a New York City hot dog vendor.

"A hot dog vendor! Can you believe it? A little more time and he might have had all the hot dog vendors in Manhattan using Blue Rhino."

But Castaneda knew that Billy was being energized by more than a road show, and that he was selling far more than shares in a company he had started. Billy was asking people to share in his dream. It was a dream that was so close it was almost real.

Billy and Castaneda ended the whirlwind road show by flying back to the West Coast to tell the Blue Rhino story to investors over breakfast at the Mandarin Hotel in San Francisco on Friday, May 14. They were running on little more than adrenaline when they finally returned home late that evening. There would be little time for rest and recuperation, however. The IPO was scheduled for 10 a.m., Monday, at the NASDAQ building in Times Square.

First, however, there remained an important chore to be accomplished, and that was for a committee to set the opening price of Blue Rhino stock. Members of the pricing committee included Billy, Castaneda, Flip, and Steve Devick. The goal from the beginning of the road show was to create demand by attracting enough investors to oversubscribe to the number of shares initially up for sale, which was 2.7 million. When Castaneda filed the IPO plans with the SEC, he announced that the offering price was expected to be between $12 and $14 a share. The committee decided on $13, at the advice of Hambrecht & Quist.

"At 13, it's way oversold," Billy said. "When it goes public, the guys who ordered 50,000 are just going to get 25,000. They're going to want to come back the next day and buy more at 14. That's the way the price goes up. You create demand."

Billy had a good feeling about number 13. Debbie was born on September 13. "That's my lucky number," he said.

Monday, May 18, 1998, dawned clear and beautiful—perfect weather for flying to New York for an IPO and realizing a dream. "It was a glorious day," he said. "It was like God had made it just for me."

Billy, accompanied by Debbie and his Blue Rhino management team, flew to New York in a private jet he had chartered for the trip. The group included Billy, Debbie, Castaneda, Belmont, Culp, and Martin—key people who had performed and directed tasks critical to Blue Rhino's development. Also present were Tom Ferrell, manager of product procurement and services who Billy later promoted to vice president, and Jerry Shadley, who had just become vice president of sales when Billy asked Belmont to concentrate solely on the crucial area of marketing.

"Billy was on top of the world," said Rick. "We all were. It was an incredible sense of accomplishment."

Billy was nervous, however. After all, as he had reiterated to Castaneda during the road show, he had looked forward to this day for many years. It was the day that he would be the first person from Yadkin County whose company was traded on Wall Street. Billy did not want anything to go wrong.

His mind eased a bit as he led the group to the NASDAQ building on Times Square and into the trading room. Billy laughed and applauded with the others when he saw how NASDAQ officials had celebrated their presence by decorating the big trading board with electronic blue rhinos with flaming horns. A NASDAQ photographer snapped their photo in front of the rhino-dominated board. Then a bell rang to start the trading and numbers raced across the big board—but no numbers signifying Blue Rhino shares.

"What's wrong?" Billy thought to himself, as he tried to appear confident and relaxed. Fifteen minutes passed, and Billy was suffering. Surely, something had gone wrong despite their hard work and meticulous planning.

Then a Blue Rhino logo charged across the board, followed by a stream of rhinos until the board was ablaze with them, and the room erupted in cheers as Billy struggled to maintain his composure.

Debbie and the entire group were jumping up and down and screaming as the numbers went from 13 to 14 and steadily higher.

"It was fantastic," Castaneda said. "I was in awe. Right there was the Blue Rhino logo with companies like Microsoft, Intel, and Yahoo, some of the largest and most respected companies in America. I thought Bill Gates must have felt like this when he went public. It was the kind of feeling I had when I went to Wrigley Field for the first time as a kid—I was in the big leagues."

NASDAQ officials popped open a bottle of champagne and presented Billy with a bull-and-bear statue. Billy, his eyes wet with tears, thanked his team and Blue Rhino employees and investors, and promised not to let them down. Everything after that was enveloped in a happy fog.

NASDAQ took the Blue Rhino team to lunch. Restaurant diners applauded when they were introduced as representatives of the newest member of NASDAQ.

Billy and his team returned home late that afternoon. It had been the day of his dreams. That night, as he drifted into a deep sleep, he was filled with thoughts of his father and grandfather. They had given him the self-confidence to build Blue Rhino and take it public on capitalism's greatest stage. Although Billy felt they were always with him, he had especially felt their presence today, and he knew they were immensely proud.

In less than a year, he would need them like never before.

King of the World

Blue Rhino was in the big leagues now, and that was both good and bad. With the prestige of being a publicly traded company came certain disquieting and often stressful responsibilities that never went away. Now, Blue Rhino had to perform for the public.

Not only that, but it had to meet or surpass quarterly projection numbers. If not, the company's stock values would fall, and Blue Rhino's relationship with the public, so harmonious now, could turn as sour as barbecue left out in the hot sun all afternoon.

"Going public was great," said Rick Belmont. "But there was apprehension, too. Now, our neighbors owned us."

No one knew this better than Billy. The IPO had generated more than $35 million, "plenty for a young, lean company ready to grow."

"Now that we're public, we have to figure out how to perform," Billy said. "How are we going to put all this money to work and do what we told people we could do?"

Billy decided to search for answers to those questions with his management team in Boca Raton, Florida.

The National Propane Gas Association's annual convention would be held there the following week, so Billy could link the two sessions, which were held at an Embassy Suites during a scorching two weeks in June about a month after the IPO.

Billy and the team would leave Boca Raton with the foundation for a strategic plan that would take the company from its position as mainly a regional player to one that was truly national, and whose rhino logo would be recognized instantly anywhere in the country. More importantly, the team members would forge a powerful bond in Boca Raton that would serve them and Blue Rhino well in troubling days to come. It was a meeting unlike any the team members had ever experienced, and one they would not forget. For some, it was a life-changing experience.

Billy had them "do their life-lines," as he called it. Basically, he instructed them to bare their souls to the group and to include all—the good, the bad, the sad, and the ugly.

"I said, 'Guys, we're in this together. We need to know each other and where we're coming from. If we're going to be a team, everybody on this team needs to know everything about you. I don't care how ugly your past was. I want you to share it openly.'"

Team members looked askance at one another. "I think we were taken aback at first," Kay Martin said.

Jerry Shadley, who had just joined Blue Rhino from McCulloch Corp., the chain saw company, was a few years older than most members of the team, and had participated in his share of executive retreat group sessions.

"I really didn't care to do anymore," he said.

But he never had participated in one quite like this one, in which the chief executive began with a story that would deeply touch everyone.

Billy told his team how close he was to his father and grandfather, how the three of them worked side-by-side in the family business, and how they taught him basic business values, beginning with hard work, honesty, and trust, and instilled in him a love of American capitalism. Billy's eyes reddened as he told them about his father dying so young from a heart attack, and how he, at nineteen, halted his college education to lead the family business with his grandfather and mother. He described his cherished relationship with his ailing grandfather, and tears welled as he told about the terrible morning that Pa Moxley committed suicide.

Those who had known Billy for any length of time knew he was sensitive and caring, but they also knew him to be a private person. This was a side they had not seen, and it had a powerful effect. Kay Martin described it as "almost scary."

"It was incredible," said Rick Belmont. "I get chills thinking about it."

"I thought that if I could be open, honest, and willing to share my feelings, then others on the team would be willing to open up and share things," Billy recalled. "I thought it was important to show them that I could be trustworthy and honest enough to disclose some very difficult things about my personal life. Bonding as a team is so powerful, but to do that you can't keep secrets from each other."

Billy's story, and the emotions he shared in telling it, profoundly affected his management team. Members broke down and wept together as they told deeply personal and emotional stories that some had kept bottled up for years. Jerry Shadley said the session was "good for the soul," and allowed him to deal with issues that he had not been able to verbalize until then. He said he believed the exercise was instrumental in his decision later to become a Christian.

"It was good for us personally and good for the company," he said.

The session allowed Billy's top management to bond as a team when Blue Rhino was about to embark on a year of tremendous growth.

"It was so important because we were taking this huge step, and we needed to take it together," Billy said. "We needed to trust each other, and to know where everyone was coming from, and all our different perspectives that we were coming from. Boca Raton bonded us together as a team, and that allowed us to go out and create something special."

That powerful bond prompted team members to believe they could actually realize the goals they set for Blue Rhino during this remarkable strategy session. They set a short-term, five-year goal of a Blue Rhino presence in forty thousand retail locations and annual sales revenue of a half-billion dollars.

The team also laid the foundation and set the strategy for the company's ultimate goal—the pinnacle of Blue Rhino's growth strategy pyramid. It was such an audacious goal that team members later would call it just that: "Our Big, Hairy, Audacious Goal," or just "Bhag," for short. Simply put, the goal was this: a Blue Rhino in every backyard, patio, and home in the United States. That would mean every household in the country would be within a few miles of a Blue Rhino retail site. They had set an audacious goal, indeed.

Billy and his team, still flush with excitement from its IPO a month before, and united by a powerful emotional bond, returned home to a rhino "herd," as employees proudly referred to themselves, that was just as excited as the management team. The big, hairy goal might have been audacious, but there wasn't one of Blue Rhino's fifty-six employees in the summer of 1998 who was cowed by it or who didn't think that Blue Rhino, led by Billy, could ultimately achieve it.

That was because Billy's personality had permeated Blue Rhino. Employees had caught his boundless optimism and passion and made them the foundation of the company's culture. That was evident in the proud way they wore caps and t-shirts with the Blue Rhino logo. Employees, men and women, searched for rhino jewelry and knick-knacks on their days off and wore them or brought them to work. They collected so many different types, shapes, and sizes of rhino jewelry that they displayed them in a case in the lobby of the administration building.

Billy's personality and leadership made people—everybody—believe they were integral parts of Blue Rhino, Mark Castaneda said, and that generated a fierce loyalty to Billy and Blue Rhino. "People would climb walls and walk through fire for him," said Castaneda.

"Billy allowed employees to take ownership as if the roles they were playing in the company were in their own companies," said Lori Hall, Blue Rhino's investment relations manager. "He encouraged you to take risks and think outside the box."

And this sense of ownership, she said, went "hand-in-hand" with the development of a sense of loyalty. "You felt good about working toward one common goal: a Blue Rhino in every backyard, patio, and home. It was that simple. That was our charge, and we were driven to achieve it."

Work was fun, said Adrianne McCollum, who joined Blue Rhino in September 1994, a few months after Billy formed the company. "Billy made it feel like a family."

Family was important to Billy.

"He took the time to learn about what was going on with your family," said Judy Smith, who worked in sales. "He even came to my bridal shower."

It was fitting and comforting, the workers said, that someone like Billy, who loved and respected family, would start and head a company that depended on and provided a service for families having fun together at home.

"Billy made coming to work a joy," said Jeff Dean. "I fell in love with my job."

It was especially fun in that exhilarating time after the IPO. The company celebrated at—what else?—a cookout in the spacious, campus-like commons area at Blue Rhino.

"Stick with me," Billy said. "If Blue Rhino does well, you could become wealthy."

That did not sound at all like boasting in the headiness of the moment. In fact, for the rest of the year after the IPO, it seemed as if the public had adopted the cute little Blue Rhino logo as its own backyard playmate. At least, that's what the stock market seemed to be saying. The stock was a little sluggish at first because the world market was down, but it took off in the fall when Blue Rhino exceeded expectations by a penny a share.

Now that Blue Rhino was a public company it had to make quarterly public projections, and Billy and Mark conducted their first quarterly conference call with market analysts not long after the IPO. The analysts make these public projections based on the numbers given to them during the conference calls. These numbers are important to the stock's well-being.

"I didn't realize how important they were," Billy said. "If you're small, the little things can impact you. It doesn't take much. Fifty thousand or a hundred thousand can affect you by a penny a share. There's not a lot of wiggle room. When you know by the end of the third month that you've got your numbers made, life is so good, but there's so much pressure until then."

A large company isn't affected so much by small unexpected expenses, he said. "If you're large, unexpected expenses may not be material to your financial statements; whereas, in a small company, they are material. A small company has to be perfect."

And Blue Rhino was perfect in 1998. "What a hell of a year! Every time we had a call our stock would go up."

But despite the excitement and prestige, there was something else about being a publicly traded company that Billy didn't like one bit. Billy is naturally, and almost irrepressibly, optimistic. It's part of his personality and charm.

Ironically, however, when Blue Rhino went public Billy had to go private. Or at least he had to turn down his optimism by several clicks.

"When you're private, you can be as optimistic as can be," he said, almost wistfully, "but when you go public, your optimism can get you in trouble. You can get sued. I had to tone it down. Really, what you have to do is learn to just state the facts, and nothing else."

Employees were aware of Blue Rhino's performance in the market. After six months with the company, they were given five hundred stock options and had the opportunity to buy stock under the company's stock purchase plan. Most took advantage of that.

"It seemed we could do no wrong," said Abbye Caudle.

By their own choice, people worked days, nights, and weekends. "I was amazed," Billy said. "I'd come by at ten o'clock at night, and all the lights would be on. There would be people here holding meetings on Saturdays and Sundays. People were challenged and excited. It was an incredible year."

Blue Rhino needed nothing less than an incredible year just to remove a little hair from the Big, Hairy, Audacious Goal. Anyone less optimistic than Billy would have probably pictured "Bhag" as some kind of angry, hairy Big Foot. Not Billy.

Bhag was a challenge—wild and formidable, maybe—but a challenge to be met, and tamed. That would take a lot of hard work and teamwork, along with boldness, originality, and thinking outside the box.

These were qualities Billy looked for in his management team, and he found them when he hired Jerry Shadley away from McCulloch Corp. a little more than a week before the IPO. A vice president of sales for McCulloch, Shadley had a reputation for aggressive and innovative salesmanship, qualities that a new publicly traded company with a huge appetite for growth would dearly need.

Rick Belmont had done a great job leading Blue Rhino's sales department; he had taken it to where Wall Street was eager to invest in the company. But Belmont's passion was not in sales; it was in marketing. When Billy offered Belmont the chance to focus on marketing alone, he didn't hesitate to accept.

A glance at Blue Rhino's annual report for 1998 shows the company came a long way in 1997, and that Billy and his team had every right to be proud. Sales for the fiscal year, which ended in July, totaled $27.4 million, almost double the amount for 1997. Retail locations more than doubled, from 4,400 stores to 9,500 in forty-six states and Puerto Rico. Those were impressive figures, but they were nowhere near the numbers represented by the Big, Hairy, Audacious Goal—forty thousand locations and $500 million in sales.

"I would certainly call that a lofty goal," Shadley said.

So did everyone else at Blue Rhino, including Billy. That's why they were taken aback, to say the least, when the first action Shadley took was to fire ten of his best salespeople.

"I think Billy thought I had lost my mind," he said.

Bhag had not caused Shadley to lose command of his senses his first few days on the job. To the contrary, he was acting on experience. Shadley, who was fifty-one in 1998, was older than most of his colleagues at Blue Rhino, including Billy. He knew from his years in sales that salespeople could not perform at the highest level if they were not focused on the product they were selling and dedicated to the company they were selling it for.

Although the people he fired were competent, experienced professionals, their first allegiance was not to Blue Rhino. They were members of a manufacturers' representative group under contract to Blue Rhino, the group also represented Char-Broil, a major grill manufacturer in Columbus, Georgia.

"We were paying them a million dollars a year, but they were not focused on Blue Rhino. I wanted people who were going to be calling on a lot of places for Blue Rhino, and who would not be distracted by anything else."

Shadley changed the structure of the sales force in about ninety days by hiring and training a cadre of ten salespeople and assigning them to specific areas. "If we needed to focus on, say, Kroger's, I wanted them to know all about Kroger's. I want the right people for the job."

Shadley was fascinated to learn how Blue Rhino built its customer base. "I had never seen a company like this. They went after the biggest customers in the world first. Most companies go after the little guys, then the medium size dealers, and then the major retailers before they take over the world. Blue Rhino did it the opposite. They went after the big boys—Wal-Mart, Home Depot, Lowe's—the biggest in the world, and then worked backwards. This was unusual. But Billy made it work."

When that method worked, it worked well because it allowed Blue Rhino to grow rapidly. But it could also cause major setbacks when a "big boy" decided to pull out, and that's what happened shortly after Shadley sent his new sales force into the field for the first time.

"Things didn't go well at all," he said. "The very first call I received was from a Home Depot buyer. I knew him. He had endorsed me to Billy. But he said, 'Jerry, I'm sorry to have to tell you this, but I'm going to have to take back from you that Tidewater group of stores because you're just not delivering.'"

Shadley assembled his sales group to stop the bleeding. "We had to find out what we were doing wrong and how to stop this before it went across the board."

He learned quickly, as Belmont had learned before him, that it was critically important to work and communicate closely with operations to make certain that new customers could be serviced on time and as promised.

To prevent future customer cancellations like the Home Depot setback, and to provide a forum for sales and operations people to blow off steam from the natural and constant friction between the two departments, Shadley and Culp established regular "slugfest" meetings attended by everyone in the two sections. That was Shadley's name for the sessions. None of them erupted into blows, he said, although the comments could get a bit caustic.

Shadley or Culp would moderate each meeting. "If I was playing moderator, I might start things off by saying something like, 'I'm just sick and tired of so and so not dealing with this situation. Now what are you going to do about it, and when?' That would definitely get things going."

Someone in operations might respond that sales didn't know what was going on in the area he was talking about, and that sales needed to get its own house in order. Sometimes tempers flared. Operations once challenged Shadley and his salespeople who were dealing with Home Depot on the way the retail giant insisted that the cylinders be delivered. Sales needed to tell Home Depot to back off from its requirements, operations said.

That was ridiculous, Shadley said. "You're forgetting who's the dog and who's the tail. Home Depot is the dog; we're the tail. If you think you can tell a $20 billion company how it should do business with a $20 million-dollar company, then you get your butt on a plane and go to Atlanta."

At some point during the meeting, complaints such as that one would join a list of others that members of the two departments would examine to identify issues and problems that prevented them from working together and keeping promises made to Blue Rhino's retail customers.

"We would go around the room and ask, 'What are the ten biggest issues keeping you from getting the job done?' After looking at them for awhile, we might decide that there were really not ten, but just four. Then we would work on priorities and schedules from there."

Shadley and Culp defended their people to the hilt, said Jeff Dean, who, as one of the BDDs, attended the sales/operations get-it-off-your-chest session. But the two men respected each other, and it showed. The members of the two departments followed suit.

"Darts were being thrown all over the place," he said. "We would call a spade a spade, and I'm sure people walked out with their feelings hurt sometimes. But it was a healthy dialogue. They were growing pains. No one stayed mad."

Those meetings were crucial to letting off steam and working out problems, and Billy recognized that, Shadley said. "Billy enabled them to happen. He knew there were meetings going on where people were yelling at each other, but he knew they were necessary to work things out. And that's what he'd say, 'Guys, work it out among yourselves. You know what you have to do. We're all in this together.'"

He and Culp worked well together and each tried to accommodate the other. Shadley would let him know that he had targeted a particular store or group of stores. "Here is where I need to be in six months," he would say. "Can you be there?"

Culp wouldn't beat around the bush. It was either yes or no, but if it was yes, it was a good bet that consumers would be exchanging Blue Rhino cylinders at that new customer retail location within that time frame.

Shadley, even when he's sitting in a restaurant booth drinking coffee, emanates a kind of energy that says he'd rather be somewhere selling something. Selling is his passion. And once he got the kinks ironed out of the new sales structure he created, and when he and Culp learned to appreciate each other's style, Shadley began to satisfy his passion with a gusto that infected his sales force.

"We started to really rack up the numbers when Jerry came in," Kay Martin said. "He was selling and stirring and stormin' and normin' all over the place all the time."

The numbers back her up. Shadley joined Blue Rhino in May 1998. At the end of fiscal year 1999, his first full year on the job, Blue Rhino's total revenues nearly doubled over the previous year's, from $27.9 million to $53.8 million.

The fired-up sales force certainly added impetus to an already hard-charging operations group, which helped establish Blue Rhino at an additional nine thousand retail locations, almost doubling the number from fiscal 1998. As Billy said, Blue Rhino had "a helluva year," and Jerry Shadley was a big part of it.

By 1998, Blue Rhino had developed a reputation as a brash, bold, hard-charging company that was considerably more than just another flash-in-the-pan with a cute logo. The big, traditional commercial propane companies were taking notice. None had cylinder exchange businesses of any significant size or scale. Billy had eliminated the only major potential competition to Blue Rhino almost four years earlier when he acquired Suburban Propane's cylinder exchange program assets, along with a noncompete agreement from Suburban.

But Blue Rhino was attracting a lot of envious attention, and Billy sensed that the virtually competition-free smooth sailing Blue Rhino had enjoyed would not last. The giant of the industry, AmeriGas, the largest propane company in the country, had a cylinder exchange program with 3,500 locations. That was considerably less than Blue Rhino's ten thousand locations in the summer of 1998, but Billy knew that AmeriGas could be a formidable enemy.

That's why he wanted Blue Rhino at full speed, charging "ahead of the herd" as the company enjoyed the excitement and attention generated by the IPO. He wanted to take advantage of Blue Rhino's position while blunting any competitive moves AmeriGas, or any other company, might have in mind. The best way to do that was to add customers.

"Sell, sell, sell," said Shadley. "Locations, locations, locations."

New locations had to have new cylinders, but they were costly, especially for independent distributors who were just beginning their association with Blue Rhino. If the company was going to grow quickly, a way would have to be found to get capital to distributors. Much of the money raised from the IPO went to pay the company's $29 million debt. A big chunk of the remaining $7.5 million was earmarked for acquisitions.

Billy wondered if a bank or leasing agency might be interested in buying Blue Rhino's tanks and leasing them back to distributors. This would allow the company and its distributors to grow at a faster clip. Billy visited NationsBank, now Bank of America, and talked with bankers Skip Brown and Carlos Evans, who had worked closely with Billy and Blue Rhino.

The bankers said their leasing division would not be able to enter into a lease arrangement with Blue Rhino. The bank would have no way of keeping track of all the cylinders, their assets, as they went from home to home around the country.

"It just didn't fit in their box," Billy said. "But they really loved the idea. They said, 'Why don't you guys set up your own leasing agency, and we'll support the whole thing?'"

That's what Billy did. He, along with Flip, Craig Duchossois, and Peer Pederson, formed USA Leasing. The idea was for Blue Rhino to buy $6.5 million worth of cylinders from the distributors and sell them to USA Leasing for exactly the same amount. USA Leasing would then lease the cylinders to distributors. USA Leasing also bought cylinders from Platinum Propane—the company Billy created in 1997 to establish distributorships—and leased them back to Platinum Propane distributors.

The lease transactions were not listed on Blue Rhino's balance sheet. "That's because they belonged to a different company," Castaneda said. Other than a tax loss, Billy and the others received nothing from the deal.

"Because we're all owners of Blue Rhino, we can't make any money from it," Billy said. "We charged Blue Rhino the exact same thing the bank charged us. Because we own the tanks, we get the depreciation, the tax loss, but that's all. It was a great deal for the company, and helping the company was the right thing to do."

In other important moves connected with its cylinders during this time, the fall of 1998 and early 1999, Blue Rhino introduced its new FuelCheck cylinder sleeve with a built-in gauge that alerted the outdoor chef when there were only two hours of fuel left—an innovation that probably saved marriages. Billy also agreed to purchase the intellectual assets of Bison Valve, the small Chicago company owned by Michael Waters who had developed plans for an overfill prevention device.

The federal government was mandating that all propane cylinders be equipped with these safety valves by April 2002. Blue Rhino had first invested in Bison Valve a few months before the IPO with a $635,000 loan. In conjunction with that investment, Billy formed an alliance with Manchester Tank, the largest manufacturer of gas grill cylinders in the country, owned by his friend, Darrel Reifschneider.

These strategic moves, especially the creation of USA Leasing, allowed Blue Rhino to grow rapidly when it had to grow rapidly, Castaneda said. "Billy was building something that had never been built before. It was a new industry. There was no road map to get us where we needed to go, and no formula for what we were trying to do—not on this scale. The only solution was for Billy to do what he's really good at: be an entrepreneur and think creatively. That's what he was doing when he created USA Leasing, and that's what he was doing when he invested in Bison Valve."

It would not be long, however, before these actions, so creative, productive, and essential to the growth of Blue Rhino, would, in Billy's words, "blow up in our faces."

Blue Rhino settled into a smooth, sustained charge that showed no signs of abating during the summer and fall of 1998. Sales and operations—though there would always be a natural conflict between the two departments—communicated well with each other, and grew to respect and even anticipate each other's needs.

It's hard to think of a rhino spreading by leaps and bounds like a gazelle, but that's what Blue Rhino was doing. New locations were being created all over the country, at the rate of almost a thousand a month.

"It was so exciting," said Judy Smith, who worked in sales. "People would come back from vacation in other parts of the country and say, 'Hey, I saw your cylinders!'"

It seemed only fitting, then, that at the height of this incredible year Billy would introduce a product designed to keep it going forever—at least well into the chilly months. It was called, appropriately, "Endless Summer."

The product was a propane-powered patio heater, which used the same type of propane cylinder as a gas grill. Billy was sure they would provide what he called a "great counter-seasonal opportunity," along with a new class of customers, consisting largely of restaurants, hotels, and resorts.

The growing number of no-smoking restrictions and ordinances had sparked a demand for more comfortable outdoor facilities, which patio heaters could help provide. Individual outdoor chefs were also interested in the new patio heaters, seeing them as an opportunity to enjoy backyard barbecues well into the fall, and even year-round in some areas, such as sections of the Southeast, Arizona, and southern California.

Billy needed to look no further than one of his own distributors in San Diego to see the popularity of patio heaters and how lucrative a patio heater cylinder exchange business could be. That distributor, Chuck Dilts, owned a cylinder exchange business called Mr. Propane, which serviced about one thousand patio heaters in southern California.

Dilts began the business in 1992, out of sheer necessity. His forklift cylinder exchange business had failed, forcing him to live on the streets. Dilts took whatever work he could find just to survive. One job was to refill a restaurant's patio heater, and this prompted him to see if there was a similar need at other restaurants. There was. His first client was a pancake house. Other restaurants, bars, and resorts followed suit, and soon his business was thriving. Blue Rhino bought those accounts in 1998, a move that immediately put the company into the patio heater business.

Billy had the Endless Summer heaters designed especially for Blue Rhino and outsourced their manufacture. He would soon have them manufactured in China through Blue Rhino's Global Sourcing Division, which would allow them to be sold at prices attractive to consumers.

The popular patio heaters, with the perfect name for Blue Rhino, were immensely complementary to the company's rapidly expanding cylinder exchange business. They helped spread the Blue Rhino name and logo at a crucial time, and added a base of winter-time customers who would soon be sorely needed.

Life was sweet for Billy and the entire Blue Rhino herd in the fall of 1998. It got sweeter as the first quarter of the new fiscal year came to a close at the end of October and Wall Street responded to Blue Rhino's numbers. Blue Rhino reported income of $422,000 on sales of $9.2 million for the first quarter, which ended October 31. That translated into earnings of 5 cents per share, as opposed to a loss of 81 cents per share for the same quarter in 1997. The stock, which had lingered in the low-to-mid-teens because of a somewhat tepid world market, began a healthy and rapid rise.

Billy installed a screen to monitor the stock in the lobby of the administration building at Blue Rhino headquarters in Winston-Salem. "It was a popular place," said Abbye Caudle. "You caught yourself going out to see how it was doing. It was so exciting."

Billy reported those numbers in November during a presentation in New York by Montgomery Securities for investment bankers. It was about that time that Mike Moe, of Montgomery, who had worked with Billy to prepare for the IPO, was hired by Merrill Lynch, one of the largest, and arguably the most widely known, financial advisory and investment institution in the world. Moe headed Merrill Lynch's small cap group, which specialized in companies with small capitalization.

Moe told Billy that it was time Blue Rhino stepped up to the big leagues of the financial world, and that Merrill Lynch stood ready to escort them through the door. Moe was quite persuasive, Billy said. Blue Rhino stock was around $18 and climbing at that point.

"He said Blue Rhino belonged in the big leagues, and the way to get there was to let Merrill Lynch lead us in a secondary offering to raise more money while our stock was on the way up. Merrill Lynch would put its stamp on it."

Moe told Billy that Merrill Lynch brokers all over the country would be talking Blue Rhino stock. Merrill Lynch analysts would perform research coverage on Blue Rhino and issue reports on Blue Rhino stock. It sounded like a no-brainer, Billy said.

"With Merrill Lynch leading the way, how could we not win? Blue Rhino can just go on forever."

Billy invited Moe to talk to Blue Rhino's board of directors.

Moe spoke to the board in December, giving members the same optimistic sales talk he had given Billy: Blue Rhino was ready for the big time, and Merrill Lynch was ready for Blue Rhino. Just before Christmas, Blue Rhino stock hit $20 a share. Board members agreed that Blue Rhino should go for a secondary offering, but made no decision on which firm should lead the company.

On the day after Christmas, Billy, Flip, and Steve Devick, their friend and fellow Blue Rhino board member, took their families to Hawaii for New Year's and the following week. It was an extraordinarily happy holiday, especially for Billy. It had been a wonderful year, and everything indicated that 1999 would be even better.

The three friends and business partners agreed that, although Hambrecht & Quist, and Montgomery, too, had performed well for Blue Rhino, Mike Moe was right.

"It was time to step up," Billy said. "We all thought it would be great to go with a powerhouse like Merrill Lynch."

Billy got in touch with the other board members, and, during a conference call, they agreed that Merrill Lynch would lead Blue Rhino in a secondary public offering.

There was no holiday hangover or blues for Blue Rhino. The stock shot to $25 on January 2, and five days later, it hit its all time high of $25⅝. So far as Billy was concerned, this had to be the greatest New Year in history.

"Good Gosh Almighty, life was good!"

He and Flip strolled down to the Maui waterfront one morning, marveling at their good fortune and admiring the oceanfront homes.

"We were thinking how we ought to buy a house on Maui just to have a place to hang out. I thought I was king of the world!" Billy recalls.

"You'll Regret This Day"

Billy had to call Dan Case, of Hambrecht & Quist, to tell him that he and his firm would not be leading Blue Rhino's secondary offering. Billy and his board decided to offer H&Q a co-manager's role with compensation the same as Blue Rhino would pay Merrill Lynch.

A former Rhodes Scholar, Dan Case was considered by many to be a boy wonder of the financial world. Case had interned at H&Q during his undergraduate years at Princeton University, and the firm hired him when he completed his studies at Oxford. He rose quickly through the ranks, becoming co-chief executive in 1992 at the age of thirty-four, and CEO two years later.

Under his leadership, H&Q invested in, or was an underwriter of, about six hundred companies, including Genentech, Adobe, and Netscape. Another was Quantum Computer Services, which was run by his brother, Steve Case, and grew into America Online. *BusinessWeek* listed Dan Case as one of Silicon Valley's top financial power brokers. *Time* included him in its list of the Top Fifty Innovators in Technology. Dan Case was forty when H&Q managed Blue Rhino's IPO. Now, less than eight months later, Billy was about to tell him that Blue Rhino had tapped Merrill Lynch to lead it to Wall Street the second time.

Billy called Case from the airport on Maui. "I told him the board had decided to let Merrill Lynch lead, but that I had good news: H&Q would be co-manager, and we're going to pay H&Q the same thing.

"Well, man, he just hit the ceiling. He said he was sick and tired of taking companies public and seeing them run off to Merrill Lynch. He told me I would 'regret this day' unless I allowed Hambrecht & Quist to be the lead manager. He said he wasn't having any part of being a co-manager behind Merrill Lynch."

Billy said he took Case's comments "as a threat." He said Abby Adlerman called a short time later. Adlerman was the Hambrecht & Quist executive under Case who led Blue Rhino's initial public offering. She left H&Q shortly after the IPO to start her own company. Billy said Adlerman told him that Case was serious and would not "play second-fiddle to Merrill Lynch any longer."

Years later, Adlerman said she vaguely recalls talking with Billy, but that she does not remember who initiated the call. She said, however, that her purpose was not to emphasize that Case was serious about a threat, because, she said, "Dan would not threaten Billy or anyone. That was not his style."

Instead, Adlerman said her purpose was to emphasize that Billy should "realize the reality" of leaving H&Q for Merrill Lynch; that he ought to weigh carefully what would be gained by going with Merrill Lynch as opposed to what would be lost in Blue Rhino's relationship with Hambrecht & Quist. She said that H&Q, Blue Rhino's "primary friend and supporter," already had completed hundreds of hours of research into Blue Rhino and knew the company and its market extremely well. Blue Rhino was one of several hundred companies at Hambrecht & Quist. "At Merrill Lynch, it would be among thousands." Although Adlerman said she did not remember the specifics of her talk with Billy, these were the points she wanted to emphasize, she said. "I wanted him to consider the implications."

Billy was not alone in thinking Case was threatening Blue Rhino. John Muehlstein, Blue Rhino board member and attorney, certainly thought so. As Merrill Lynch began the due diligence process, Muehlstein continued talking with Case, still trying to get Hambrecht & Quist involved. Case would have none of it, Muehlstein said.

"He said he was not going to take this lying down, and that he intended to protect his turf." Muehlstein was flabbergasted. "I spoke to him very directly," he said.

Billy, meanwhile, tried to work things out until the last minute. "Essentially, we were going to pay them for nothing," said Castaneda. "I think it was all about ego. We couldn't believe anybody could be so arrogant. Billy just wanted it to work out, and for everybody to be happy."

But that was not to be.

On January 10, *Wall Street Journal* reporter Robert McGough interviewed Castaneda by telephone. "He was real positive," Castaneda said. "He said, 'Hey, you guys are really doing great!'"

A number of his questions focused on USA Leasing, the company Billy, Flip, Duchossois, and Pederson organized in October to buy cylinders from the company and lease them back to Blue Rhino.

The next morning, Blue Rhino board member Richard Brenner was scanning the *Wall Street Journal* headlines when he stopped abruptly at the "Heard on the Street" column on page B2. His jaw dropped, and his heart sank.

The headline read, "Blue Rhino's Complex Business Maneuvers May Put a Damper on the Red-Hot Shares."

Brenner, a highly successful Winston-Salem businessman, knew instantly that the headline itself would put a damper on Blue Rhino shares. But his concern was not just for the money that Blue Rhino and its stockholders could lose. It was for the company's reputation, and for Billy's.

"Billy is a man of so much integrity," Brenner said. "I knew this would hurt him deeply."

The story questioned the propriety of the USA Leasing transaction and that of Platinum Propane as well, and suggested that Blue Rhino manipulated its October report to inflate its earnings report and make its stock more attractive to investors in its secondary offering. It cited unnamed "skeptics" as arguing that USA Leasing allowed Blue Rhino to move "some of the burden of growing its business off its balance sheet, and (who) contend the stock is overpriced at 50 times projected earnings of 49 cents a share for the year ending July 1999."

One anonymous investor was betting against Blue Rhino stock, saying that the sale of the cylinders to USA Leasing actually masked "a negative cash flow of $3.4 million for the company's October 31 quarter."

The column quoted Castaneda indirectly as saying that Blue Rhino cylinders were sold to USA Leasing to assist distributors and free up their capital; that, otherwise, Blue Rhino wouldn't have held such a large inventory ($6.5 million) of cylinders. Referring to Platinum Propane, the article stated that Blue Rhino "insiders," in some instances, had "big stakes in distributors, as well." It noted that Billy and Flip "own 40 percent of a partnership (Platinum Propane) that accounts for 37 percent of Blue Rhino sales."

The column did not quote Billy directly, although it did note that "Mr. Prim says business with the distributors he owns is conducted in the same arm's-length manner as with all other distributors, and that he is taking on risk to help finance Blue Rhino's growth."

Castaneda read the column about the same time Brenner was reading it. He was shocked. This was no positive article, as the reporter had indicated by his demeanor and attitude that it would be. Castaneda saw almost immediately that the article implied that Blue Rhino was deceptively recording money from the cylinders to make it appear, shortly before a second public offering, that Blue Rhino revenues were higher than they actually were. Blue Rhino absolutely did not do that, he said.

"We were very open about what we did."

He was stunned at what he considered to be a slap at his integrity and reputation, as well as that of the entire company. Like Brenner, he knew this would hurt Billy. He picked up the phone to call him about the same time Brenner picked up his.

The phone rang about 7:30 a.m. at Billy's house. It was Brenner. His message was terse and to the point. "You better read the *Wall Street Journal*, Billy."

Then came a deluge of calls, beginning with Castaneda's.

"My day from hell had begun," Billy said.

It seemed as if the day would never end, and it got worse as it went along. Call after call came in—from friends wanting to know what was going on, from worried stockholders, from stockholders wondering if they ought to be worried, and from business writers wondering what was going on. As the day wore on, other publications and Internet business sites picked up on the column from the prestigious *Wall Street Journal*. Most, such as this one from *TheStreet.com*, were painfully sarcastic, unable to resist the gas analogy:

"Short-sellers are betting Blue Rhino could take on gas if investors were to focus on how the company reduced its inventory not long ago, thereby bumping its results before announcing plans last week to sell two million additional shares, today's Heard on the Street column in the *Wall Street Journal* said."

(The term "short-sellers" describes speculators who seek to profit from the decline of a security. Most investors buy a security, such as a stock, hoping that it will rise in value. To profit from a stock on the way down, short-sellers borrow it and immediately sell it, hoping it will decrease in value so they can buy it back at a lower price and keep the difference. For example, if the shares in ABC Corp. are at $20 a share, a short-seller would borrow one hundred shares and immediately sell them for $2,000. If the price of ABC Corp. falls to $10, the short-seller could buy them back for $1,000 and return them to their original owner, while pocketing a profit of $1,000.)

When Blue Rhino, listed as RINO, on the NASDAQ board, began the day January 11, 1999, it bore an impressive price of $24. The price fell quickly. By the end of the day, it had fallen $5\frac{5}{8}$, to $18\frac{5}{8}$. Billy soon found out why in a phone call from his friend, C.J. Lett, a Blue Rhino investor from whom Billy had purchased distributorships. Lett wanted to know what was going on. He told Billy that he had just received a call from his H&Q broker who told Lett that Hambrecht & Quist was dropping research coverage of Blue Rhino. Lett said his broker told him that Hambrecht & Quist was questioning some of Blue Rhino's actions, and that his broker advised him to put his money elsewhere.

Billy said brokers were being told essentially the same story that was in the *Wall Street Journal* column: "That I had a conflict of interest because I owned the distributors and USA Leasing and Platinum Propane, and Blue Rhino; that I was selling to myself and booking the revenue, and Blue Rhino's financials were not credible." It was just the day before, Billy said, that Dan Case hung up the phone after saying Billy would regret going with Merrill Lynch.

Craig Duchossois knew Case from having done a considerable amount of business with Hambrecht & Quist. Like Billy, he believed that Case planted the article, causing PWC, as he put it, "to do a one-eighty on Billy." As Duchossois watched Blue Rhino's stock slide, he picked up the phone and called Case.

"I said, 'Dan, you've got to help me. What the heck is going on, and what can we do? This is absolutely ridiculous. There's got to be something you can do.' Case said he believed he had been stabbed in the back, and he just couldn't tolerate it, and there was nothing he could do. But he said he had no idea how that article got in the *Wall Street Journal*."

Flip recalls Case and other Hambrecht & Quist people saying that Hambrecht & Quist would suffer few, if any, consequences if it retaliated against Blue Rhino.

"They said the amount of bad blood it would generate against them would be like that generated by a gnat on an elephant's ass. But it would create a huge example for anyone to see who might consider mistreating them like that in the future."

Yes, Billy said, "I do believe Dan Case planted that article."

However, Abby Adlerman, now the manager of a large executive recruiting firm in San Francisco, said it was "unimaginable" to her that Case would do such a thing. "He had too much integrity to do something like that," she said. "And it just wasn't his style."

Billy was furious with Case, but it wouldn't be long before his anger cooled, and he felt sorry for the man he believed sabotaged Blue Rhino after managing its initial public offering. A few months after the disastrous Heard on the Street column, Case, the man the *San Francisco Chronicle* dubbed the "scholar of venture capitalism," became ill with brain cancer. He died in June of 2002.

But in the days immediately after the article appeared, it didn't matter who planted the seed. Billy simply didn't have time to play detective; he was too busy concentrating on how to stop the bleeding. Blue Rhino was bleeding green—as in money—all over the big NASDAQ board. Billy turned to Merrill Lynch. Investors would surely listen to what the prestigious firm had to say about Blue Rhino. Billy and other board members urged Merrill Lynch to issue its own report to counter H&Q's sell recommendation.

"I said, 'Please, people are losing millions of dollars.' I was losing money. But, more importantly, we were getting ready to sell stock to the public, and it's going to hurt the company to sell at a much lower price."

Merrill Lynch said it wouldn't be proper, and would perhaps even be illegal, to issue a rebuttal before the secondary stock offering. "But they told me not to worry," Billy said. "They said, 'We're Merrill Lynch, and people will listen to us.'"

As the phone rang incessantly and Blue Rhino stock continued to reel, Billy and Castaneda had to decide—in the midst of what felt like an attack by a hostile force—whether to go on with the road show.

"There were major questions we had to answer," Castaneda said. "Was our accounting wrong in some way? Should we still go for the offering?"

Billy and Castaneda felt strongly that Blue Rhino had nothing to hide or, for that matter, had nothing that had been hidden. They knew the USA Leasing and Platinum Propane transactions had been carried out and recorded in ways that were completely above board. They also felt strongly that they could answer any questions, and calm any concerns, investors had about the *Wall Street Journal* column. "We thought the stock would rebound once we got out there and told our story," Billy said.

He and Castaneda wanted to assure investors that Blue Rhino was the company of integrity that they had always known it to be, and they needed the capital that the $42 million offering would bring to ensure Blue Rhino could continue to grow.

Mike Moe, who was familiar with Billy's powers of persuasion, also expected the stock to rebound when Billy and Castaneda hit the investment capital houses. Moe and his firm's financial sleuths performed some extra due diligence, focused mainly on USA Leasing and Platinum Propane, and the suggestions raised in the newspaper column. "They checked out every allegation and found them to be false," Billy said.

Blue Rhino stock had dropped to about 15 when Billy and Castaneda started the two-week, cross-country road show in late January. It was a tense and stressful trip. Every investor at every stop had the *Wall Street Journal* column, often underlined and highlighted, and accompanied by a list of questions. But Castaneda and Billy were ready.

They made Blue Rhino's response to the column part of their presentation. Before the questions began, Castaneda explained to investors what USA Leasing was and why it was formed—which was to assist Blue Rhino distributors and free up their capital. He told investors that Blue Rhino realized "absolutely no additional revenue or gain" from the deal. Billy explained that neither he nor anyone else who helped organize USA Leasing made any money from it, and never expected to. He and Castaneda emphasized that their auditor, prestigious PricewaterhouseCoopers, approved the transaction.

Investors listened to what they were saying. And they did more than listen—they bought. Blue Rhino's stock halted its decline just before hitting 14, and began to climb back. Billy began to feel pretty good. Blue Rhino's second appearance on the Wall Street stage was going to be successful after all.

Jim Lattanzi, a partner in the Greensboro office of PricewaterhouseCoopers, called Billy and Castaneda when they were about midway through the road show. There was nothing to worry about, he said, but he wanted to let Billy and Castaneda know that the *Wall Street Journal* column was prompting PricewaterhouseCoopers' main office to take a look at Blue Rhino and its secondary offering. But there's no problem, he assured them, no need to worry.

The Securities and Exchange Commission called on the last day of the road show. SEC officials also had read the article, and they had a couple of questions. Castaneda cut the day short to make some word changes in documents associated with the secondary offering. "The SEC said fine and signed off on it. We're ready to go."

Billy was happy.

"We were able to answer everybody's questions, just like we thought we would. Our goal was two million shares, and we received orders for more than four million. Our stock had climbed back to almost $19.

"I'm feeling good."

Billy needed just one more thing to clear the way for the second offering—a letter from PricewaterhouseCoopers.

Billy still felt good, and he had plenty of reasons. The road show had closed, and the reviews were great, considering the huge problem they faced at the start. He and Castaneda had just turned around a potentially disastrous situation brought on by the *Wall Street Journal* article. The previous year, 1998, had been fantastic, but this year, now that the fallout from the column fiasco had died down, promised to be even better. And the next day, February 5, was his birthday. He would be forty-three. It would be good to celebrate it knowing Blue Rhino should have a successful secondary stock offering.

All that remained was for the pricing committee to meet and set an opening price for the stock. That would happen as soon as PricewaterhouseCoopers' Lattanzi supplied Merrill Lynch with a "comfort letter" declaring that all the company's financial statements were in order and everything was good to go for the offering.

The road show had ended in Chicago, and Billy and Castaneda were still there talking by conference phone with the pricing committee. The committee was ready to proceed. It and Merrill Lynch were waiting for Lattanzi and the cover letter. By mid-morning, Lattanzi had not arrived or called. That was odd, because he knew how important the cover letter was. The stock offering could not take place without it.

Morning dissolved into afternoon, and still no Lattanzi. Billy, Castaneda, Merrill Lynch, and the pricing committee were getting nervous, because they knew that investors would soon be getting nervous. Billy and Castaneda began to work the phones. No one at Lattanzi's office in Greensboro knew where he was. No one at the giant auditing firm's corporate headquarters in New Jersey was available. Castaneda and Billy called everybody they knew to call, and left messages everywhere.

Finally, at 5:30 p.m., Lattanzi called. His account manager was also on the phone.

"Jim, what's going on? Where are you?" Billy asked.

Lattanzi replied that he was at PricewaterhouseCoopers' corporate office near Florham Park, New Jersey. He said he had been instructed not to talk with Billy or anyone else at Blue Rhino. Lattanzi's account manager told Billy that PricewaterhouseCoopers "was not prepared to provide a comfort letter" and that the firm's attorney had told him and Lattanzi not to talk with Billy again.

"Whoa, wait a minute!" Billy said, in a voice as calm as he could make it. "What has happened?"

Blue Rhino attorneys and others, who were also on the phone, were not quite so calm. "What's going on here?" they demanded. "This is outrageous!"

Someone from PWC would be in touch, said Lattanzi's account manager, and then he ended the conversation.

Several years later, Lattanzi declined to be interviewed about the incident or his association with PricewaterhouseCoopers and Blue Rhino.

"Merrill Lynch was just stunned, and so was I," said Billy. "We've sold all this stock, and we can't do a thing and none of our own auditors will even talk to us. It was just unbelievable, a totally, helpless situation."

Castaneda and Billy caught a flight home that night from Chicago. They agreed to stay home and not take any calls, Castaneda said, "because we had no answers to give anybody." Meanwhile, investment bankers "are going crazy," he said. "They want to know what to do, what to tell people. Hours and minutes are important—not days. It's very stressful."

Billy spent his birthday trying to contact someone in a top executive position at PricewaterhouseCoopers. He had phone numbers, including numbers for the CEO, but no one would return his calls. Finally, the accountant in charge of PWC's Raleigh office, who headed the firm's operations in the state, called Billy about 6 p.m.

"I think we can get this thing straightened out," he said.

The *Wall Street Journal* column had spooked executives in PWC's corporate office, he said. When they realized Blue Rhino was a PWC client, they examined figures questioned in the article and decided that some of the accounting should have been handled differently—even though PWC's own agent, Lattanzi, had approved it.

The PWC agent in charge of North Carolina began his examination of the accounting issues, a process that took three days. Meanwhile, the offering was delayed. Merrill Lynch told increasingly nervous investment bankers that there was just a minor glitch that had to be worked out.

The stock began to fall.

Billy and Castaneda breathed a bit more easily when PWC's Raleigh chief called to say he didn't see a problem with Blue Rhino's accounting. But that relief was short-lived. The home office didn't agree with its Raleigh office. In fact, the PWC corporate office not only had a problem with the way Blue Rhino dealt with the USA Leasing transaction, it also wanted Blue Rhino to revise the way it accounted for the Bison Valve transaction, a deal that amounted to only $635,000.

PricewaterhouseCoopers was now saying that Blue Rhino should have consolidated USA Leasing's financial statements with its own, maintaining that its owners—Billy, Flip, Duchossois and Pederson—had not provided sufficient equity. So far as the Bison Valve deal was concerned, PWC's corporate office said Blue Rhino should have recorded it as an equity investment and not a loan. Because Blue Rhino was committed to buying the assets of Bison Valve, PWC said any Bison Valve losses should have been recorded on Blue Rhino's books.

Billy and Castaneda were shocked. The PWC local office, in filing after filing, had approved the way Blue Rhino had recorded each of the transactions. In fact, regarding the USA Leasing transaction, they said PWC had advised Blue Rhino to purchase the $6.5 million worth of cylinders from its distributors. Blue Rhino then sold the cylinders to USA Leasing for the same amount, and USA Leasing leased them back to distributors.

Billy told PWC that Blue Rhino's accounting had been exactly the way that PricewaterhouseCoopers advised. But Blue Rhino's stock was deteriorating rapidly, and orders for the offering were rapidly being lost. If they were going to salvage anything from what had looked to be a lucrative offering, despite the *Wall Street Journal* column, they were going to have to comply with PWC's instructions. "We said we'd do whatever they wanted us to do," Castaneda said. "They said don't change the audit, because that's what they're on the hook for. They said changes should be in the first quarter, the period they didn't audit."

Castaneda made the changes and submitted them to the Securities and Exchange Commission. And then an already bizarre situation became even more bizarre. The SEC rejected them.

"They said they'd already approved it once, and they liked the way it was originally," Castaneda said. "It was unbelievable. It was crazy, just crazy. PWC said they would take it to the highest levels of the SEC. I think egos came into play."

The SEC and PWC debated for a day, and "about half our orders fall out, and our stock goes down again," Billy said. "And, boy, I'm getting nervous. Thank God it was Friday. I tell the SEC guy we have to get this thing settled this weekend. I said, 'You just don't know how damn important this is.'"

But it was not settled over the weekend. The two sides remained at loggerheads until Monday when the PWC corporate office took its argument to a higher level in the SEC and persuaded the agency to require the changes the way PWC wanted them. They included a one-time write-off for the Bison Valve transaction. The decision required Blue Rhino to restate earnings for two quarters. The result was devastating—a net loss of $70,000 for the first quarter of fiscal 1999—that compared to what had been a profit of $422,000. The restatement also adversely affected earnings for 1998. Blue Rhino stock plummeted to 9. "From 18⅝ to 9!" Billy exclaimed.

The secondary offering was cancelled, and Merrill Lynch severed its relationship with Blue Rhino, saying that its policy was not to provide coverage or analyst reports on any company whose stock was under $10. "They did take my phone calls and treated us nice," Billy said. "They said to call when we got things straightened out. That's just the way it was."

Billy, Castaneda, and the Blue Rhino board demanded answers from PWC but got none. The head of PWC's Raleigh office attended a Blue Rhino board meeting but declined to answer the board's questions, saying PWC's lawyers instructed him not to say anything.

"They wouldn't even return our phone calls," said Muehlstein. "It was outrageous, unbelievable conduct."

The board fired PricewaterhouseCoopers, replacing it later with Ernst & Young, another of the country's leading accounting firms.

Blue Rhino, a company that prided itself on its integrity, had seen the ugly side of business. "Our reputation was sullied," said board member Richard Brenner. "That hurt me more than anything." The only remaining question concerning PWC was whether to immediately sue the company's former auditing firm. The board decided it was wiser, Brenner said, to "concentrate on sustaining Blue Rhino." A lawsuit could wait. Blue Rhino couldn't.

Less than a year after realizing his dream to build a company and take it public, Billy was again going to have to summon all his strength and business savvy just to save it.

It had been an incredible five or six weeks, unlike any that anyone associated with Blue Rhino could have imagined. Words such as "shocking," "unbelievable," and "bizarre" could not convey how extraordinary they had been. Years later, Billy and Castaneda struggled to find words to describe the range of emotions they experienced during this short period that began with such promise.

It was the "worst point" Castaneda had experienced in his career. He felt "helpless, terrible. Yet, we couldn't have done anything differently."

Christmas and New Year's, when everything was wonderful and promising, were only a few weeks past, but could just as well have been a hundred years ago. It hardly seemed possible, Billy thought, that it had been only a little more than a month since Blue Rhino stock was flirting with $25, and he was looking out over the waterfront on Maui feeling like he was king of the world.

"And I believe I would have been king of the world if I had let Dan Case manage the offering. The *Wall Street Journal* article would have never come out, and PricewaterhouseCoopers would never have looked at us. The future was bright then, and suddenly it was dark."

How quickly everything changed. As the new year began, there was nothing but praise for Blue Rhino, and it appeared to be almost a certainty that 1999 would be another marvelous year. Six weeks later, rumors alleged that the company countenanced improper accounting practices. As its stock fell with each passing rumor, the only certainty was that no one knew how bad it was going to get.

Though life had battle-tested him as a young man, and he had suffered his share of setbacks, Billy would consider this chapter in his and Blue Rhino's life as "a huge learning experience. It was a revelation of just how unfair the world can be. You learn to cut your losses and move on."

But it was far from easy. Billy estimated that the loss of the secondary offering, combined with the collapse of its stock, cost Blue Rhino more than $100 million. "And there's the compounding effect it has on everything else. Number one, your internal employees. They're wondering what's going to happen to their jobs. All these stock options and now they're all worthless. Your competitors start going to your customers and your customers start asking, 'Hey, are you going to be all right?' You spend all your time putting out fires."

A few months earlier, Billy and his management team had set a lofty goal of becoming a $500 million company in five years. There had been so much excitement and passion throughout Blue Rhino that few employees thought the company wouldn't reach that goal. Now, there was another, unspoken, goal—survival.

Gone, too, was the excitement and passion that had permeated Blue Rhino. In their place was a kind of uncertain numbness, something akin to shell-shock. Abbye Caudle said employees would seek out her and Lori Hall for assurance that everything would be alright. "They knew we worked with Billy and Mark, so they looked to us for reassurance," she said. "We told them not to worry, that it was just a little something that they have under control. But we were worrying, too."

Everyone at Blue Rhino needed reassuring, from the management team to office clerks. They wanted to hear Billy tell them it was going to be okay; that Blue Rhino might have stumbled just a little, but would soon be charging again.

Billy called an all-hands meeting and told them just that, but he didn't downplay the seriousness of the situation, and he didn't mince words.

"I told them the truth. I didn't blame it on, or even mention, Dan Case. I told them the PWC national office didn't like the way we accounted for some items, although the local office had approved them, and that we felt we had done everything as we should. I said it didn't hurt our financials, but it did hurt our credibility in the marketplace, which hurt our stock and ability to raise money, especially growth money."

As the company's employees listened to him intently, Billy told them that Blue Rhino was still the best cylinder exchange company in the world, and that they should be just as proud and passionate as they were a few weeks ago when its stock was at $25.

"That hasn't changed, and won't," he said. "We're going to rally and grow out of this together."

Billy also talked one-on-one to nervous employees and anxious investors, who were calling by the droves.

"Billy wanted to talk with every investor who called in, and the phone was ringing off the hook," Caudle said. "I can hear Billy talking to them now," she said, chuckling at the memory. "He told them not to worry. He'd say, 'We dropped the price of the stock just for you.'"

Tony Golding, president of Golding Farm Foods in Clemmons, called at least once a week. She said he would ask, "Abby, what's going on? Do I need to be worried?" Golding said he was concerned from the minute he read the *Wall Street Journal* article.

"It hit me right in the stomach," he said. "My heart just sank."

Nevertheless, Golding said he never lost faith in the company or its leadership. "Sure I was concerned when it fell all the way to 2, but not enough to keep me from buying up a bunch of the stock."

Billy never failed to reassure him, Golding said.

Castaneda said Billy was always outwardly positive and cheerful during this period, which encompassed almost all of 1999 and much of 2000 as well. "It was a tough time, really tough, but he would always try to make you feel better, no matter what."

But Castaneda and others close to Billy said they knew he was aching inside.

"People were calling from all over who had bought the stock at 17 or 18, and now it was at 9. They'd say, 'What are you guys doing?' They'd say we were cheap, terrible, and called us names. It got pretty bad."

It would get worse. Billy would later call it a year spent "fighting the wolves" unleashed by Dan Case and the *Wall Street Journal* column.

Perception is everything in business, and that's what hurt so much, personally as well as corporately. It was maddening to Billy, Castaneda, and everyone else who knew Blue Rhino, to witness its stock's sudden and inexorable decline. They knew that Blue Rhino was an excellent company, and that business was good. What it needed was capital to grow.

That was the reason for going for the $42 million second public offering—to get capital to expand into other Wal-Marts, Home Depots, and Lowe's, as those large retailers, and others, wanted Blue Rhino to do. If it didn't, they would get someone who would, and Blue Rhino would die. It was that simple. It was critically important to stop the stock's hemorrhaging, and to turn it around.

That would not be easy. Perception and momentum were on the side of the wolves.

"We had been such a bright and shining star," Caudle said. "Now, some people, outside Blue Rhino, were saying we cooked the books. They wanted to see us go down."

Blue Rhino immediately lost credibility the moment the "Heard on the Street" column hit Wall Street. Billy and Castaneda won back a considerable amount on the road show, an indication of how strong the company was, but it could not withstand the negative reaction ensuing from the refusal of its own auditors to approve its books for a second public offering.

"The perception was that the company had bad guys in it," Castaneda said.

That perception grew and gained momentum as the stock fell. Share-holders who had applauded the decision to create USA Leasing and Platinum Propane now called to ask why Billy and Flip personally owned and did business with distributorships. "The tide turned and the perception changed," Castaneda said. "They began seeing things in a negative way." Before the article and the PWC fiasco, shareholders considered those companies beneficial to Blue Rhino, their stock holdings, and their pocketbooks. Now, everything was turned on its head. The perception was that Billy was "making money off distributors at the expense of the shareholders."

Billy knew it would be difficult to slow the momentum of the stock's decline, much less turn it around, but he knew he had to try. The alternative was unacceptable. He had the backing of his board, thanks especially to Flip, Duchossois, Muehlstein, and Brenner. Each believed strongly that Billy, in Duchossois' words, "had been stabbed in the back." They calmed nervous investors and let Billy know that he had their support and backing to try to find the capital it would take to prevent Blue Rhino from going under.

"We knew it would be tough, and I was really concerned," Brenner said. "But we knew Blue Rhino wa a good company. The locations were growing, and business was good. All the fundamentals were there. And when you know what's good and what's evil, you know good is going to win. But it was scary."

It was scary, Flip said, because of "the whole range of reactions precipitated by the actions of Dan Case and PricewaterhouseCoopers." Blue Rhino's lack of capital was forcing it to "run on fumes," he said. "Because we couldn't raise the money in the offering, we were relying entirely on debt, and we were about to violate our covenants. There was little hope of coming back without a cash infusion."

But a cash infusion would be difficult to come by in the wake of the momentum generated by Blue Rhino's collapsed credibility and plummeting stock. Momentum can be crucial, in business and in life, Billy said. It's important to recognize it early, and to be able to discern when and in what direction it is about to change.

"One year your momentum can be going exactly the way you want it to go, and before you can know it, or anticipate it, you are headed in the opposite direction. When that happens, you had better catch it, fast—because it's extremely tough to turn around."

Scrambling and Ratcheting

Raising money would definitely be difficult. Few investors would want a stock that had lost almost two-thirds of its value in six months. The stock was trading at 18⅝ on February 5, 1999. It had fallen to $6.88 on August 10. Counting from January 5, when the stock was at almost $25, the loss was closer to 75 percent. But if anyone could do it, Billy could, declared Caudle, who had seen him raise millions of dollars numerous times—although not under circumstances as difficult as these.

"Nobody, but nobody, can raise money like Billy. It just blows you away. People believe in him. What you see is what you get with Billy."

Before Billy could scramble, there were a couple of items under the heading of damage control that had to be taken care of. They involved the sale of USA Leasing and Platinum Propane, the companies mentioned or referred to in the *Wall Street Journal* column. Perhaps selling those companies wouldn't stop the stock slide, but it might slow it, and it would stop the talk about Billy and Flip being involved in or controlling companies that dealt closely with Blue Rhino.

Billy and Flip sold their portion of Platinum Propane in August 1999, to a group of business people headed by his friend, Dick Hardin. "I wanted to do everything I could to repair the damage, so I announced to the whole world that I sold it. I sold Platinum Propane even though the SEC had once looked at it and blessed it. The saying was then, 'Billy believes in it so much he's investing in distributors.' Everybody had blessed it, including the distributors."

Blue Rhino, itself, bought USA Leasing, "because of perception, because some people thought it looked bad," Castaneda said. Even so, several major accounting firms, including their new auditor, Ernst & Young, "were incredulous that this had happened to us." Accountants performing due diligence for a teachers retirement investment group, TIAA-CREF, which was considering investing in Blue Rhino at that time, told Castaneda that Blue Rhino "got screwed."

Castaneda and Billy held their breath, hoping the respected organization would invest in Blue Rhino, but that didn't happen. The SEC made an informal inquiry into the issues raised by PricewaterhouseCoopers and the *Wall Street Journal* column, and that was enough to prevent the teachers fund from investing.

That rejection hurt because the stock kept slipping. It was down to about 6 in September when Billy hooked up with an investment management firm in New York called Promethean Capital Group, a firm that dealt in convertible and equity-linked securities. Promethean was willing to loan a substantial amount of money to a company whose stock was in decline, but it would be, Billy said, through "a deal that we were extremely lucky to survive."

Promethean loaned Blue Rhino $10 million, but required a "ratchet clause" that obligated Blue Rhino to continue issuing warrants to Promethean at about $6 a share, or lower if the stock declined further, until the loan was satisfied. "You just keep giving them more shares," Billy said.

That was an example, Castaneda said, of the continuing adverse effect of the *Wall Street Journal* article and PricewaterhouseCoopers' refusal to provide a green light for the second public offering. When the teachers group, TIAA-CREF, declined to invest in Blue Rhino because of the informal SEC inquiry, it forced Blue Rhino to enter into a "more desperate" type of deal that could quickly decimate the company. Billy got $10 million that the company dearly needed, but he would have to scramble to pay it back and hope the stock didn't sink lower.

Billy also received an infusion of cash from his board and friends. He, Flip, Duchossois, Len Carlson, Bob Lunn, Castaneda, and several others bought about $8 million worth of stock at $8 a share. Billy then turned to his friend Peer Pederson, the cagey attorney and deal maker in Chicago. Lunn and Pederson put together a group that invested another $6 million in Blue Rhino.

Billy had raised about $25 million—not close to the amount Blue Rhino most likely would have raised from the aborted $42 million offering, which he and Castaneda had oversold considerably, and there were numerous troubling and tightly knotted strings to the Promethean money.

But the money helped stanch the bleeding. The stock halted its slide and even performed a quick little bounce back to $10, and then $10.44. It wasn't a turnaround toward the heady environs of $20 and $25 prices where Blue Rhino had resided recently, but now seemed so long ago, but it was a hopeful start. And there was now cash to pay a mounting debt and generate more capital that would allow Blue Rhino to grow—all the way to China.

People familiar with Billy's entrepreneurial and business talents talk admiringly about his vision, his money-raising skills, and a managerial style and personality that elicit loyalty and respect. There's another—less specific, perhaps, but no less real—and that's his uncanny ability to find and hire the right person for the right job at the right time.

He demonstrated that talent time after time in moves that greatly improved the company, and perhaps at times even saved it. Just when he needed someone with a superb knowledge of retail markets and merchandising, he found and hired Rick Belmont; just when he needed someone who could create a state-of-the art information system, he found Kay Martin; just when he needed a top-notch retail sales director, he hired Jerry Shadley; and just when he needed an excellent CFO to lead the company to Wall Street, he found Castaneda and convinced him to come to Blue Rhino. The list could go on and on: Dave Slone, Dick Arthur, Jeff Dean, Chris Holden, Bob Travatello—people with special abilities Blue Rhino needed, then and there.

Malcolm "Mac" McQuilkin—entrepreneur, salesman extraordinaire, and raconteur—was one of Billy's finest, most important, hires, and certainly one of the most interesting and unusual. Billy not only got McQuilkin, the "Marco Polo of the world," as Billy would call him, but he got McQuilkin's company, Uniflame. Neither could have come at a better time.

Encouraged by the modest stock rebound, Billy began to look around for a business to acquire that would complement Blue Rhino while allowing it to diversify and not be so dependent on seasonal sales. Billy was also interested in establishing a foothold in the Far East. He learned that a company called Uniflame, which imported grills, patio heaters, fireplace accessories, and garden art, and which had extensive interests in China and the Far East, might be for sale. Its corporate office was in Zion, Illinois, where the company also had a large warehouse. Uniflame's customers included large retailers, such as Wal-Mart, Home Depot, Lowe's, and Sears. The list could have been a carbon copy of Blue Rhino's major customers. Uniflame was earning about $2 million a year from revenues of about $22 million. Billy was intrigued. He met McQuilkin, Uniflame's founder and principal owner, in November at the hotel where he had planned and negotiated numerous other business deals, the Four Seasons in Chicago.

Billy was even more intrigued when he met McQuilkin. If there was ever a born entrepreneurial free spirit, McQuilkin is one, and Billy sensed it. He could have been talking to Flip. McQuilkin and Flip have similar styles— from their ponytails to their penchant for doing business over their cell phones, to their proclivity to take risks and to say and do what is on their minds.

Billy is his chosen brother, Flip said, but if he ever chooses another it will be McQuilkin. "Mac has tremendous ability and maturity, but he's been able to keep a youthful, exuberant personality. That's a tremendous asset. His life has been very colorful. This is a guy who has been through many hardships, but he never gets unraveled. He doesn't live by dogma; he lives by reality."

McQuilkin was born in London in 1947 and grew up with dreams of becoming a professional soccer star. The dream evaporated when he broke his leg. McQuilkin left home when he was eighteen and got a job with Cunard, the cruise ship line. "I was at loose ends, because I couldn't play soccer," he said in a down-to-earth British accent that spoke of the sea, numerous ports-of-call, and bawdy nights. "So I got a job on the *Queen Mary* and *Queen Elizabeth*."

Indeed, McQuilkin worked on each of those luxury ocean liners, performing various jobs, such as working with the ship's chefs or bartending when he "was good" and nastier jobs when he was not—the nasty jobs usually coming after he struck up an unauthorized relationship with a passenger.

McQuilkin decided to go into business for himself in New York City in the late '60s and early '70s. He and a friend transformed a bar into a small disco to catch the overflow from New York's first discotheque, the famous "Murray the K's Dance Your Ass Off." He stayed in the disco-bar business until 1974, when he got into the concessions business at sports events and concerts for major rock groups such as UFO, Rush, and Billy Joel. He eventually began working concessions for the rock band KISS and toured with that group throughout the country and much of the world.

By about 1980, McQuilkin had decided the rock and roll business was making him "jaded," and that he needed a change. He moved to California and got into the flea market business, working in the San Diego area and along the Mexican border. When the peso devalued, his business suffered, and he had to find something else. That's when he met and fell in love with Sheri, who was assisting her father in a fireplace accessory business.

McQuilkin took a cue from them. He, with Sheri's help, started his own fireplace accessory business, concentrating on specialty stores so he wouldn't be competing with his father-in-law. He compiled a customer list by collecting phone books from around the country and copying in longhand the specialty fireplace stores listed in the yellow pages.

McQuilkin obtained a $2 million line of credit and began importing fireplace equipment from Taiwan. Sheri came up with the name "Uniflame," McQuilkin said. "We just thought it sounded good."

McQuilkin moved his company to Illinois in 1990, first to Skokie, where he had received financing from a partner, and then to Zion in 1995, after buying out his partners. By 1995, Uniflame was one of the major importers and wholesale suppliers of fireplace accessory equipment in the country. It had expanded to three divisions: mail order, supplying businesses such as Spiegel and J.C. Penny; large mass merchandise retailers on the order of Home Depot and Wal-Mart; and about 1,500 specialty stores around the country. McQuilkin was spending much of his time overseas dealing with his suppliers and large retailers with a presence there, such as Wal-Mart.

McQuilkin had been on an overseas trip for about a month in April 1999, when disaster struck. He suffered an aneurysm in Bangkok, Thailand, and had to have emergency brain surgery. The surgery was successful, but he developed bacterial meningitis, and it almost killed him. He remembers almost nothing of that time but the long needles used to give him spinal taps. Finally, after six months, seventeen spinal taps, and a half-dozen operations he awoke to see Sheri and his grown children, Leanda and Brandon, standing beside his hospital bed at Northwestern University.

"They finally put me back in my body," he said.

But there was still considerable doubt that McQuilkin would ever get back completely. He would require weeks of rehabilitation and relearning basic skills and tasks, such as driving a car around his neighborhood without getting lost. It was doubtful that he would be able to go back to work.

Uniflame had received several inquiries from potential buyers when McQuilkin was lying in the hospital gravely ill. Blue Rhino's was among them. McQuilkin and his attorney looked up Blue Rhino on the Internet. "I thought, 'Hey, these guys look pretty good.'"

McQuilkin called Billy, who said he was planning to be in Chicago next week, anyway.

Billy and McQuilkin met at the Four Seasons and walked to Spiaggia, a high-end Italian restaurant, where they basically settled the deal over dinner, although it wasn't finalized until April, five months later. They agreed that Blue Rhino would acquire Uniflame for $13.3 million. The deal would consist of about $4.3 million in cash, $6.7 million in stock, and $2.3 million in deferred cash payments. Billy told McQuilkin that if and when his health returned, he would have a job with Uniflame—which would be a subsidiary of Blue Rhino—if and when he wanted it.

"If you don't want one, that's okay, too," Billy said.

Before he finalized the deal with McQuilkin, Billy acquired a company that complemented Uniflame and increased its value to Blue Rhino. He bought International Propane Products, a manufacturer of patio heaters and owner of a patent for OPD valves, for $2.9 million in cash plus stock worth $1.1 million. Billy believed that purchasing IPP would allow Blue Rhino to lower the price of patio heaters, thereby increasing the demand for Blue Rhino's cylinder exchange services.

McQuilkin was back in the office and in control of his company by January. Soon, he was back in Taiwan and China, repairing relationships that had rusted during the months of his illness, and creating new deals. McQuilkin was his old self again, maybe even better. When the day came in April to finalize the sale of Uniflame to Blue Rhino, McQuilkin was in Taiwan conducting a line review with Wal-Mart representatives, who were placing orders for grills, patio heaters, and other items for the coming season. He authorized his attorney to complete the sale in his absence. As the deal was being finalized, McQuilkin was completing the largest order he ever had written.

He called Billy the next day, barely able to contain his excitement. He had a commitment from Wal-Mart for $25 million worth of barbecue grills.

"And Billy!" he said, excitedly. "They want patio heaters!"

And want them they did—about forty thousand of them. McQuilkin was back, really back, from his long illness, and Billy knew it. He asked McQuilkin to take charge of patio heaters and OPD valves, and to keep doing what he was doing. McQuilkin said he was happy to oblige.

McQuilkin accepted a salary of only $30,000 the first year as a consultant, although he retained his title of CEO of Uniflame, and he became CEO of Blue Rhino Global Sourcing, the company's expanded import division that grew out of the success of Uniflame. In its first year as a subsidiary of Blue Rhino, sales of Uniflame jumped from $22 million to more than $60 million.

Before the year was out Uniflame would live up to its name. It was to remain a visibly bright and shining segment of the company during Blue Rhino's darkest and most difficult days. Only months after he sold his company in a deal consisting of 50 percent cash and 50 percent stock, McQuilkin watched as Blue Rhino stock again began a plummet that would take it from $14 to $2 before the end of the year.

McQuilkin never complained, and for that, he won Billy's undying respect and appreciation. "He never said how stupid it was to get hooked up with me or Blue Rhino or anything like that, even though he could have. Uniflame was doing well. It was Blue Rhino that was hurting. All Mac did was work tirelessly every day to make us all better."

Uniflame was able to "help shore up Blue Rhino when it was under attack," McQuilkin said. "I'm glad we could do that. Billy and I always understood we were working toward a common goal, and that we were in it together." McQuilkin said Billy liked to say that Blue Rhino was like Gillette. "He'd say Gillette makes a lot of razors and razor blades. Well, I was the razor, and he was the blade. We worked together, and well."

When Billy and Castaneda flew to Chicago early in April of 2000 to buy Uniflame, they took with them Blue Rhino's new director of human resources, Robin Manley, who spent a good deal of the flight pinching herself.

That was because she wanted to be sure she wasn't just dreaming that she was flying to Chicago on her first day on the job to buy a company. She might have had her head in the clouds, but they were real clouds, and she really was Blue Rhino's new human resources director. Billy wanted her along to help Uniflame employees start a smooth assimilation into the Blue Rhino herd.

Billy was confident Manley would be up to that immediate task; he was familiar with her work. But he also was counting on her for something far more important—to make the Rhino herd feel good about itself again.

Billy had met Manley a few years earlier when she worked for Boston

Market in Chicago, where her job's stated mission was to make the company "an amazing place to work." Manley had done that, he thought. Until recently, it had never entered Billy's mind that he might need to hire someone to teach employees that Blue Rhino was an amazing place to work. That was almost self-evident, or it had been until all the problems precipitated by the *Wall Street Journal* article, and the stock slide brought on by the refusal of PricewaterhouseCoopers to provide a green light for the second offering.

Now, it was not so evident. A malaise had crept in and threatened to embed itself into what had been a wonderful Blue Rhino culture. Billy believed the reservoir of can-do optimism and entrepreneurial spirit that had fed the Blue Rhino culture was still there. It had just slipped beneath the surface, and Billy needed someone who could tap it. He placed an ad in local newspapers for a human relations director. In addition to recapturing the Blue Rhino spirit, the new director would have to build a human resources department. Until then, the company had outsourced the work required to maintain its recruitment and benefits programs.

It had been several years since Manley had seen Billy or Flip when she was with Boston Market in Chicago. She had moved to Colorado where she had met her husband, who was from Greensboro. When the couple came to Greensboro, a friend showed Manley Billy's ad in the *Winston-Salem Journal*, which did not mention his name or Blue Rhino's. But it read as if it had been written just for her. When Billy saw her résumé, he hired her immediately.

"It was meant to be," she said. "I believe in fate. Things happen for a reason."

By her own description, Manley is a whirling dervish of optimism. She doesn't just light up the room; she bathes it in neon.

"I'm like a hurricane," she said. "You hear me before you see me."

It didn't take long for Blue Rhino employees to know she was around. As soon as she got back from Chicago, she began to try to make them fall in love with Blue Rhino again. Like Billy, she was convinced that the feeling was still there. It had just become a little numb—perhaps still shell-shocked from all that had happened in such a short time.

One of the first things she did was buy "a really good camera" and start taking pictures of people. First, she took a picture of every employee and arranged them all around a big Blue Rhino logo in the lobby of the administration building. "The idea was to say, 'This is your company, something wonderful to be proud of.'"

Manley also took action shots of employees and set them to music, producing a show that was a huge hit at quarterly meetings and holiday events.

Manley had been with Blue Rhino for only about a week when the company hosted a major corporate meeting of a hundred people or so. She doesn't remember exactly what the meeting was about or who was there, but what was indelibly imprinted in her memory was what was missing.

"There were no hamburgers or hot dogs. It was catered by Boston Market, for goodness sakes. I said, 'Where are the hamburgers? Where are the hot dogs? Where are the grills?' We were saying we wanted to be the king of backyard, but where was our backyard?"

Manley began pushing for a deck with ready-to-fire-up grills, and tables and chairs to accommodate about a hundred people. She went to Castaneda who, as CFO, would have to approve spending the money for such a venture, and money was tight. But Castaneda liked the idea, and he found $6,500 to build and equip the deck. There was a pretty, grassy commons-like area in Blue Rhino's campus-like setting that seemed to be waiting for what Manley had in mind. The $6,500 was enough to build the deck and supply it with grills and patio heaters. It was an instant demonstration of how complementary Blue Rhino and Uniflame were. It also became the perfect place to act out the Blue Rhino motto: "Spark Something Fun!"

To Manley's surprise, however, employees didn't take to the deck right away. "I don't know why. It was almost like they had to be shown it was all right to have fun."

Gradually, though, they did embrace it, especially after people like Rick Belmont and Bud Kiger began using it regularly. Manley described them as veritable grill aficionados who prepared mouth-watering concoctions that prompted others to try to emulate. Belmont had an amazing number of dishes with unusual and exotic marinades, Manley said. His Caribbean jerk chicken was a real winner, and he could prepare a medley of pineapple, pears, apples, and other fruit that "was to die for." And speaking of items to die for, Kiger could somehow actually bake a chocolate cake on the grill.

Following their expert lead, other employees began to bring chicken breasts, hamburgers, even steak, to grill for lunch, and the deck became a popular, fun place. Manley organized family-oriented events around the deck, such as "Bring Your Kids to Work" days when they would do the cooking.

Rarely did a week go by that Manley didn't organize some type of fun event, like an ice cream social, for employees, and often for their families as well.

"The idea was to create an environment where kids and the family would like to be, and be proud of. I think we did that, and it made our people feel important and valued. It restored the feeling that they had all along—that anything was possible with this company."

Manley did exactly that, and more, Billy said. "She was one of the best cheerleaders for a company I had ever seen. She did an outstanding job of reviving Blue Rhino's upbeat culture. She was a good ambassador for the company to employees and distributors in the field. Robin made people feel good again about being with Blue Rhino."

Spiked! But Where's the Sympathy?

The outlook was bullish for Blue Rhino at the dawn of the new millennium. Billy's scrambling in late summer and fall and board members' willingness to provide the company with a much-needed infusion of cash had halted the stock's hemorrhaging and actually turned it around. By ACC tournament time, it was back up to $15 and climbing. And truly astounding was how quickly the number of Blue Rhino locations was growing.

As the twentieth century drew to a close, there were 21,777 stores—including retail giants such as Wal-Mart, convenience stores, and little mom-and-pop groceries—where backyard chefs could exchange their cylinders. By April, the month that Billy acquired Uniflame, that number had jumped to more than twenty-three thousand. It appeared that Blue Rhino was back and preparing for a long, powerful, and productive charge into the twenty-first century.

But that charge would have to wait. Even when the stock surged upward in early 2000 as Billy and his board took steps to acquire Uniflame, powerful market forces were about to present Blue Rhino with the most serious challenge yet to its existence, and send Billy scrambling again to try to save his company.

The threat was a sudden steep rise in the price of propane. It was as unexpected as the allegations in the *Wall Street Journal* article and PricewaterhouseCoopers' refusal to support the company's second offering. Potentially, this threat was far more serious than either of those because it involved the price of propane, the company's life blood.

Later, in hindsight, Billy and the board would say they should have seen it coming and should have been prepared with a price hedging program in place to protect the company from just such a devastating occurrence. But there had been little or no indication in previous years that a hedging program would be necessary. There had been almost no volatility in the price of propane in the summer. "I had been dealing with propane since I was a kid, literally," Billy said, "and propane had always been cheap in the summer. I never thought the price would increase in the summer."

There had been little advance indication. Early in the year, the price of natural gas began to climb. In April, the price of propane, a by-product of natural gas and crude oil, began to rise noticeably when petroleum refineries, in a price-saving move, began to use propane to fuel their refining processes instead of natural gas. By the Fourth of July, propane prices had spiked to historic levels—more than double, from about 30 cents a gallon to almost 70 cents.

"I had thought there was no way possible that this could happen," Billy said. "But it did, and here I am, about the only guy in the country really using propane in the summertime. It crushes us."

Blue Rhino distributors were caught in the middle. "We agreed to pay them more, or they couldn't have survived," Castaneda said. "But our margin went to nothing."

Blue Rhino began to break its covenants, and nervous bankers began insisting on stricter terms. Billy explained it this way. "Let's say the way the bank agreement was set up that we anticipated seven thousand new locations for the year 1999, and that they would require $7 million in capital expenditures. Now, let's say we only have capital for three thousand locations, so the bank gets nervous. So the bank says, 'Where you were paying 8 percent on this $15 million, you are now going to have to pay 10 percent and a one-time fee of $500,000, and we're going to charge you $100,000 a month to monitor what you're doing.' I started thinking, 'My God, I'm going to be working for the bank.'"

The banks certainly didn't do anything wrong, Billy said. "That's just the way it is. It was the normal course of business. They could have demanded full payment immediately. But they didn't. They just charged me a lot."

Billy had to scramble, hard and fast, and he had to do it on two fronts. He needed to raise prices, and to do that he had to renegotiate agreements with his major retailers—Home Depot, Wal-Mart, and Lowe's. And second, he had to raise capital quickly.

Home Depot, Wal-Mart, and Lowe's were Blue Rhino's "Big Three" of retailers, accounting for 60 percent of the company's business. In the summer of 2000, when the propane spike began to really skewer Blue Rhino, the company was operating under fixed price-per-tank agreements for the year that it had negotiated with each of the major retailers.

"They were paying us a fixed amount," Billy said, "and I was out there buying propane at variable prices every day when it jumps from 30 cents a gallon to 70 cents. I needed to change what I was charging."

Billy put Brent Boydston in charge of getting a price increase. Ordinarily, that would have been the job of Jerry Shadley, vice president of sales, but Billy had recently promoted Shadley to the presidency of QuickShip, Inc., an in-store, retail shipping service company that Blue Rhino acquired in October 2000. Shadley had hired Boydston a year earlier as the company's national accounts manager. Boydston, a former buyer for Sears, knew that a price increase in the middle of the year was practically unheard of.

"It almost never happened." In fact, he said it was one of his "credos" in retail to never grant a price increase to a vendor.

But he had never been in a situation like this, in which his company's very survival rested in large part on whether its three main retail customers would grant it a price increase. Boydston had watched Blue Rhino's stock begin its slide two quarters earlier, tied to the rapidly rising price of propane.

"I think everybody kind of ignored it, or tried to, hoping it would go back down to where it had been for at least the past ten years, between 28 cents a gallon and 33 cents, " he said. "But they didn't, and we soon needed a price increase in the worst way."

Billy and Castaneda went with Boydston when he called on Home Depot. Boydston did the only thing he could do, and that was show Home Depot the history of propane prices for the past ten years, and the figures were on his side. The price had risen to "historic highs," Castaneda said.

"Look what has happened to us—we need this," Billy told Boydston. "The figures are there."

"We can't survive without an increase," Boydston told the Home Depot buyers.

Home Depot didn't like it, but Boydston, Billy, and Castaneda were able to obtain a $1.10 increase from the big retailer. Boydston got a $1 increase from Lowe's, and he finally squeezed 75 cents out of Wal-Mart, which probably liked it least of all. Wal-Mart reasoned, ominously, that if Blue Rhino could not manage its resources any better, it would soon be time for Wal-Mart to find another supplier.

That attitude surprised Billy. "Our cost has doubled. Yet, they want to keep it at the same price. They didn't have any sympathy. That was a huge learning experience."

It was quite a learning experience for Boydston, too, a virtual baptism by fire. Shortly after he obtained the price increases, Billy appointed him vice president of sales for Blue Rhino.

The price increases, though modest considering that Blue Rhino's propane costs had more than doubled, were significant, nevertheless. "They helped sustain the company, and I'm proud I played a part in that," said Boydston.

They also did something else critically important. They provided Billy with some time and room to do what he does best: scramble for capital. And scramble he did—like a quarterback down six points in the red zone with time running out. And like the best quarterbacks, those who thrive in game winning, do-or-die situations, Billy wants the ball when everything is on the line. That's when he's at his best, and he exults in it.

"There isn't any bigger rush for me than getting up before a group of investors and talking about our company. I enjoy being challenged with questions, hard questions. I love to tell my story and then challenge them to tell me where the holes are."

He had to be at his best in the fall of 2000. Time was running out, and he was about to be sacked. That's when Billy, as he so often does in a crisis, met the person he needed to meet. This time it was Dick Kiphart, a managing partner and head of corporate finance for the prestigious William Blair & Co., an independent investment firm with offices in major cities in the United States, Europe, and the Far East. Kiphart was with the firm's Chicago head-quarters, and it was one or more of Billy's Chicago buddies—Flip, Duchossois, or maybe Robert Lunn—who introduced them.

"We hit it off right away," Billy said. "He's a Harvard MBA, but with the common sense to go along with the smarts."

Billy told Kiphart the Blue Rhino story—including the *Wall Street Journal* column, the PricewaterhouseCoopers debacle, and the sudden, crippling spike in the price of propane—and how demand for Blue Rhino's services continued to grow in spite of all those crises, any one of which might have killed a lesser company.

Kiphart said he knew just the person Billy ought to meet. His name was David Warnock, head of a firm in Baltimore called Camden Partners. The firm managed investment capital of about a half-billion dollars. It liked to invest in companies with good management teams but that, for whatever reason, needed infusions of capital. Almost by definition, Blue Rhino fit that description.

Kiphart told Warnock that he thought Blue Rhino was an extremely interesting company, one that was having stock and earnings difficulties brought on by the sudden heavy spike in propane prices. Kiphart arranged a conference call in which he introduced Billy and Castaneda to Warnock. Billy and Castaneda then gave their investment sales presentation to Warnock.

"I had never met David," Billy said. "We explained what had happened. That's all you can do. You can't expect sympathy. Everybody has a story, and everybody has an excuse. But I knew the business fundamentals were solid."

But it must have been a heck of a sales job. "How much do you need? " Warnock asked when Billy and Castaneda completed their presentation. "About $10 million," Billy replied. Then Kiphart, who had stayed with the call, said he liked what he had heard, and that he would put in another million.

Actually, Warnock said he did take the time to check with Blue Rhino's major customers, including Home Depot, Lowe's, and Wal-Mart, and that each gave Blue Rhino high marks. They were especially impressed with the company's inventory management system. "They really liked the product, and they liked the way it was delivered," Warnock said. "It appeared unlikely that anyone would be able to take business away from Billy."

Warnock said Camden Partners invested $9 million in purchases of stock and warrants, and brought in several other people who bought about $3 million worth, for a total of around $12 million. "We must have done a good sales job," Billy said, "because the stock was at $4 and he bought it at $6. I told him I wouldn't sell it at $4."

Shortly after Warnock and Camden Partners invested in Blue Rhino, the stock resumed its slide. "It went right down to $3 and then $2," Warnock said. "I didn't lose faith in Billy or the company. But we bought it at half of what it was and it's still going down. That got my attention, I can tell you."

As part of the deal, Warnock was given a seat on the Blue Rhino board, where he served for the next four years. He could watch the stock languish in the cellar from close up, and wonder if it would ever go back up.

But he could help, too. Warnock had a lot of contacts in the financial world, and he introduced Billy to Allied Capital of Washington, DC. Allied billed itself as a "leader in the private finance industry (that) provides debt and equity financing to primarily private, middle market companies—the backbone of the American entrepreneurial economy."

Billy needed another round of cash to pay off Promethean, the firm that loaned him $10 million under a risky ratchet clause. Because Blue Rhino's stock had deteriorated, Billy literally risked losing the company unless he satisfied the debt to Promethean quickly. It was Dan Case coming back to haunt him. "He said we would regret it. Those were his words."

Billy used the money from Warnock to pay Promethean, and he borrowed an additional $10 million from Allied Capital under a subordinated debt arrangement. It was expensive, but it gave Billy and Blue Rhino some precious breathing room.

Basically, what Billy had done was recapitalize his company. Although the propane price spike ate quickly and heavily into the company's earnings, Blue Rhino, "like a hungry beast, was still growing," he said, "and I had to somehow keep feeding it. That's what I was really doing."

Meanwhile, Billy wanted to make sure that the beast would never again go hungry because of an unexpected rise in the price of propane. To ensure that, he put together a hedging program to cover the costs of supplying propane to his Big Three: Home Depot, Wal-Mart, and Lowe's. He explained how it worked.

"At the end of 2000, we work out an agreement with Wal-Mart for 2001. We estimate that we think we'll sell a million cylinders, with four gallons of propane a cylinder, in 1,500 Wal-Mart stores. That's four million gallons of propane.

"Then we agree on a price, and we get an increase for the coming year of 20 to 30 percent. Then I immediately go to the marketplace and pre-purchase the propane. So, I'm able to fix my margin for the coming year. Now, I know how much I'm paying for my gas, and I know what I'm going to sell it for to

Wal-Mart next year. And we cut similar deals with Lowe's and Home Depot, and I'm locked in to the price on the futures market."

Billy negotiated his propane price hedging program with Duke Energy Co., one of the largest suppliers of natural gas in the country. Former North Carolina Governor Jim Martin, who was on the Duke Energy board, introduced Billy to Rick Priory, CEO of Duke Energy. Billy had met Martin, who served two terms as governor from 1985-1993, during Martin's first gubernatorial campaign.

Martin, like Billy, is an avid golfer. They played together in the Crosby Celebrity National Golf Tournament when it was played at Bermuda Run, about fifteen miles west of Winston-Salem. Martin also played in Billy's annual charity golf tournament named for Billy's father, the Dean Prim Classic. Former Vice President Dan Quayle played in their foursome. Martin and Billy later flew to Scottsdale, Arizona, to play golf with Quayle on Quayle's fiftieth birthday. It was on that flight that Billy and Martin talked about Blue Rhino, which Billy was preparing to take public. Martin said he'd like to invest in the company. Billy said, "Governor, I'd be proud to have you as an investor."

A few years later, Martin introduced Billy to Priory. The three were playing a round of golf in Charlotte when Priory directed Billy to Duke Energy people in Houston who could put together a hedging program for him.

Martin said all he did was introduce Billy to the person who could hook him up with people with the knowledge and skill to help him. "That's all I could, or should, do. Any more would have been a conflict of interest." But he was happy to do it, Martin said, because Billy is a "remarkable person who built a remarkable company. He has proven himself in business and in the community."

Billy said the goodwill and good deeds directed toward him by Martin and others have had a tremendous impact on him. "I believe this is a big part in life, knowing people willing and able to help you when you need help. I meet Jim in politics, and we play together in charity golf tournaments and become friends. Then he helps me out by introducing me to Rick Priory. You never know when little things can cause a turn in the road."

Billy turned to other friends, Gordon Regan and Ashnead Pringle, to manage his hedging program. The two owned and operated Propane Partners of Atlanta, a firm Regan started after leaving AmeriGas, where he was working when Billy met him. Propane Partners dealt with Blue Rhino distributors, managing propane purchases and hedges for the entire Blue Rhino network.

There had been a turn in the road for Billy, all right, but as the warm and beautiful Carolina days of autumn yielded to the cold winds of winter, it was not at all apparent that the turn was for the better. In fact, judging from the performance of Blue Rhino's stock, and the reaction from some stockholders to its performance, Billy must have wondered at times why he had ever taken that road. "He tried not to show it," said Bob Travatello. "And I think he did a great job of shielding employees, but you could see he was under tremendous stress. He was taking a pounding every day."

Those closest to Billy—Debbie; his mother, Mayo; and sisters, Jeannie and Luanne—could tell he was under tremendous stress. Mayo had a sensitive antenna, and she knew when Billy was going through a particularly rough time. "Mayo would call and say, 'Call your brother. He's had a rough day,'" Jeannie said. "Debbie would do the same thing. We all knew."

Family members were concerned about Billy. Debbie and others knew about the phone calls he was getting from angry stockholders, and the toll they were taking on him.

"I heard from Debbie about those calls," Jeannie said. "He knew all those people had invested money in the company, and he didn't want to let them down. I could tell he was stressed out, and I know he felt he had the weight of the world on his shoulders."

It was with him everywhere—at work, at home, when he went out to dinner, even on the Internet. Especially on the Internet. "This was about the time they started creating message boards on Yahoo, and they were really tearing me up, calling me a crook and telling me how stupid I was, and so on. It really hurt. I had to keep myself from reading that negative crap. I had to try to keep positive."

But that was hard to do, especially in a town the size of Winston-Salem where many people knew Billy, and what happened to Blue Rhino was big news. Stories about Blue Rhino's woes that might have made a briefs column in the *Chicago Tribune* led local and business fronts in Winston-Salem and nearby Greensboro.

If Billy and Debbie sought solace at a quiet restaurant, someone was almost certain to recognize him and try to start a conversation about the company's troubles. It was hard for Billy to avoid or ignore people who wanted to talk about Blue Rhino.

"When things go bad, you become a big fish in a very small pond."

He might have added, "a lonely fish," because, although Castaneda got some calls, too, it was usually Billy to whom people insisted on talking.

"What happens is, you turn into the company," he said. "At least I did. Blue Rhino was what I was. It was hard to separate myself from it—even when I was out to dinner with Debbie."

Christmas of 2000 was a sad time. Calls from disheartened, disgruntled, or even seemingly disturbed stockholders intensified in number and emotion as Christmas neared. Billy took every one of them personally. One, in particular, bothered him. A man called him at home, sounding morose and upset, very close to Christmas Day.

"He told me he was looking over his portfolio, and that he didn't know whether to get drunk or shoot himself. He said, 'Do you know how much money you've lost me?' I tried to tell him to hang in there, and explained what we were doing, but it didn't do any good. He kept saying, 'I've lost so much money.' It made me feel terrible. It just wore me out."

But as much as that encounter, and all the others during this time, weighed on him emotionally, and although he was deeply concerned for the future of Blue Rhino employees and stockholders, Billy refused to get down on himself. He knew that he had done his best to save his company.

"There's only about 50 percent of business you can really control," he said. "You do that by hiring the right people, initiating hedging programs, and so on. You need luck with the other 50 percent. Sometimes you're going to have bad luck, but you can't sit in your office and sulk about it. You can influence that luck by continuing to surround yourself with the right people and doing the right things. But, even then, sometimes you can have bad luck and there will be nothing you can do about it."

Bad luck had hit Blue Rhino. If doing the right things didn't turn it around, Billy wasn't going to sulk, and he certainly was not going to be frightened of the future. "There's no way I'm going to be afraid after the things that had already happened to me in my lifetime."

What he was going through with Blue Rhino was difficult, but not nearly as difficult as experiencing the deaths of his father and grandfather, and guiding the family business without them. "I felt like my father and Pa left me with an inner strength. All this was bothering me, and bothering me something terrible. But I always knew I would get through it."

Turnaround in 2001

There is an art to scrambling for money. Few people are inclined to lend money to someone desperate enough to have to scramble for it. On the other hand, you can't raise money when you're desperate for it unless you're scrambling. The secret then is to be able to conceal your desperation while moving fast and being convincing.

In other words, know what you're talking about and never let them see you sweat. People probably saw Billy sweat when he unloaded fertilizer from a tractor-trailer, but never when he was making a pitch for money for Blue Rhino. That's because he believed in the company, and he loved to tell the Blue Rhino story. He could be as passionate as an itinerant preacher—and considerably more convincing. He had to be convincing; the people he had to convert were natural skeptics with tight grips on their wallets.

"Billy was always well prepared and well informed, and he did an excellent job of telling the story of his company," said David Warnock of Camden Partners. Warnock's investment, coupled with the loan from Allied Capital, had kept the wolves from the door temporarily, and allowed Billy to initiate a hedging program. But the wolves resumed their snarling as 2001 began, and Blue Rhino's stock teetered around $2. Billy knew he would have to convince other investors to buy his company's stock, or it could become worthless, and there would be no Blue Rhino at all.

Warnock had done more than invest in Blue Rhino; he also introduced Billy to other leading and influential investors. One was Allied Capital in Washington, DC. Another was Paul Stephens, a highly respected San Francisco trader. With the stock in the low single digits, Billy had no analyst coverage. He would have to rely on his passion for Blue Rhino, his knowledge of the market, and his powers of persuasion to convince one of the most knowledgeable and sophisticated investors in the country that he should put his money in Blue Rhino, a stock that had resided in or near the cellar for a good part of the past year.

That was all he needed. Billy told him the Blue Rhino story and showed him his growth plans for the year. "I told him, 'Paul, if you will invest with me, I can tell you that we have a solid plan for growth, and we're going to hit every one of our numbers. If we don't, I'll let you know.' He bought more than a million shares."

Stephens did more than that. He also introduced Billy to Jon Gruber of Gruber & McBaine Capital Management, a major San Francisco investment firm. Billy told the Blue Rhino story to Gruber, and his firm also bought more than a million shares. And Stephens wasn't through. He was so impressed with Billy's presentation and the potential of Blue Rhino that he began telling everybody about it. "He's telling everybody in the world," Billy said. "He even called me and said he wanted to introduce me to Peter Lynch."

Peter Lynch, sixty-two, is arguably the best stock-picker in the world. He earned that reputation with Fidelity Investments where, in 1977, he was placed in charge of the firm's obscure Magellan Fund, which at that time had about $18 million in assets. By the time Lynch resigned as fund manager in 1990, the fund had more than $18 billion in assets. During Lynch's thirteen years as its manager, the Magellan Fund averaged an incredible 29.2 percent annualized return.

In midsummer of 2001, Billy was invited to give a Blue Rhino presentation to a growth conference in Boston, administered by CIBC Oppenheimer, the Canadian investment and banking firm. Blue Rhino stock, bolstered by purchases from Stevens and Gruber & McBaine, had edged up to between $6 and $7.

Billy was in a conference room of the Four Seasons Hotel, preparing for his presentation. "I'm getting my microphone and notes ready when this guy walks in and takes a seat on the front row. He looks familiar to me, and I keep thinking that I've seen that guy before. And then, five minutes into my presentation, I recognize who he is. It's Peter Lynch. I've seen him on TV."

Billy finished his presentation and opened the floor to questions. Lynch asked four or five, and Billy answered them all. Billy then walked to the elevator and, as he was about to get in it, Lynch arrived and got in the elevator with him. Lynch looked at Billy for a moment, and said, "I like what you had to say in there. Can you do a conference call tomorrow?"

"Why, yes, Mr. Lynch," Billy replied. "I certainly can."

The next day Billy and Lynch participated in a two-hour conference call that covered every aspect of Blue Rhino. "I mean everything," Billy said. "Customers, hedging program, everything. He really gets involved personally."

As the call was winding down, Billy asked Lynch a question.

"I say, 'Mr. Lynch, does this mean you're going to buy some of my stock?'

"And he said, 'The truck is backing up to the dock as we speak.'

"I said, 'Are you going to buy a truckload, Mr. Lynch?'

"He said, 'The truck is backing up.'"

It was never disclosed how many shares Lynch bought, but it had to be "a real big truckload," Billy said. He called every couple of months to get an update on Blue Rhino from Billy, and then he started telling everybody about Blue Rhino.

"That's what really got the momentum going. And he would tell me to talk to so-and-so at T. Rowe Price or Wellington or Fidelity or wherever."

Lynch purchased the stock gradually, over a period of about eight months. The stock began edging upward. It faltered momentarily on 9/11, and then Blue Rhino surged forward. Although other industries suffered in the aftermath of the 9/11 terrorist attacks, the backyard barbecue industry did not.

"People started staying home a lot more," Billy said. "Instead of going out and spending a lot of money on a steak dinner, people stayed home and saved money. I think they felt better being at home in their own backyards."

The sales of gas grills began to increase, and with them the sales of propane cylinders.

"Pretty soon, Blue Rhino gas began to fly off the shelves. Nine-eleven had a big impact on our business."

The biggest impact, however, and the major factor in the turnaround of Blue Rhino stock, was created by Billy's success in persuading these prominent and respected traders and investment managers to take a chance on Blue Rhino.

"We were able to get in the right network, and that made all the difference," he said. "That's how the stock got from under 4 to a legitimate trading price. I meet Dick Kiphart, and Kiphart introduces me to David Warnock, and Warnock introduces me to Paul Stephens, and through Stephens I meet John Gruber and Peter Lynch. These were some of the most respected traders of all times."

Once again, Billy had met the right people at the right time and had been able to win them over to his side. "Even when things seem to be about as bad as they can get, I know they can get better. You have to believe it. You have to believe that hard work, resilience, and never giving up can, and will, turn things around."

That type of attitude and work ethic attracts people who can and want to help. There were many people who helped during Blue Rhino's times of crisis, and many became more than just investors to Billy. They became his friends, who stay in touch by calling or visiting regularly.

One is Mickey Straus of Straus Capital Management in New York. Billy met Straus at the Pierre Hotel on one of his road shows. "Mickey's a character. He manages several hundred million dollars, but he's never had an office. I always met him at the Pierre or some such place."

On one occasion, Straus wanted to meet Billy at the Harvard Club in Manhattan. Billy arrived before Straus and was trying to call him on his cell phone when Straus walked into the club. "My goodness," he kidded. "You haven't been using that cell phone in the Harvard Club, have you? That just isn't done!"

Whether it's at the Pierre, Harvard Club, Four Seasons in Chicago, or downtown Winston-Salem, Billy strives to maintain relationships with Straus,

Stephens, and others with whom he has become involved in financial dealings. "You know when you connect or not, and when you do, you want to maintain and improve the relationship. You do that through life. I think it's one of my better characteristics."

But Billy has also learned there are some people with whom he would be better off not to have a relationship—even if it means he won't complete a business deal. "If I don't like the way the relationship feels, I know how to walk away from a deal. If I don't have a good feeling about the relationship and the person, then I have to question the quality of the business deal.

"Life's going to take a lot of turns. You want people who are going to stay with you and try to make it work—people like Mac McQuilkin, for instance. You want people who will stick with you through good and bad. Those are the people you want to surround yourself with, whether they are investors, employees, friends, or neighbors." There's a foolproof way, Billy says, to determine whether to enter into a business relationship—or any kind of relationship, really—with someone. "It's easy. Just look at how they treat other people."

Billy was often on the road scrambling for capital between 1999 and 2002, and he made it a point to keep his management team informed. Team members knew where he was going, who he was going to see, and why. "You have to be honest and open with your employees. You don't go behind closed doors with the board and let the employees read about it in the newspaper."

Billy liked to mix his crisis communication with good cooking. He would call a meeting in the commons area while one of Blue Rhino's excellent barbecue chefs prepared lunch or dinner. News of a lawsuit or the ramifications of skyrocketing propane prices went down a lot easier when it was accompanied by good food. "I'd say, 'Okay, guys, here's exactly what's going on.' Otherwise, they would have to read it in the newspaper, and often it was wrong or full of half-truths."

Billy focused on the truth of whatever the growing crisis was. He asked employees to trust him to deal with it and told them the best way they could help him was to concentrate on their jobs. "You've got to make sure more than six million cylinders get delivered to customers. Let me concentrate on everything else. You guys focus on your customers."

Employees were more than willing to do that. "We trusted Billy because everybody knew he trusted and respected us," said Jeff Dean. "The culture he built here—the optimism and the passion that made it fun to come to work—survived even the bleakest times."

That culture allowed the company to grow even as steep wholesale propane prices decimated Blue Rhino's balance sheet. The company lost

41 cents a share in 2000–2001, and posted a $4 million loss in revenues. Yet, Blue Rhino kept growing. By July 31, 2001, the Blue Rhino logo was arguably as recognizable as McDonald's golden arches; it was certainly at more locations. In fact, Blue Rhino's twenty-seven thousand were more than the 26,538 locations of Wendy's, Burger King, and McDonald's, combined. Blue Rhino added about two thousand locations in 2000–2001, despite the spike in propane costs. The increase in the number of cylinder transactions was considerably more impressive, and encouraging—from 5 million to 6.2 million.

Boydston, who became vice president of sales in the fall of 2000, concentrated on establishing Blue Rhino in every one of a major retailer's stores in a particular buying area of that retailer. For instance, if Home Depot had seventy-five stores in its Denver area, Boydston would push to get every one. "It was the domino theory. Get one or a couple of the big ones, and the rest would be likely to come in. I wanted to get deeper and deeper into the area with each one."

Sometimes he didn't know how deep into an area he would have to go. For example, Home Depot's Southern California area included a store in Yuma, Arizona—about a four-hour drive for the local distributor, who was losing money on the trip. He refused to service the store, saying it cost him more to drive the distance to replace three or four cylinders than the money he was making on the sales.

Home Depot wouldn't have it. Store executives told Boydston that if Blue Rhino didn't service the Yuma store the way Home Depot wanted it serviced, Home Depot would remove Blue Rhino from all of its approximately 125 stores in that area. "They meant it," Boydston said. "I knew that if we didn't do Yuma, we'd lose them all. So we wound up paying the distributor ourselves to make the trip to Yuma and back, even if it was to replace two cylinders. We either paid him, or we lost all the stores in the area."

It was a no-brainer, Boydston said.

That kind of initiative, focus, and willingness to sacrifice helped turn Blue Rhino around. Sales never slackened. No matter what its stock price, consumers continued to believe Blue Rhino was a good buy. By the end of calendar year 2001, about six months after Lynch made his first Blue Rhino stock purchase, the stock was at $10. It appeared that Blue Rhino was on the way back.

Helping fuel that turnaround was the new state-of-the-art cylinder distribution center that Blue Rhino and Manchester Tank Co. built in the Yadkin County town of Hamptonville, thirty-two miles west of Winston-Salem. It opened in the spring of 2000 and was named the R4 Tech Center (for Regional, Recertification, Refilling and Refurbishment). The center was built on thirty-four acres at a cost of about $7 million.

The plant receives thousands of cylinders a day from retail locations up and down the East Coast. In an almost completely automated process, the tanks are inspected for safety, refurbished, repainted, and refilled with propane. The tanks, some showing their age with grime and rust, move like squat little robots at attention on fast-moving conveyer belts that deliver them from station to station. Each is sandblasted to remove all traces of rust and repainted. They are automatically refilled and weighed on electronic scales with minute tolerances.

When they are reshipped for redistribution to retail centers, they're like brand new cylinders in every way. The plant, with a capacity of refurbishing and returning to stores thousands of cylinders a day, took over the work of at least ten distributors. The faster the tanks were available for exchange at retail displays, the faster they could be sold.

But there was another reason the Hamptonville plant spurred Blue Rhino's rebound. In April 2002, federal regulations required that all propane cylinders be equipped with overfill protection devices—known as OPD valves. Blue Rhino had the valves because of steps that Billy had taken in purchasing the intellectual property of Bison Valve and International Propane Products. Mac McQuilkin oversaw their production in China and their shipment to Blue Rhino. As backyard chefs learned of the new regulation, many turned to Blue Rhino, which was, by far, the largest cylinder exchange service in the country.

The Hamptonville plant produces about 2.8 million cylinders a year, an average of almost eleven thousand a day. It produced many more during the period of OPD compliance. "When Blue Rhino first started, if you could do 350 or 400 a day, you were doing pretty good," said Dave Slone.

The R4 Tech Center was Slone's baby. He was involved in its construction from the planning stages, including visiting plants in Europe where the technology had been in place for about ten years. The Hamptonville plant would be the first of five of its type that Blue Rhino would build, although the R4 Tech Center would remain the largest, by far.

Few things on Earth are as brilliant as the first rays of sunshine enveloping dogwoods in full bloom on a Carolina morning in the springtime. But two came close in the spring of 2002. Those were the smiles of Billy and Castaneda as they announced Blue Rhino spring quarter earnings of $1.8 million, up dramatically from a loss of $2.3 million a year earlier. The company had truly turned the corner. Blue Rhino's long, dark nightmare appeared to be over.

"We see nothing but increased revenue and earnings in the future," said Billy, beaming and fairly bursting with confidence.

He had reason to beam. Everything was finally coming together as they should, like the flavors of a Brunswick stew melding perfectly on the grill. His scrambling for capital, the hedging program, the R4 Tech Center, and the hard work to comply with the OPD valve replacements—everything was finally working and coalescing as they should.

Best of all, he thought, as analysts pressed him for predictions for next quarter, the Blue Rhino herd—from his board, to his management team, to workers and distributors in the field and across the country—had never quit, had never lost faith, even when the nightmare was darkest. That was when the stock bottomed out at $2 in 2000–2001.

Billy knew that many employees, such as Susie Simpson and Adrianne McCollum, continued to buy the stock at rock-bottom prices. It pleased him immensely that they would profit from their faith in the company, and in him. In fact, the last time Billy had been this pleased was on another sun-splashed spring day almost four years ago to the day, May 18, 1998, when he took Blue Rhino public.

Billy's smile might have been even a little wider a few months later when he and Castaneda announced even more dramatic end-of-the-year numbers showing Blue Rhino's astounding turnaround. Blue Rhino posted revenues of $205.59 million in fiscal 2002, up from $137.96 million in 2001. That gave the company a net income of $8.03 million, compared with a net loss of $4.72 million in fiscal 2001, a huge upswing. Blue Rhino stock closed at $15.84 on September 16, 2002. A year earlier, on September 17, 2002, the company's stock closed at $3.20.

The turnaround was sparked by an 81 percent increase in cylinder sales, and a 32 percent jump in sales of Blue Rhino propane-fueled products, especially patio heaters.

As he released the numbers for the remarkable success story of 2002, Billy announced that a new Blue Rhino product with the catchy moniker of "SkeeterVac" would be introduced in 2003. As its name implies, SkeeterVac is a propane-powered mosquito zapper. It attracts mosquitoes using carbon dioxide generated by the propane and a bait-induced scent by tricking the insects into thinking a warm-blooded mammal is in or around the device. When they fly too close, a vacuum sucks them in, where they are trapped and die.

SkeeterVac was an ideal Blue Rhino product because it used propane, and a lot of it—about twice as much as a typical grill, Billy told analysts. The average backyard cook will empty two cylinders a year. The SkeeterVac, however, was designed to run constantly during the bug-biting season—twenty-four hours a day, seven days a week, emptying a twenty-pound cylinder of propane in three weeks.

In 1998, brimming with confidence and basking in the glow of the IPO, Billy and his management team developed a strategy session for Blue Rhino's long-term growth and goal of "A Blue Rhino in every backyard, patio, and home." It became known as "The Big, Hairy, Audacious Goal," or, simply, "Bhag" for short. Because of the setbacks that began just a few months after that meeting—the devastating *Wall Street Journal* column, the pull-out by PricewaterhouseCoopers, the aborted secondary offering, and the propane price spike—Blue Rhino was unable to realize that goal.

But it survived, and in 2003, Billy and his management team updated the goal—a Blue Rhino in every backyard, patio, and home, an estimated 100 million households, by 2014. The prize for obtaining the goal would be the $2 billion in revenue generated by sales to those households. The strategy that would get Blue Rhino to that lofty goal would be the same strategy that Billy and his team devised in 1998. It also was the same strategy that allowed the company to survive against formidable odds while expanding by tens of thousands of retail locations into almost every state in the country.

The strategy was simple, but powerful. Its foundation was built on basic entrepreneurial values, such as competitiveness, innovation, flexibility, and, above all, integrity. Billy added a couple more—fun and loyalty. Blue Rhino is a company dedicated to making backyards fun, so it stands to reason that it ought to be a fun place to work. "Spark something fun," became the company motto. Finally, loyalty occupied a major position in Billy's and Blue Rhino's foundation of values. "If you're part of Blue Rhino," he said, "I want you to bleed rhino blue."

There were three main strategic areas: converting refillers to exchange customers (for example, by making cylinders with OPD valves readily available); increasing market demand by introducing products, such as SkeeterVac, that use propane; and leveraging the company's $100 million state-of-the-art infrastructure that Billy had been building for eight years.

"If it didn't fall within one of those areas, we didn't do it," he said.

Although the strategy had not gotten Blue Rhino to its Big, Hairy, Audacious Goal by 2003, it had led the company to a position where Billy and the board felt comfortable in taking care of some old but unforgotten and festering business. It was time to sue PricewaterhouseCoopers.

The company had first filed suit against PWC in late 1999 about ten months after PricewaterhouseCoopers refused to issue Blue Rhino a "comfort letter," which would have cleared the way for the company's $42 million secondary offering. The stock plummeted from $25 to $6, costing the company untold millions. Blue Rhino withdrew the suit about a year later, when its stock had fallen to about $2 and Billy was scrambling to keep the company afloat. There was no time to prepare for a lawsuit. Now, in 2002, the stock was headed upward, and Blue Rhino was thriving. Billy could give the case his full attention, and he thought it deserved it. Billy and his board believed strongly that Blue Rhino had been wronged and done great harm by the actions of PricewaterhouseCoopers.

Blue Rhino's lead attorney was William F. Maready of Winston-Salem, a scrappy former U.S. Army Green Beret soldier who was "tough as nails, and exactly the right lawyer for us," Billy said. "He thought we were absolutely right, and that the case was a no-brainer."

The trial began in January 2003, in Forsyth County Superior Court in Winston-Salem. The relationship between business and the public was different from what it had been in 1999. Enron, the former Houston-based energy trading giant, was under a federal criminal investigation related to its swift decline into bankruptcy. Enron's accounting firm, Arthur Anderson, had been indicted a few months earlier in connection with the Enron investigation. "This affected the trial greatly," Billy said. "I think the public probably thought CEOs and accountants alike were crooks and liars."

The trial focused on how PricewaterhouseCoopers changed its opinion regarding how Blue Rhino should account for its relationship with Bison Valve and USA Leasing. Billy was the first witness called. He testified that Blue Rhino's accounting for both transactions was exactly the way PricewaterhouseCoopers' local office advised. He said PWC had never complained that Blue Rhino was not providing enough information for the accounting firm to do its job—as PricewaterhouseCoopers alleged in court documents and its lawyers' remarks to the court.

"Blue Rhino accounted for the transactions and disclosed them to the public the way it had been advised to do so by Jim Lattanzi of PricewaterhouseCoopers," Billly said. "Later, the PWC national office over-ruled Lattanzi, and Blue Rhino suffered the consequences. There was never a dispute with the PWC local office on how to account for Bison Valve or USA Leasing. We did what we were told to do by PWC in Greensboro."

PricewaterhouseCoopers made its strategy plain in opening remarks by claiming that Blue Rhino deliberately withheld information from the accounting firm in order to prevent a loss in the quarter prior to the secondary offering.

"They said we weren't credible management," Billy said. "It seemed that their main strategy was to attack and insult me. They said we misled them and misled the public. But we disclosed everything. PricewaterhouseCoopers looked at it and agreed with it, and then they later changed their opinion."

Blue Rhino stock dipped a little lower each day Billy testified. His testimony was positive so far as Blue Rhino was concerned, but that was not apparent in the media outside North Carolina.

"The only thing in the national media was that Blue Rhino was in a trial fighting with its auditors. With institutional investors, that's not a good thing, and it's not good for the stock at all."

Billy was into his third day of testimony when he and Castaneda decided to heed the judge's advice to Blue Rhino and PWC to try to settle the case. "We knew we had a good business and that we had it back on track, and we had done a good job of getting our points out, so we gave Bill Maready instructions to see what kind of settlement we could get."

Maready, who believed Blue Rhino had an excellent chance of winning the case, wanted to continue with the trial. But he negotiated with PWC lawyers and came back with a "nice check," Billy said, although not close to the $50 million to $100 million that Blue Rhino lost in market value because of the stock plunge and being forced to abort the secondary offering. Both sides agreed not to disclose the amount of the settlement, although there were reports that PricewaterhouseCoopers paid Blue Rhino between $2.5 million and $3 million, plus legal fees.

Billy said that to this day he still isn't sure what prompted PWC to change its opinion, although the adverse publicity concerning Enron and Arthur Anderson must have had a great deal to do with it. He said, "Everything we did was fair and disclosed, and PWC approved it. I think in the final analysis it was about policies, procedures, and people's egos, and very little to do with business."

Travels with Billy

In 1994, when Billy decided to name his new company Blue Rhino, he dared to dream that when he took it to Wall Street its name and logo would be as recognizable as the ubiquitous Pink Panther. He envisioned a map with a virtual herd of Blue Rhinos stretching from North Carolina to California, from Maine to Florida, and from Texas to the Dakotas. That didn't quite happen in 1998, the year he took Blue Rhino public, but by 2003 that was pretty much how a Blue Rhino map of the United States would look. Blue Rhino and its flaming horn were in more than twenty-seven thousand retail locations in forty-eight states and Puerto Rico, and Billy was looking around for room to grow.

He thought he had found it in Brazil. Wal-Mart was making a tremendous push in that big South American country where almost every family used gas. Wal-Mart named Blue Rhino its International Vendor of the Year in 2003 and invited Billy to come to Brazil. "They were opening stores there like crazy," said Billy, "and they really wanted us in them."

Praxair, a large industrial gas company doing business in forty countries, had a major presence in Brazil. Billy arranged to meet Dennis Reilley, Praxair's president and CEO, through one of his friends, Gordon Regan, who owned a firm that handled the hedges for propane companies, including Blue Rhino. Billy and Reilley, during a golfing weekend on Kiawah Island near Charleston, South Carolina, talked about the possibility of Blue Rhino moving into Brazil. Reilley arranged for Billy and members of his management team to visit Praxair operations there.

Billy, along with Mac McQuilkin, Operations Chief Tim Scronce, and SkeeterVac head David Pearsley toured Praxair plants and facilities for a week in Sao Paulo, Rio de Janeiro, and other cities. A number of things stood out, Billy said.

"Everybody had a little gas tank they used. Companies would do home delivery and switch them out—people used them under the kitchen stove, for cooking—or a driver would come by in something that looked like an ice cream truck and blow the horn, and you go out and tell him you needed an exchange."

Billy also noticed that every company in the gas cylinder distributing business was also in the bottled water business.

Although there was a strong market in Brazil, Billy was reluctant to enter it because he thought the Brazilian government had far too much control over the sale of propane in the country. "The government controlled the entire energy busines—prices, everything. Praxair would have been a good, strong partner, but I thought it best that we not get involved."

Billy checked out Mexico with a businessman by the name of Jesus Zaragoza, whose family owned a company called Texas Oil and Gas. Zaragoza, who lived in San Diego, was president. It was the largest propane gas business in Mexico, more than a billion dollars a year in sales. Billy was interested in touring his Mexican operations because Wal-Mart had just moved into Mexico.

"It was already one of the country's biggest players. They said, 'Come on to Mexico if you can make it work.'"

Billy and Zaragoza met in San Diego, just across the border. Billy was a little apprehensive because Zaragoza's family had been mentioned in a segment on the television news show *60 Minutes* about drugs smuggled across the border in propane trucks. "Jesus said the driver disappeared and they hadn't seen him since."

Zaragoza picked Billy up in a big SUV with a driver and bodyguard. "And there's a vehicle in front of us and another behind. I said, 'What's wrong? Why do we need all this security? Is this going to be dangerous?' He said, 'We're a little concerned about kidnapping. My family is always worried about it. My brother was kidnapped last year, but I don't think you have to worry.' I said, 'What happened?' He said, 'We paid the ransom.'"

Billy was considerably more apprehensive and much more appreciative of the bodyguard cars as they sped through Tijuana "like the president in a military convoy, guns and all."

Billy visited two plants, one in Tijuana and another south of that city. He saw workers filling cylinders by hand all day, while customers stood in line with their cylinders to refill them. "The workers were being paid about $2 a day or something like that. It was the largest propane company in Mexico, but they were selling it for less than I could buy it, a dollar a tank or some ridiculous amount. I asked Jesus how he could sell it that cheap. He said the government subsidizes it and tells them how much to sell it for."

Again, as in Brazil, the government was paying for and subsidizing propane. "It's all about relationships," Billy said. "Unless you're one of the chosen, you have no chance. How are you going to wean the public from paying $1 for a tank of propane to paying $10 for a tank?"

Billy traveled the world looking for places Blue Rhino could grow—China, where Blue Rhino already had a presence with McQuilkin and Uniflame, but no cylinder-exchange business; Southeast Asia; and Australia.

"There were a lot of places we looked at that had a lot of potential volume, but also carried a lot of risks and complexities."

Australia was especially attractive, but there was another company so eager for the business that Billy felt the cost would have been too prohibitive.

Billy did establish an agreement to buy tanks from a vendor in Thailand. His old friend, Darrel Reifschneider, from whom Billy had purchased tanks for years, sold Manchester Tank and Equipment Co. to the McWane Corp. in 1999. McWane decided to restructure Manchester, and Reifschneider, who had led Manchester for fifty years, was let go, and McWane raised the price of the tanks.

That did not sit well with Billy. He withdrew Blue Rhino's business, which was one of Manchester's largest accounts, and moved it to Thailand, where he bought tanks at a much less expensive price than he could have gotten them from McWane. "I didn't like the way my buddy was treated," he said.

Ultimately, Billy decided to strike a deal with Praxair in Canada. The agreement, which would become effective in the spring of 2004, was for the Connecticut-based Praxair to act as Blue Rhino's exclusive independent distributor, providing filling and distribution services across all six Canadian provinces. Plans called for full implementation with Blue Rhino cylinders available at major retail stores in all provinces before the end of the 2004 summer outdoor barbecue season. The deal represented the first move outside the United States and Puerto Rico for its tank exchange service. Billy had made Blue Rhino cylinder exchange an international business.

If it were possible to prove, it would be a darn good bet that the politicians who were cussed most often in boardrooms during the past seventy-five years or so were not any of the well-known liberals or organized labor supporters such as Teddy Kennedy, Lyndon Johnson, Hubert Humphrey, or even Franklin D. Roosevelt. Instead, they are two members of Congress whose names, spoken individually, ring few bells of recognition outside their home states. But spoken together, as in "Sarbanes-Oxley," they are recognized far beyond their home turfs. The recognition can be painful, especially among business groups.

And that's probably unfair to Senator Paul Sarbanes, D-Maryland, and Representative Michael Oxley, R-Ohio, sponsors of the Sarbanes-Oxley Act of 2002, the most sweeping federal legislation affecting corporations since FDR and the New Deal of the 1930s. For good or ill, their names are attached to the law for the ages, but they were joined overwhelmingly by their colleagues in enacting it in July, 2002, in the wake of a series of high-profile corporate accounting scandals, such as those at WorldCom and Enron.

Backed by major business groups such as the Business Roundtable, the law passed the Senate by a vote of 99–0, and in the House by 423–3. It wasn't long, however, before businesspeople, especially medium-size corporations with entrepreneurial cultures like Blue Rhino's, began to realize that Sarbanes-Oxley might be a cure that could choke them to death if they weren't careful. It was a law, opined an article in *USA Today*, mandating that all companies "undergo financial root canals to take care of a few rotten teeth."

The law required companies to look into every nook, cranny, and crevice to make certain that internal controls were present and working. That sounds all fine and good, but it quickly became obvious to Billy, and many other entrepreneurs, that compliance with the legislation would be incredibly expensive, even stultifying, for rapidly growing companies like Blue Rhino. "You had to have auditors check your auditors. You had to have external auditors and then get another firm to audit your procedures."

This was the infamous—many entrepreneurs called it odious—Section 404. "It cost every firm another million or so to put in the proper software and procedures, and an ongoing cost to check those procedures every year. It was just so ridiculous to me that a company like us, with maybe a $200 million or $250 million business, fell under the same requirements as a $10 billion company."

Billy sensed that Sarbanes-Oxley could easily douse Blue Rhino's entrepreneurial spirit and culture, as well as its way of conducting business. Billy abhorred bureaucracy and micromanaging. From Blue Rhino's earliest beginning, he had hired people who could act on their own—often, like Billy, at a moment's notice. Indeed, much of Blue Rhino's extraordinarily rapid rise was due to the company's ability to make decisions and turn deals quickly. Moment's notice deals and decision making were anathema to the spirit of Sarbanes-Oxley. Every decision had to be checked and approved, and rechecked and approved again, before becoming finalized.

The monumental task of preparing for the new law, which was scheduled to become fully effective in June, 2004, fell mainly to Bob Travatello, the company's chief information officer. He received help from CFO Mark Castaneda and Blue Rhino's new president, Tim Scronce.

Billy hired Scronce, who had held executive positions with Frito-Lay and Diageo, in 2001, when Joe Culp left the company. Impressed with Scronce's leadership skills and business sophistication, Billy tapped Scronce, who was only thirty-six at the time, to become president of Blue Rhino in November 2002. By then Travatello was buried in Sarbanes-Oxley.

Travatello and his team had one thing going for them. They had begun a project to improve and streamline the company's financial data and inventory control systems before Sarbanes-Oxley. Travatello and Castaneda said Blue Rhino would have initiated the necessary improvements anyway—without legislation that added layers of bureaucracy and put a crimp in the company's spirited entrepreneurial style. In an interview with the business journal *CIO Insight*, Travatello described the effects of that crimp.

"The mentality at Blue Rhino was always to beat the market," Travatello said. "If a major retailer wanted us to do something, and that would get us the business, we would do it right away. We basically looked at ourselves as a speedboat going through the water. If someone said we had to make a left turn, we were able to make a left turn on a dime. What we see happening now with Sarbanes is that we can't make that turn on a dime anymore."

Sarbanes-Oxley, along with the need to add to Blue Rhino's size and scale, were the main reasons Billy traveled the world in 2002–2003 searching for places Blue Rhino could grow. Another had to do with his only real competitor, AmeriGas, the largest propane company in the country. AmeriGas, with home offices in King of Prussia, Pennsylvania, was a $2 billion-a-year company. But it cost Billy just as much or more, percentage wise, to comply with Sarbanes-Oxley as it cost AmeriGas.

AmeriGas' cylinder exchange program accounted for a fraction of its total business revenue, but cylinder exchange produced the bulk of Blue Rhino's earnings. Furthermore, when Blue Rhino submitted its required quarterly and annual financial reports, they were, to a great extent, reflections of the performance of the company's cylinder exchange business, and the numbers were there for the world to see. The AmeriGas numbers for its cylinder exchange program were dwarfed by the figures accounting for the overall performance of AmeriGas' many divisions.

AmeriGas, with its almost 1.3 million commercial, industrial, agricultural, and wholesale customers, and almost six thousand employees, was Blue Rhino's proverbial elephant in the living room. It was always there, and everybody knew it. The elephant wasn't usually disruptive, but the potential was ever-present. It was like a ticking clock was draped around its neck.

Billy knew that cylinder exchange accounted for less than 5 percent of AmeriGas' profits. "But it was 90 percent of mine. I knew they could cut my legs out from under me any day they wanted to—and that was a terrible position for me to be in. That's why I was looking to link up with other companies and expand into other countries."

Sarbanes-Oxley and the big gaseous elephant in the living room were forcing Billy to take action.

AmeriGas started to compete with Billy when the big company saw Blue Rhino take off in 2001–2002. In 2003, AmeriGas cylinders were available for exchange in about eighteen thousand locations, compared with Blue Rhino's almost thirty thousand. Some of the big national retailers then began to play Blue Rhino against AmeriGas. "It gave them a choice," Billy said.

"They would go to AmeriGas to try to keep prices down." Those large national stores—Lowe's, Home Depot, and Wal-Mart—were 60 percent of Blue Rhino's business. "They were our core," Billy said. "They were critical."

AmeriGas was led by a fifty-three-year-old former Philadelphia lawyer by the name of Lon R. Greenberg. Billy approached Greenberg several times about buying AmeriGas' cylinder exchange business. Sometimes Greenberg appeared interested, other times not. Billy also tried to work out a deal in which AmeriGas and Blue Rhino would form a joint venture. AmeriGas would distribute the cylinders, and Blue Rhino would be the brand marketing company dealing with retailers. It didn't happen. Either Greenberg wasn't interested, or he was one of the few people with whom Billy was unable to develop a rapport.

"Every time I thought we were making progress, I was wrong. It just didn't happen. The comfort level wasn't there like it was with Dennis Reilley. It's too bad. We would have made a lot of money."

Billy finally concluded it was useless trying to reach an agreement with Greenberg, although he knew that AmeriGas could run him "into the ground anytime it wanted to."

Although Blue Rhino was vulnerable, Billy was an entrepreneur in the classic sense of the word, which made him, by definition, an optimist and a risk taker. He and Blue Rhino had weathered storm after storm. He had taken on-the-chin blows that would have knocked most people out of the ring, and the arena as well. He not only got back on his feet each time; he prevailed.

Now, it was time to take a moment and savor what he and the employees and independent distributors of Blue Rhino—many of whom had been with him almost from the beginning—had accomplished. Figures in the annual report for the fiscal year ending July 31, 2003, said it all. Blue Rhino had come back from the abyss in fine fashion. Sales for 2003 topped $258 million. Those revenues generated $33 million in profits. In less than a decade, and at times against tremendous odds, Billy and Blue Rhino had revolutionized the industry.

Actually, they had done more than that; they had created a new industry. Cylinder exchange had existed only as small, local ventures until Billy—leveraging off the Blue Rhino brand, a top-notch information technology system, and a network of independent distributors—expanded across the country. Large propane companies took notice.

"I was taking part of their business away, and it was the only growing part of the industry. They saw that. Then our revenues grew to $258 million. That's real money, and we made $33 million in profits. People saw that."

They certainly did. Billy was named Ernst and Young's Entrepreneur of the Year for the Carolinas in 2003, and was awarded lifetime membership in the Entrepreneur of the Year Hall of Fame.

Billy's accomplishment left CEOs of propane companies many times larger than Blue Rhino shaking their heads in envy and amazement. James E. Ferrell of Ferrellgas was one. Ferrellgas, with headquarters in Overland Park, Kansas, rivals AmeriGas as the country's leading propane retailer.

Ferrell, a slim and trim sixty-six, has run the company since 1965 when he returned home to Atchinson, Kansas, from a two-year stint in the U.S. Army. When he took the reins from his father, the company owed more money than it was worth. Almost forty years later in 2003, Ferrellgas was a billion-dollar company, and Ferrell was an icon in the propane industry. Although a millionaire many times over, Ferrell is known for his frugality, which he expects from his executives as well.

"If it's a choice between a four-star hotel and a Hampton Inn, he'll choose a Hampton and eat at McDonald's, and ask why you didn't," said one. Those who know him, however, agree he is an interesting and complicated man.

For instance, he and his wife, Elizabeth, have amassed an impressive collection of rare, antique bibles and manuscripts.

Billy has a lot of respect for him. Their backgrounds are similar. Each took over ailing family businesses at a tender age, and each built them into major players in the industry. "He basically started with nothing. I admire his accomplishments and his integrity," Billy said.

So far as Ferrell is concerned, the feeling is mutual. He, along with the rest of the bulk propane industry, watched Billy build a business that almost no one thought could advance further than a local or regional level, until it stood alone as a national leader. "I guess I was like everybody else who was watching him," Ferrell said. "At first I thought it was a screwball idea that would never work. Then I got envious."

Ferrellgas, like most bulk propane companies, with the exception of AmeriGas, had no cylinder exchange business. It had a few filling stations where a backyard cook could refill his empty cylinder, but that was it.

Blue Rhino's annual report for fiscal 2003 stirred Ferrell's envy, as well as his admiration, and prompted him to give Billy a call. He said he was coming to Winston-Salem and would like to visit.

The two talked business, a subject they both loved, easily and informally over dinner at Noble's Grille in Winston-Salem.

"What's your end game, Billy?" Ferrell asked, meaning, did Billy plan to sell Blue Rhino. "When are you going to cash out?"

Billy said he had just started. "I'm still growing," he said. "I want to be like Ferrellgas some day—over a billion dollars a year."

"That's fine," said Ferrell. "But if you're ever interested in cashing out, give me a call."

Angering a Giant Sparks a Painful Decision

It was late summer of 2003, time for line review with the major retailers to determine, among other things, prices for the coming year. Lowe's, whose corporate office was in North Wilkesboro, about an hour's drive west of Winston-Salem, was up first for review. Lowe's and Blue Rhino had an excellent relationship. Blue Rhino had brought thousands of customers to Lowe's since the big retailer became Blue Rhino's first major customer almost ten years before.

Blue Rhino, bolstered by its fantastic year, asked Lowe's for all its cylinder exchange business. In other words, Blue Rhino asked Lowe's to kick out AmeriGas, which had about 40 percent of the retailer's cylinder exchange business. The Blue Rhino sales team emphasized how much business Blue Rhino had attracted for Lowe's. Lowe's agreed and gave Blue Rhino all of its business.

"They wouldn't even take AmeriGas' calls," Billy said.

A couple of weeks later, in September, the sales team was in Atlanta negotiating with Home Depot. Right away, the big store's executives said Blue Rhino had a major problem. "You have an aggressive competitor who just dropped the price two dollars a cylinder," they said. "We feel obligated to go with them. We are going to give more of the business to AmeriGas."

Blue Rhino was stunned. It had pissed off a giant.

Once again, what had been wonderful news and a time of immense satisfaction and celebration had turned into a nightmare. AmeriGas had taken in every word when Billy proudly announced Blue Rhino's record year of $258 million in sales and $33 million in profits. AmeriGas was so impressed that it quoted Blue Rhino's year-end numbers to Home Depot—but in a different way, Billy said, and with a different goal in mind.

"They went in there right after I made my announcement, and said, 'Look how much Blue Rhino made off you. Just look at all that money. It's way too much. Go with us, and we'll get the price down where it ought to be.'"

Although Lowe's wouldn't talk to AmeriGas, Wal-Mart would, and did, the very next week, and Wal-Mart's reaction was the same as Home Depot's. Although the chain had enjoyed an excellent relationship with Blue Rhino, it felt obligated to go with AmeriGas, and the much lower price.

"I'm being forced out of business," Billy said. "These guys could give the gas away, and it wouldn't have a major impact on their overall company. To me, it means everything."

Once again, it was scramble time, and everything was on the line. What Billy had feared could happen with AmeriGas was happening, and it was happening fast. Billy hurried to Bentonville, Arkansas, and walked into the office of Gordon Erickson, Wal-Mart's senior vice president in charge of merchandising.

"I show him how his sales had gone from zero to about $70 million in less than ten years, and how he wouldn't even have this part of his business if it hadn't been for Blue Rhino. I tell him how I had been loyal to him in building the business. I ask him not to make a quick decision because what they'll do is give you a low-ball price just to force me out and get in the door, and then when they get inside, they'll raise prices again. I've known them to do that for years."

The next day Billy flew to Atlanta and made the same argument to Steve Jansen, vice president of merchandising for Home Depot. "I'm selling my ass off. I'm giving the best sales pitch I possibly can to be able to keep my business. That's what was on the line. I do this for two or three weeks."

Billy's best was good enough, barely, and for the moment. He was able to retain Blue Rhino's share of the big retail stores' business at a price that would allow Blue Rhino to stay in business and grow. But Billy knew that the agreements he negotiated, after completing the best sales jobs of his life, amounted to no more than buying a little time.

Billy's heart was heavy when he boarded the plane in Atlanta for the flight to Winston-Salem. "I knew I had fired every one of my bullets, and that it would be impossible to survive another year the way we were. AmeriGas could, and I knew would, pull the ground out from under us."

Billy knew he had to do one of three things for Blue Rhino to survive.

Number one, he could go private. That way it wouldn't be so easy for a big company to undercut him because he wouldn't have to announce his numbers.

Number two, he could make acquisitions in order to diversify the company.

Or, number three, he could sell or merge Blue Rhino with another company. Going private was the most palatable of the three, but he knew it would probably be prohibitively expensive.

As the plane made its approach to Winston-Salem, Billy came to the sad realization that he might have to sell Blue Rhino.

Billy spoke with Flip shortly after he returned to Winston-Salem. "I'm not sure I can stand it, " he said, "but it looks like I'm going to have to merge or sell the company."

Flip knew what Billy was going through. He had been there himself. Flip knew what a deep, personal connection Billy had with Blue Rhino, its employees, and its customers.

"He felt that tremendously," Flip said. "This, of all his trials and tribulations, brought him to tears."

Flip told Billy he would support whatever decision he made. "You know Blue Rhino better than anybody. I know this is emotional and tough for you, but think about what's right for everyone. Take your time and do what you think is best. I'm with you all the way."

Castaneda told Billy almost exactly the same thing. He and Billy had been through numerous financial wars and crises together, and were battle-tested. They knew how each other thought, and each trusted the other completely.

Billy asked Bank of America to analyze the option of going private. That was his favorite option, by far.

"This was my baby. I really wanted to try to take it private. It'd be nice to own it all, anyway. I know I've got to change the structure. I couldn't figure out how going private was going to work, but I felt like I had to get Bank of America to look at it.'

Bank of America told him that going private would require hooking up with a private equity group, "and leveraging the company, big time. They said I'd have to borrow all the money the banks would allow me to borrow, and I'd need a private equity firm to put equity into the business, and that they would end up calling the shots. We estimated we'd need to borrow more than $200 million."

Reluctantly, Billy realized that going private didn't make a lot of sense. "If I put myself in a leverage position, I'd be more vulnerable to a price war. The only advantage would be to not have to reveal my numbers."

Sadly, it had become apparent that Billy would either have to merge Blue Rhino with another company, or sell it outright. He took Debbie out to dinner and told her, over a glass of wine, that the only way to save the company was to sell it.

"We got emotional," Debbie said. "It was his baby."

Billy called his new friend, Dennis Reilley of Praxair, and told him he needed to talk. Reilley was preparing to leave for China the next day, but told Billy he would meet him at the airport in White Plains, New York, if Billy could get there in time. Billy did, and the two men drove to a diner and talked over coffee. Billy got to the point right away. "Would you be interested in merging with or purchasing Blue Rhino?" he asked. "If we're a part of Praxair, we can continue to grow and kick AmeriGas' butt. But with their size, I'm not sure Blue Rhino can do it alone."

Reilley said he was interested, and he'd send a team to Winston-Salem within the next week to begin the discussions.

It was time to bring other key people in on the plans, including Blue

Rhino President and COO Tim Scronce, and General Counsel Scott Coward. Billy also spoke personally to each member of his board about what he was doing and why. They all understood and backed him solidly.

This was in October. Less than three months after Blue Rhino posted record sales and profits, Billy and his team of Castaneda, Scronce and Coward began a series of due diligence meetings with Praxair CEO Dennis Reilley's team. The meetings were to afford Praxair the opportunity to learn everything it could about Blue Rhino before deciding what kind of an offer, if any, to extend to Blue Rhino. The teams met secretly in a conference room at Southern Community Bank for three weeks.

Billy and the Blue Rhino board met in November in Palm Springs, California. Billy decided to have his board meeting there because he was in the running for the 2003 National Entrepreneur of the Year Award, whose winner would be announced in Palm Springs during an event hosted by Jay Leno.

Billy, anxious to hear what Praxair would offer, asked Reilley to call him in Palm Springs. Reilley called immediately before Billy's board meeting, and the news was not that good. Reilley told Billy he couldn't offer him more than $14 a share. The stock was trading at about $12 at that point.

Although he had not yet presented it to the Praxair board, Reilley said he knew that some of his board members were concerned about Blue Rhino's reliance on stores such as Wal-Mart and their pressures to keep costs down.

Billy was disappointed. He told his board that, considering the cost and adverse effects of Sarbanes-Oxley, he did not feel comfortable continuing for another year as an independent, publicly held company. Neither did he feel comfortable about accepting an offer as low as $14. The board agreed, and Billy asked Bank of America to compile a list of likely candidates.

Bank of America's list included a name with which he was familiar—Ferrellgas. Another candidate was Shell Oil in London. There had been rumors that Shell's London office might be interested in a venture such as Blue Rhino's in the United States. As Billy was going down the list with Bank of America, he mentioned Ferrell's visit in August and the interest he had expressed in Blue Rhino.

"Then you should talk to Ferrell, CEO to CEO," the Bank of America investment bankers told Billy. "We'll go to London and talk to Shell. You talk to Jim Ferrell."

As it turned out, the rumor about Shell of London was little more than a rumor. Shell said it wasn't interested; that Blue Rhino stock, which had jumped from $12 to $14, was "overpriced." Jim Ferrell, however, was for real.

Super Sunday

Billy called Jim Ferrell in the first week of December. He had no idea whether Ferrell could come to Winston-Salem, or would even want to talk with him. After all, it was only in August that Billy had told Ferrell that he was not interested in "cashing in."

He certainly didn't want to sound desperate now, or too specific, but he did want to extend enough of a carrot to entice him. Billy asked Ferrell if he would like to come back for a visit and continue their discussion of four months earlier.

"How about Saturday?" Ferrell replied.

The two CEOs—each a self-made millionaire who had pulled himself up by his bootstraps—met at the Forsyth Country Club, not far from Blue Rhino headquarters in Winston-Salem.

As usual, Billy had done his homework. He already knew that his and Ferrell's backgrounds were similar in that each had built their businesses from an early age. But Billy also had learned that their management philosophies were similar. A profile on Ferrell in the *Kansas City Star*, in which he offered suggestions to eager entrepreneurs and budding business owners, could have been a profile of Billy. Much of his advice also was espoused by Billy:

> Be resilient. Get over setbacks. Don't let them push you off course.
>
> Fall in love with the business so you can get over the humps, but be able to cut your losses when it's not working.
>
> Use what comes from this part of the world—values, respect for people.
>
> Conduct business so you can have repeat customers. If you sell something for $2 and the customer finds out it should have been $1, you can't go back and sell another one.
>
> You'll always be judged by the people you surround yourself with. Pick employees carefully.
>
> Find things you like to do, not just for money, but to contribute something to the world.

Billy didn't want to sell or merge his business, but, if he had to, he thought he could live with Jim Ferrell and Ferrellgas. Billy, however, did not want to let on at first that Blue Rhino might be for sale. He began by asking Ferrell questions similar to those Ferrell asked him in August. When was Ferrell going to "cash in"—what was his end plan?

"Do you have a successor, Jim?"

Ferrell said, no, he really didn't have a successor in mind. "I know I'll have to retire sometime. Now, if I had young talent like you...."

The two were courting each other, and Billy knew it.

"I'm dating him, and he's dating me. I'm smart enough to see that, and so is he."

Billy explained how the problems and costs generated by complying with the requirements of Sarbanes-Oxley were especially severe to a young and growing public company such as Blue Rhino. In fact, he told Ferrell, "In this day and time, a company needs to be of a size and scale" larger than Blue Rhino's.

Billy said that since August, when he and Ferrell talked, he had done "a lot of thinking about this whole thing, and I think I might be better off being part of a much larger entity." And Ferrellgas, he said—with more than a million customers in forty-five states, sales of almost 900 million gallons of propane, and revenues of $1.22 billion in fiscal 2003—just might be the right larger entity for Blue Rhino. "I think we could make it work, and we'd be pretty powerful. We could kick AmeriGas' butt."

Billy could see that Ferrell was more than a little interested. But Ferrell wanted to know more; particularly, he wanted to know where Billy figured into the scheme of this larger entity. "I don't think we can do it if you don't stay on," he said.

Billy said that since Ferrell had no one to hand the company down to, he wanted to stay on and see if there was a possibility of "becoming CEO of the whole thing."

"Billy, I like your thinking," Ferrell said. "I need somebody like you."

Ferrell was extremely interested now. He wanted to know how much it would take to purchase the company. The stock was at about $14 then. "But shareholders aren't going to accept it at $15 or $16," Billy told him. "We've been at $25."

Ferrell was silent for a moment. Billy wanted him to act, to take the game to the next level. "The board might want me to put it out for bids," Billy said.

"No. No. Don't do that," Ferrell said. "I can move pretty fast."

And he did. Ferrell had a team of people in Winston-Salem the next week looking at Blue Rhino's books. The dating was over. It was time to work out the prenuptials.

Ferrell and Billy talked through the holidays and into January. It was a painful and difficult time for Billy, and for others involved in the process from Blue Rhino. Not because Ferrell and his team were difficult and demanding. They were not. It was painful because they were participating in radically changing the structure and culture of a company they had created, nurtured, and loved.

It was especially painful for Billy, participating in the due diligence discussions—which were again held at Southern Community Bank—and discussing the futures of employees and distributors who had helped him build the company. Knowing in his mind that what he was doing was right didn't help the hurt in his heart.

"It was just a very difficult period."

Ferrell's and Billy's teams conducted two day-long sessions under a tight veil of secrecy. Ferrellgas, of course, wanted to know everything about Blue Rhino before agreeing to buy it. Who were its best customers? Its largest customers? What were the gross margins? What kind of management agreements are in place?

"Basically, they want to know what can go wrong," Billy said. "And they want to know what costs they can cut out if they decide to come in."

Companies merging or considering merger look for "synergies," or areas they can combine to increase savings or productivity. "We knew right away we could save a million or more from required filings, public documentations, and so on," Billy said. "Insurance was another area where there were savings for the combined companies. Are there places we can distribute the product more cheaply? Can they use any of their own warehouses?"

Personnel was another area, although Billy pressed hard for as few Blue Rhino casualties as possible in this area. "I could just see them looking around the room, and I know they penciled in, 'What's your salary, Scott? What do you make, Castaneda?'"

The teams also used this time to examine each other's culture and philosophy. Are they similar? How are they going to get along? Can they get along? Most organizations take on the personalities of their CEOs. Ferrell runs a company based on accountability to each other, Billy said. "He didn't believe in a lot of corporate structure. You earn your merits. He and I were alike in that respect."

Ferrell took all the information he and his team gleaned from meetings with Billy and his team and mulled it over through most of January. Billy and his management team attended the annual distributor conference in Orlando and discussed plans and goals for the coming year. Meanwhile, he talked with Ferrell by phone "about every hour or so."

This was the year the Carolina Panthers National Football League team made it to the Super Bowl. Billy, an avid Panthers fan, planned to go to the game, which would be played in Houston, where Ferrell lives. Billy asked Ferrell if he wanted to go with him. He didn't, but he invited Billy to breakfast at his home on Super Sunday, the morning of the game.

It was then and there over breakfast that Ferrell agreed to a price of $17 a share. He also agreed to honor Blue Rhino's employee agreements and promised that Blue Rhino headquarters would remain in Winston Salem. The Panthers lost the Super Bowl in a thriller, 32–29, but Billy believed Blue Rhino and its employees and shareholders were winners. His board agreed when he informed members in a conference call the next day.

Billy and Ferrell shook hands and agreed they were going to make a great pair. The deal, however, was far from finalized. Still ahead were days and days of negotiating the details and fine print of the merger agreement before it could be announced. Sarbanes-Oxley governed much of this process as well. Billy was required to step away from the procedure entirely. This was because some of the points to be negotiated were specific to management. The idea behind the law was to prevent top executives from negotiating excessive packages for themselves.

An independent committee of Blue Rhino directors, chaired by Richard Brenner, took over the negotiations for Blue Rhino. The committee, in addition to Brenner, included David Warnock, John Muehlstein, Steve Devick, and Bob Lunn. The committee hired its own counsel, along with Bank of America, to perform an independent evaluation of the company. Every procedure had to be meticulously followed and recorded. The cost was in excess of a million dollars, and Billy questioned the necessity of the expensive procedures. It was money that could have gone to the shareholders.

"They said we needed to go strictly by the books. If we did, we still might get sued, but if we followed all these procedures, we'd win. If we didn't, we would lose. And we did get sued."

As the committee members and lawyers negotiated the financial side of the merger, detail by detail, Billy and Ferrell hammered out what Billy's new position would entail. Every day was emotionally exhausting for Billy. "I've always acted with my head and not my heart, but it was hard to separate them this time. In my head, I knew this was the right thing to do. But emotionally, it was hard to sell my baby."

Billy went home each night with a heavy heart and recounted the day's negotiations with Debbie. "I know we're doing the right thing, honey," he said. She assured him that he was.

Billy called his friend, Craig Duchossois, one of Blue Rhino's original investors, over the weekend before the announcement of the sale Monday morning. Duchossois had left the board about three years earlier to pay closer attention to his businesses, but he and Billy had remained close friends. "I was pleased that he called me," Duchossois said. "Unlike a lot of CEOs,

Billy does not base his decision on ego. There was never any whining from Billy, but I felt a great deal of empathy for him, and I told him so. Blue Rhino was his baby and he loved it, but he felt a strong responsibility to his shareholders."

Duchossois said Ferrellgas appeared to be a "win-win situation" for Blue Rhino and its shareholders. He told Billy that he should be proud. He had taken a company with "zero value, and in less than ten years turned it into a $250 million corporation. That's quite an achievement."

Words of support from Duchossois and others, such as Flip and Brenner, in the tight circle of acquaintances and associates who knew what was happening, helped bolster Billy's spirits as the negotiations dragged on. They lasted almost two weeks, from the last week in January through the first week of February, including Saturday and Sunday. After the final legal phrases were agreed to, and the documents dated and signed, the deal was pretty much what Billy and Ferrell decided it would be over breakfast in Houston before the Super Bowl game.

The agreement, contingent upon the approval of stockholders, called for Ferrellgas to pay $17 a share for Blue Rhino stock, a total of $343 million to shareholders, and Ferrellgas would assume $52 million in Blue Rhino debt. It was a deal amounting to almost $400 million.

Blue Rhino would become a division of Ferrellgas. To the outside observer, however, there would appear to be little, if anything changed. Its headquarters would remain in Winston-Salem; its brand name and logo, recognizable throughout the country, would be retained; and its founder and CEO, Billy Prim, would remain at the helm. Few key employees would lose their jobs, although Castaneda and Coward, the company's general counsel, would eventually be bought out.

The agreement also called for Billy to become a member of the Ferrellgas board. Public filings showed that his yearly salary plus incentives would total $1.2 million, and if he stayed at least three years, he would receive an extra $2 million. Billy and Flip each agreed to buy $15 million worth of Ferrellgas stock "to show our support for the new company," Billy said, "and help it out on Wall Street."

All in all, the final agreement for the merger of Blue Rhino and Ferrellgas was what Craig Duchossois said it would be—a winning situation for everybody.

There was one part, however, that was particularly upsetting to Billy. Selling Blue Rhino was already tearing at his heartstrings, but then Ferrell insisted that Billy sell part of the family property that was especially dear to him—the old fertilizer warehouse. It was a building brimming with memories of his father and grandfather. It was where they taught him the fundamentals and values of business, and so much more. It was where

Blue Rhino began. Blue Rhino was still using the building as a cylinder refurbishing and refilling station, and there was a propane storage tank on the site. Billy had leased the property to the company.

When Billy showed him the site, Ferrell immediately told him that it had to be included in the sale. There could be no related party activities or conflicts of interest, he said. The property was developed to be part of Blue Rhino and was being used as a part of Blue Rhino. "Somebody could come in and start competing against us," Ferrell said. "We've got to have it."

Billy understood Ferrell's position, and he finally agreed to sell. The terms of the sale were not disclosed, but he said he received a "substantial amount," along with the right of first refusal to repurchase it if the property ever ceased to be a part of Blue Rhino. It was comforting to know that it could be back in the family again.

Now, it was time to tell his family about the impending sale. He had already told Debbie, of course, and had been confiding in her for weeks. But the rest of his family—his mother, Mayo, and sisters Luanne and Jeannie and their families—did not know, not even Luanne's husband, Chris, who worked at Blue Rhino. It would be a momentous change in their lives because all owned significant amounts of Blue Rhino stock.

It also would be a momentous change in the lives of Billy's Blue Rhino family, not only because of the new owner, but because most employees owned Blue Rhino stock. Some employees had bought stock through the company's option and ownership plans since the company's beginning. The official announcement at Blue Rhino was scheduled for Monday morning, February 9. Billy's announcement to his family would be a couple of days earlier.

Announcing the Marriage

Abbye Caudle loved Blue Rhino, and she loved working for Billy as his executive assistant. That's why she felt a sudden stab of dread at the words Billy spoke to her shortly after Jim Ferrell called late in November 2003.

"Let's keep it on the low that Mr. Ferrell called," he said. "Let's keep it quiet." That's all Billy said, but it was enough. There was something about the way he said it.

"I think I knew then he was going to sell the company," she said.

A few days later, Billy confirmed her fears. He called her into his office and told her he was going to sell Blue Rhino to Ferrellgas.

"He needed me to help call people and set up meetings, and so on. He told me it was going to be like always. Nothing would change. He was going to stay and be the CEO of Blue Rhino. He asked me to keep everything quiet, not to tell even my husband."

Caudle swallowed her dread and tried to believe nothing was going to change. She didn't say a word to anyone, not to her husband and not even to her friend, Lori Hall, the company's investor relations manager, and they usually shared everything.

Billy called her into his office again about five weeks later, on the afternoon of Friday, February 6. This time Human Resources Director Robin Manley was there, too. Manley knew nothing about the sale to Ferrellgas. She was stunned when Billy told her, and that the news would be announced to the entire company on Monday.

Manley had worked for a company before that had been sold, and she had found the process painful. It took a moment for the news to sink in.

Once it did, Manley said, "I think my exact words to Billy were, 'I hope I live long enough to forgive you for this.' I think he was worried that it would break my heart. And then I laughed, and Billy laughed, and I asked him what I could do to help him get ready for Monday."

Billy told Caudle and Manley that he wanted Monday to be a day of celebration, not sadness. "I want it to be a party," he said. "I want people to think this is a good thing, which it is."

The two recruited several other employees to help them, although they couldn't tell them why they were getting ready to celebrate. They worked all weekend.

Meanwhile, Billy and his personal family were celebrating that weekend. Billy turned forty-eight on Thursday, February 5, and the following day was Mayo Prim's birthday. The entire family planned to celebrate by attending the Wake Forest-North Carolina basketball game Saturday afternoon at Lawrence Joel Coliseum in Winston-Salem, and then going out to dinner that evening. The game was a good one, although Luanne, a Carolina fan, was probably the only member of the family to enjoy the outcome, since the Tar Heels won by a 79–73 score.

The family packed into Billy's car after the game to go to dinner—Billy and Mayo; Jeannie and her husband, Ron Cannon; and Luanne and Chris Holden. Billy started the car, and then half-turned in his seat and told the family he had an announcement to make. He got right to the point.

"Ferrellgas has offered us a nice price for the company, and we've decided to merge with them. We're going to announce it publicly Monday, so you can't tell anybody until then."

All the chatter about the Wake-Carolina basketball game stopped. Nobody was talking.

"Everybody's mouth dropped," Jeannie said. "It was a huge shock."

Finally, Mayo Prim said, "You're doing what? Why?"

Billy told his family that the time was right for the merger. "The company will still be here, and it will still be Blue Rhino. It will be good for Blue Rhino, and since the family has a good deal of Blue Rhino stock, it will be good for the family."

They peppered him with questions. What was he going to do? Was he going to still be head of Blue Rhino? Billy told them that his specific roles were still being decided, but that he would remain as CEO of Blue Rhino and assume additional duties with Ferrellgas.

After the initial shock wore off, the family took the news well. "Billy knows his business," Mayo said. "We trusted his judgment."

Chris Holden, like Abbye Caudle, expected Billy to sell at some point, "but I didn't expect it to come so quickly." But Holden learned long ago that Billy's business timing was exquisite. "If Billy said the time was right, you can take it to the bank. The time was right."

Jeannie said the timing was also good for Billy personally, too. She knew that he had agonized for friends and family members during the times that Blue Rhino stock plummeted to almost nothing. "He felt the weight of the world on his shoulders then. He wasn't going to let them down."

When Blue Rhino employees arrived at work Monday morning, February 9, 2004—a date most will never forget—they all did double-takes, and some might have wondered if they had taken a wrong turn into a neighborhood carnival or street festival. Colorful balloons and smiling faces were everywhere. They drove under three big blue and white balloon arches along the driveway, and balloons festooned the entrance to each of the four buildings. Continental breakfast buffets of bagels and pastries awaited them in each building. They surely thought that something incredibly wonderful and pleasing had occurred or was about to occur.

That's exactly what Manley and Caudle wanted them to think. The women had worked through the weekend to create the celebratory atmosphere that Billy wanted to surround the announcement that would profoundly affect every Blue Rhino employee. Caudle had worked through the night, getting home at 5 a.m., barely enough time to shower, dress, and get back to work as the first bewildered employees began to arrive.

When workers got past the tables of bagels, pastries, and other breakfast goodies; sat down at their desks; and turned on their computers, they were teased with a message that exciting news was imminent. Caudle and Manley sent the e-mail announcement about 8:30 a.m., as soon as they knew that the press release, scheduled to be issued that morning had been sent over the news wires. Billy wanted Blue Rhino employees to be the first to hear the news, and to hear it before the market opened.

The company e-mail message emphasized the positive—that Blue Rhino was merging with Ferrellgas, and that it was a good thing. Everything, including Billy as CEO, would remain the same. The only thing different would be more opportunity for Blue Rhino to grow and realize its goals. The message invited all employees to attend an all-hands meeting at 1 p.m. with Billy and Jim Ferrell.

A hush descended over the company as employees began receiving and reading the e-mail announcement. "It was no longer a festive atmosphere," Caudle said. "Everybody was shocked. It was not happy news."

Meanwhile, Billy and Ferrell were holding a news conference with Winston-Salem Mayor Allen Joines at the downtown Piedmont Club. Billy wanted to assure the mayor and city that "we weren't going anywhere. Blue Rhino was staying right here in Winston-Salem."

Billy had briefed his senior managers Sunday afternoon and early Monday morning. "They were all blown away, of course. I told them I wanted them to act as if this was a good thing, which it was. I told them we had ten times the brand recognition of Ferrellgas and that we get to keep that recognition. I said the only difference is that, as a part of Ferrellgas, we'll be operating on a much larger platform—and this is a good thing."

This was the theme that both Billy and Ferrell continued to stress at the all-hands meeting that afternoon. It was held in the auditorium at SECCA, the Southeastern Center for Contemporary Art, in Winston-Salem. Blue Rhino often held meetings there. Billy again emphasized that the merger presented

Blue Rhino with a great opportunity to grow and realize its goal of a Blue Rhino in every backyard in America, and he would be with them as they obtained that goal. Blue Rhino might be a part of Ferrellgas, but it was still going to be his baby.

Billy's eyes glistened as he told the assembled Blue Rhino herd that the company was born from a "handful of stores, a little money, and not much else." He considered Blue Rhino his baby from the start.

"It was very much like being given a new baby girl at the hospital. You're happy because this little girl is yours, and you've been waiting for this moment all your life. You have tremendous plans as to how this little girl is going to accomplish amazing things. You're going to take really good care of her, make sure she gets what she needs, and nothing but the best is going to be good enough for her. At the same time, you're intimidated—because you've never been a parent before. It's more responsibility than you've ever had in your life."

But the happy father accepts the responsibility and embarks on a fantastic adventure, Billy told the hushed Rhino herd. "You have big wins—a smile, the first step, the first tooth, and the first birthday party. But, you also have tears, skinned knees, and the occasional bad report card.

"As your little girl gets older, she begins to experience the outside world. She makes friends, has a personality of her own, and develops habits, some good and some not so good. As a parent, you try to guide her to do the right thing. You make safe and thoughtful decisions on her behalf. You love her, and you want nothing but the best for her."

Then almost before the bewildered dad can realize it, Billy said, his little girl has blossomed into a beautiful young woman. "It happens in the blink of an eye," he said, smiling wistfully. "She's suddenly independent, smart, and fun. Everyone wants to be around her. And then the dating begins. As a parent, you look at the boys who come calling as aliens from another planet! They're nice enough, but who could ever be good enough for your little girl?

"And time moves on. Somehow you manage to get through the dating years, the college years. And then just when you think you are out of the woods, it happens. Your little girl drops a major news flash. Your little girl is going to get married."

An announcement like that can certainly take the wind out of your sails, Billy said. "But even though you might not like to admit it, you start to like the guy. As the wedding approaches, you get excited because it's not the loss of a little girl, but the gaining of a son and a whole new family, joined with yours, sharing the same values, the same dreams, together."

That's the way it was with Blue Rhino, he said. "We were first-time parents when it came to running cylinder exchange. We started this amazing company, and each of us had a vested interest in how she grew up. Nothing was too good or too challenging for our company. When opportunities presented themselves, we seized them! At times, when it would have been easier to have slow, modest growth, we never settled. In fact, we did just the opposite —we pushed her! We pushed her because we knew what she was capable of. We were not interested in baby steps, learning to crawl, and then walking. No, not us! We wanted to run! We wanted to charge! And charge we did!

"We signed up America's finest retailers on a national basis before we even had the infrastructure in place. In fact, we figured out the infrastructure on our way to install Wal-Mart and Home Depot. We were fearless, and we always welcomed trying something new! We always embraced change. Today, thanks to those early years and the right investments, we have state-of-the-art technology that's given us valuable information to grow."

But Blue Rhino's most valuable asset has always been its herd—its employees and distributors, Billy said. "We're surrounded at Blue Rhino with incredibly talented and smart people. I believe that's why Blue Rhino is where we are today—because of the innovation, creativity, and courage that are in this room. Blue Rhino has accomplished more in ten years than most companies accomplish in a lifetime."

Then Billy said he was proud to announce that Ferrellgas had acquired Blue Rhino.

"I want you to think of this partnership as a marriage," he said. "It's a union that we both welcome with open arms, and one that we believe will allow all of us to grow and flourish."

Billy introduced Ferrell and his team to the employees. "Gentlemen, welcome to the herd!"

Ferrell told the anxious employees that he had no intention of moving Blue Rhino out of Winston-Salem or changing anything about the company. "We like Blue Rhino the way you and Billy built it. That's why we bought it. Why would we change anything?"

What Billy and Ferrell said calmed some fears, but not all. A lot of employees still felt the way Jeff Dean did when he heard the news: "I thought somebody had shot my horse out from under me."

A Warm and Special Place, Always

The third week of April, 2004, was a week Billy will long remember. First, a judge threw out a lawsuit against Blue Rhino, filed by the New York law firm Milberg Weiss on behalf of a shareholder who objected to the sale. Milberg Weiss, called by some, in a not-always complimentary manner, as the "king of torts," was known for its class-action lawsuits filed on behalf of disgruntled shareholders. The firm was often successful in persuading companies, which wanted to get along with taking care of business and shareholders, to settle cases just before trial.

Billy refused an offer from Milberg Weiss over the weekend to settle the case, and the judge then ruled, in Blue Rhino's favor, that the case was too weak to try. Meanwhile, short-sellers who bet against Blue Rhino stock had been caught with their pants down when Ferrellgas bought Blue Rhino for a premium price of $17 a share. On Wednesday, April 21, Blue Rhino stockholders met in Winston-Salem and approved the sale. Their action made it official.

"What a fantastic week!" Billy exclaimed to Brenner. "We beat Milberg Weiss, we screwed the short-sellers, and our shareholders came out big winners. It just doesn't get any better!"

The shareholders' approval paved the way for delivery of a powerful antidote against the uneasy and foreboding feeling many Blue Rhino employees had about the sale. It might not cure the feeling entirely, but it would certainly assuage it. This wonderful salve was known as cash.

At $17 a share, some members of the Blue Rhino herd—including office workers, drivers, and other rank-and-file employees who had been with the company since its formative years—were about to receive substantial amounts. Quite a few of those employees had continued to buy Blue Rhino stock when its price had fallen as low as $2. "We thought that was a good time to buy," said Adrianne McCollum.

And it was, said Judy Smith. "We knew it would go back up."

Although most declined to say how much they received from the sale, some described amounts large enough to pay off mortgages and finance college educations—with enough left over to help out with retirement years.

It was immensely satisfying to Billy that many of Blue Rhino's loyal, long-term employees, such as Travatello, Belmont, and others received substantial amounts. Some checks were as high as seven figures.

"Sometimes nice guys do finish first," Billy said.

With $343 million to go around, more than a few nice guys and girls would finish in the money—even after the major shareholders were paid.

Billy felt a sense of pride, too, knowing that investors outside the company, large and small, made money off the sale. It was especially satisfying after those critical, and sometimes nasty, calls he received from people just three years earlier accusing him of causing them financial ruin.

After the sale to Ferrellgas became official, small-time investors often recognized Billy and would ask him, excitedly, when they were going to get their money. He loved to tell them it was on the way.

"I was in the airport, and this little guy came running up to me. He said, 'I read about that deal! When's my check coming? When's my check coming?' I said, 'It's coming. Don't worry about it one bit.'"

It was also good to see rewards going to major investors, such as Craig Duchossois and Flip, who supported him early. They were rewarded handsomely—tens of millions of dollars. "We had done our best to get a win for shareholders, a win for employees, a win for the company, a win for Ferrellgas, and a win for our customers. I think we did all that.'"

Mark Castaneda became a millionaire "a couple of times over." Blue Rhino "went out on top, negotiating from strength," he said proudly. "Billy had a marvelous sense of timing, and I'm forever grateful to him. I loved every part of my job."

It was also a win for Billy. He made "tens of millions more" than he ever thought he would want or need.

Billy's sister, Jeannie, knew it wouldn't work just as soon as Billy told her that he was going to work for Ferrellgas. Not that it had anything to do with Jim Ferrell. It was just that she didn't think Billy was cut out to be an employee. He already had worked for the only people he would ever work for, his dad and his grandfather. There would be no more bosses for Billy. He was an entrepreneur, not an employee, and everybody who knew him knew that.

"He won't last a month," said her husband, Ron Cannon, as they drove back to their home in Raleigh on February 7, the day Billy told the family about Blue Rhino's sale.

Actually, Billy lasted longer than a month, although not much longer—almost nine months, counting from the day the sale was announced in February; just over six from April 21, the day shareholders voted to make it official.

But he tried. He really did. Billy thought for a while that he soon would run all of Ferrellgas. After all, Ferrell had hinted that he might retire soon, and he said he would like to have someone just like Billy to hand the reins.

Billy went out to Kansas City and Houston and absorbed everything he could about the big company's operations.

But it didn't take him long, three or four months at the most, to realize that he could be waiting a long time before he touched the reins to the company.

"Once I really understood Mr. Ferrell, I could see how much he loves running Ferrellgas—so much so that he might go to his grave still running it. I was fine with that. There's nothing wrong with that at all. It's his company. But I wanted to do something different."

By early summer, four months after he sold Blue Rhino, Billy knew he was not going to be able to stay with Ferrellgas, not even as the head of Blue Rhino. It wasn't that he felt like an employee, exactly. Ferrell gave him plenty of autonomy. But Billy felt that he had stopped growing. He was not creating, and that was something he couldn't stand.

"In no way was I dissatisfied about Ferrellgas or Mr. Ferrell, but I just didn't see myself growing. I was in the role of managing a business rather than growing something."

Billy's entrepreneurial spirit was burning, and he was powerless to ignore it. "I needed to grow other things. It might sound funny, but to me, the bigger deal in my life was buying that business from Tyra Hobson back in 1981, and putting those oil companies together when I didn't have any money. For me, I feel there's always a bigger plan, a bigger deal, and I was having trouble seeing how that was going to happen from where I was sitting."

Billy made certain that Blue Rhino was operating smoothly within Ferrellgas and that Blue Rhino employees were secure in their jobs, and "everybody was doing the right thing." Then he went to Ferrell and told him Ferrellgas didn't need two CEOs. Ferrell said he wasn't going anywhere, that he liked what he was doing.

Billy said that was fine, and he understood. "But I told you, Mr. Ferrell, that I can't be an employee. I don't know how to be an employee, and you don't need another CEO. I'm going to have to do something else."

Why? Ferrell wanted to know. Counting his Ferrellgas stock, Billy would make more money than he could spend. "I don't even call you most weeks," Ferrell said. "Why?"

Billy told Ferrell that, at forty-eight, he was in the prime of his business life, with contacts around the world—"major business contacts for whom I've made a lot of money, and they know my abilities and skills. I can't see myself with all these opportunities sitting here and managing a business unit from within an organization. My skills are putting people together to make deals and grow things. I feel my skills would be wasted here. I think I've finished this chapter, and it's time to start a new one."

Billy said he thought Ferrell would have done the same if someone had bought him out when he was forty-eight. "I want to look back at my $400 million

Blue Rhino deal as my small one, and do a $10 billion deal when I'm sixty."

Ferrell said he understood, but he wanted Billy to maintain an association with Blue Rhino and Ferrellgas. He restructured his agreement with Billy, making him a "special adviser to the chairman." Billy also retains a seat on the Ferrellgas board. Ferrell wanted to tap into what he calls "Billy's classic entrepreneurialism. He has the ability to have a vision, keep it organized, and have people follow him. He has a Pied Piper quality. You can't teach what Billy has."

Billy called his final all-hands meeting to announce he was leaving. Jeff Dean said almost everybody in the room had tears in their eyes. "We've talked about him every day since," said Adrianne McCollum.

Billy's last day was November 1, 2004. He took Abbye Caudle with him to be his executive assistant in a new entrepreneurial venture he began the next day called Primo Water. It focuses on the bulk bottled-water market, and its concept is modeled after the cylinder exchange business. It will be as popular as Blue Rhino in stores throughout the country, he said with the same unbridled optimism that created Blue Rhino. It's the second of "many Blue Rhinos I have in me," Billy said.

But the first one—with its brightly burning horn, slightly mischievous grin, obviously about to "spark some fun"—will always warm a special place in his heart. It was his baby.

INDEX

Continuation of Dedication

Blue Rhino employees when the company merged with Ferrellgas on Feb. 9, 2004:

Rich Achor, BRC, Sr. Director Product Innovation; Alfonso Alcantar, CARIBOU, Production; Guillermo Alegria, PLAT LA, Blue Rhino Delivery Driver; Scott Alfson, BRC, Patio Heater Tech; Abimael Alvarez, R4, Operator; Reina Alvarez, R4, Operator; Maria Anaya, PLAT LA, Office Administrator; Raymond Anderson, PLAT CHIC, Blue Rhino Delivery Driver; Marianne Anderson, BRC, Customer Care Spec.; Manuel Angon, BUFFALO, Production; Thomas Angsten, PLAT GA, General Manager; Bernabe Aniceto-Dircio, R4, Operator; Ken Arnold, BRC, Systems Analyst I; Oscar Arriaza, PLAT LA, Supervisor; Aaron Arroyo, UNIFLAME, Warehouse; Ricardo Arroyo, UNIFLAME, Warehouse; Dick Arthur, BRC, Dir. of Skills Training & Reg; Roberto Arzate, PLAT LA, Production; Marvin Austin, RAVEN, Blue Rhino Delivery Driver; Gabriel Avila Aguilar, R4, Operator; Lewis Bailey, PLAT GA, Blue Rhino Delivery Driver; Perry Baker, PLAT VA, Office Administrator; Manuel Barrios, R4, Operator; Claude Batchelor, CARIBOU, Blue Rhino Delivery Driver; Bob Batton, BRC, Customer Care Spec.; Fred Baumann, BRC, Sr Dir Regional Accounts; Magdaleno Bautista, R4, Operator; Blanca Baylon, BUFFALO, Production; Dana Beach, PLAT NC, Installer; Marc Beegun, UNIFLAME, Account Executive; Rick Belmont, BRC, VP Mktg; Kevin Bennion, CARIBOU, Blue Rhino Delivery Driver; Stacey Benson, BRC, Customer Care Spec.; David Bentley, R4, Controller; Kathy Benton, BRC, Accounting; Allison Birmingham, BRC, Regional VP; James Blankenship, R4, Maint.Tech; William Blankenship, R4, Operator; Mady Blue, R4, Shipping Clerk; Carolyn Boak, BRC, Dist Svcs Acctg Spec; Michael Bock, RAVEN, Yard; Tom Bock, RAVEN, General Manager; Thomas Bock Jr., RAVEN, Production;

Wayne Boise, RAVEN, Blue Rhino Delivery Driver; Antonio Bolanos, PLAT LA, Production; Claudio Bolivar, PLAT GA, Route Supervisor; Gary Bonsangue, PLAT LA, Development Manager; Chris Bonsangue, PLAT SD, Blue Rhino Delivery Driver; Larry Boone, PLAT VA, Forklift Operator; Linda Booth, BRC, Collection Spec; Martin Bossler, BRC, Executive Vice President; Tom Boursaw, CARIBOU, Production Supervisor; Napoleon Bouvier, RAVEN, Yard; Jeremy Bowen, CARIBOU, Production; Michael Bressler, PLAT SD, Blue Rhino Delivery Driver; Julia Brewer, BRC, Compliance Manager; Kay Brickley, BRC, Strategic Acct Mgr; Harold Brisbane, PLAT SC, Blue Rhino Delivery Driver; Michael Brock, CARIBOU, Blue Rhino Delivery Driver; Kevin Brogden, PLAT VA, Blue Rhino Delivery Driver; Brian Brown, BUFFALO, Warehouse; Quintus Brown, BRC, Regional VP; Tod Brown, BRC, Executive; Chris Browning, BRC, Sr. Director of Sales - West; Jonathan Bryant, PLAT FL, Blue Rhino Delivery Driver; Tony Byrd, PLAT NC,

Blue Rhino Delivery Driver; Bruce Byrd, PLAT SC, Blue Rhino Delivery Driver; Rafael Caballero, R4, Operator; Edgar Cables, PLAT MIAMI, Blue Rhino Delivery Driver; Troy Calvert, BUFFALO, Blue Rhino Delivery Driver; Oscar Camacho-Santana, PLAT LA, Production; Joseph Candra, PLAT CHIC, Maintenence; Antonio Cantu, PLAT MIAMI, Yard; Daniel Carpenter, BRC VEGAS, SR Blue Rhino Delivery Driver; Mike Carr, RAVEN, Office Administrator; Brent Casstevens, R4, Maint.Tech; Mark Castaneda, BRC, EVP/CFO; Pedro Castillo, PLAT LA, Production; Rosendo Castillo, UNIFLAME, Warehouse; Abbye Caudle, BRC, Executive Asst.; Michael Cauthen, BRC, Dir of Fin Rptg/A.C.; Rafael Cervantes, R4, Operator; Jerry Chaffin, JAYHAWK, Blue Rhino Delivery Driver; Jamie Chamberlain, PLAT CHIC, Production; Charles Chapman, RAVEN, Blue Rhino Delivery Driver; Bonnie Chewning, R4, Operator; AlexChurchill, PLAT NC, General Manager; Doug Clark, BRC, Safari Tour Guide/Office Manager;

Dan Coffman, CARIBOU, Blue Rhino Delivery Driver; John Coldiron, CARIBOU, Production; David Collins, R4, Truck Driver; Anne Combs, BRC, Communications Manager; Donnie Couch, PLAT NC, Blue Rhino Delivery Driver; Scott Coward, BRC, Legal Counsel; David Cox, PLAT NC, Blue Rhino Delivery Driver; LeeCox, BRC, Customer Care Superv; Antonio Cruz, R4, Operator; Jose Cruz, R4, Supervisor; Mario Cruz, R4, Operator; Roman Cruz, R4, Supervisor; Ubaldo Cruz, PLAT GA, Yard; Martha Cruz, PLAT FL, Office Administrator; Benedicto Cruz-Figueroa, R4, Forklift Operator; Robert Cummings, PLAT VA, Blue Rhino Delivery Driver; Richard Dahl, PLAT MN, Blue Rhino Delivery Driver; Anissa Daniels, BRC, Cash Receipts Coord; Elliot Darden, PLAT MN, DSD Scheduler; Jeff Dean, BRC, Sr. Dir., Dist Svcs; Juan DeArmas, PLAT LA, Blue Rhino Delivery Driver; Liza Decelle, R4, Quality Control; James Dees, PLAT FL, Blue Rhino Delivery Driver; Dalmacio Deguzman, UNIFLAME, Controller; Alfredo DeLeon, PLAT LA, Production; Gwendolyn Dervin, BRC, Customer Care Spec.; Craig Diggs, PLAT LA, Blue Rhino Delivery Driver; Teddy Doohan, BRC, Desk Top Analyst; Charles Dorris, PLAT FL, Blue Rhino Delivery Driver; Michael Doss, PLAT NC, Blue Rhino Delivery Driver; Jimmy Dotts, PLAT SC, Blue Rhino Delivery Driver; Jonathan Drabik, BRC SLC, General Manager; Pete Duchene, PLAT MN, Blue Rhino Delivery Driver; William Dull, BRC, VP Finance/Controller; Jennifer Dunn, BRC, Acct. Srvs. Coordinator; Cheri Edwards, CARIBOU, Office Administrator; Mark Elam, PLAT NC, DSD Scheduler; Chris Elledge, BRC, Cash Receipts Coord; Frank Enriquez, PLAT LA, Production; Ramon Espinoza, PLAT LA, Production; Charles Evans, PLAT LA, Blue Rhino Delivery Driver; Hugh Evans, PLAT NC, Maint. Tech; Adalid Fajardo, R4, Operator; Paula Farley, BRC, Legal Assistant; Michael Fasel, BRC, President/ COO Global Sourcing; Charles Ferguson, PLAT NC, Blue Rhino Delivery Driver;

Jeffrey Finch, PLAT FL, Blue Rhino Delivery Driver; Ellery Finch, CARIBOU, Blue Rhino Delivery Driver; John Fitzgerald, PLAT FL, Blue Rhino Delivery Driver; Joseph Fitzgerald, BRC, Warehouse; Mike Fleming, BRC, Director H&S, WC, Erg; Michelle Flynt, PLAT NC, Office Administrator; Antonio Forte, BUFFALO, Production; Daryn Fox, BRC, Wal-Mart KAM; Chris Fredrick, PLAT GA, Blue Rhino Delivery Driver; Paul Friduss, BRC, VP Sales, Global Sourcing; Brian Fryer, PLAT SC, Blue Rhino Delivery Driver; Oscar Fuentes, R4, Operator; Doug Fullerton, BRC, VP, FutureWorks; Aaron Funderburg, RAVEN, Blue Rhino Delivery Driver; Julio

Galinda, BUFFALO, Production; Henry Gallegos, BRC SLC, Blue Rhino Delivery Driver; Mark Galy, PLAT VA, Blue Rhino Delivery Driver; Aban Garcia, R4, Operator; Erasto Garcia, R4, Quality Control; Jose Garcia, PLAT LA, Production; Marcos Garcia, UNIFLAME, Warehouse; Ryan Gardner, BRC, Desk Top Analyst; Kurt Gehsmann, BRC, ; Sean Geraty, UNIFLAME, MIS Technician; Andrew Gillespie, PLAT GA, Blue Rhino Delivery Driver; Clarence Gipson, BUFFALO, Delivery and Install Supervisor; Kevin Glass, PLAT CHIC, Production; Jose GodInez, PLAT CHIC, Production; Octavio Godinez, UNIFLAME, Warehouse; Carlos Gomez, PLAT FL, Development Manager; Santos Gonzales, PLAT LA, Production; Alfredo Gonzales-Flores, R4, Operator; Salomon Gonzalez, R4, Operator; Javier Gonzalez, PLAT FL, Operator; Jesus Grande, R4, Forklift Operator; Loretta Gregory, R4, Operator; Jennifer Griffin, BRC, A/P Coor; Samuel Groce, PLAT NC, Blue Rhino Delivery Driver; Richard Guillen, BUFFALO, Production; MickGunter, BRC, Dir, Blue Rhino FutureWorks; Leonard Guyton, PLAT GA, Blue Rhino Delivery Driver; LoriHall, BRC, Investor Relations Mgr.; Janice Hamburg, PLAT GA, Office Administrator;

Robert Hansen, PLAT FL, General Manager; Amy Hargette, BRC, Cash Receipts Coord; Lisa Harris, R4, Lead Operator; Bud Harris, UNIFLAME, General Manager; Robert Harrison, PLAT SC, Blue Rhino Delivery Driver; Eric Harrison, BRC, Wal-Mart KAM; Melinda Hartgrove, BRC, Sr Accountant; Chris Hartley, BRC, Dir, Adv/Promo; George Hayek, PLAT NC, Blue Rhino Delivery Driver; Angela Healey, PLAT SD, Office Administrator; Bryan Heckler, PLAT CHIC, ; Jeff Heinz, BRC, Inv Control Mgr.; Fred Hendrick, PLAT FL, Installer; Jose Hernandez, R4, Forklift Operator; Steve Hershey, R4, Maintenance Supervisor-A Shift; Lisa Hicks, BRC, Customer Bill Spec; Daniel Hill, BUFFALO, Blue Rhino Delivery Driver; Eric Hite, JAYHAWK, Delivery/Installation Supervisor; Adam Hodge, R4, Lead Operator; Jennifer Hodges, BRC, Customer Care Spec.; Jesse Holbrook, CARIBOU, Production; Chris Holden, BRC, Regional Sales Mgr- East; Robert Holland, PLAT GA, Blue Rhino Delivery Driver; Patrick Holland, PLAT NC, Blue Rhino Delivery Driver; Timothy Holmes, CARIBOU, Blue Rhino Delivery Driver; Carolyn Hood, BRC, Dir. Nat. Conv. Stor; Rebecca Hoover, UNIFLAME, Operations Manager; Darren Howanietz, UNIFLAME, VP of Operations; Catherine Howe, BRC, HR Comm & Culture Mgr; Kevin Hudson, BRC, Dist Svcs Acctg Spec; Richard Huffman, JAYHAWK, Blue Rhino Delivery Driver; John Huggins, PLAT SC, Blue Rhino Delivery Driver; Tracy Hunt, R4, Blue Rhino Delivery Driver; Todd Hurst, BRC, Junior Engineer; Mary Hutchens, PLAT NC, Office Administrator; Jesus Ibarra, PLAT LA, Production; Clifford Ingles, CARIBOU, Production; Joel Ireland, R4, Blue Rhino Delivery Driver; Mike Isgett, PLAT SC, Distribution Supervisor; Michael Jackson, PLAT VA, Blue Rhino Delivery Driver; Charles Jacobs, PLAT SC, Blue Rhino Delivery Driver; Amy Jarvis, BRC, Field Sales Spec; Michael Jefferson, PLAT VA, Blue Rhino Delivery Driver; Donavon Jenson, CARIBOU, Blue Rhino Delivery Driver; Mark Johnson, PLAT GA, Blue Rhino Delivery Driver;

Alfred Johnson, PLAT MN, Blue Rhino Delivery Driver; Jesse Johnson, PLAT VA, Blue Rhino Delivery Driver; Mark Johnson, BRC, EDI/EFT Project Mgr; Roger Jolly, PLAT NC, Blue Rhino Delivery Driver; Tarra Jolly, BRC, A/P Coor; Richard Jones, RAVEN, Blue Rhino Delivery Driver; William Jones, RAVEN, Blue Rhino Delivery Driver; Nicole Jones-Sutton, BRC, Executive Asst.; Deborah Jordan, R4,

Operator; Mateo Juan, R4, Operator; Daniel Juarez, PLAT LA, Blue Rhino Delivery Driver; Robert Juarez, PLAT LA, Blue Rhino Delivery Driver; Juan Juarez, PLAT NC, Yard; Lisa Keen, BRC, Purch Spec/asst; Bud Kiger, BRC, Regional VP; Richard Kmiecik, PLAT CHIC, Production; James Ladd, CARIBOU, Production; David Landers, PLAT GA, Blue Rhino Delivery Driver; Victoria Langford, BRC, Customer Service and Sales Specialist; Jason Larsen, BRC SLC, Blue Rhino Delivery Driver; Cecil Lawrence, R4, Production Mgr; Darrell Lee, PLAT GA, Yard; Patrick Lee, BUFFALO, Yard; Celia Leffler, BRC, Customer Care Spec.; Kenneth Leon, RAVEN, Blue Rhino Delivery Driver; Nicholas Lewis, PLAT CHIC, Blue Rhino Delivery Driver; Amy Lineberry, R4, Operator; Oscar Lizama, UNIFLAME, Asst Warehouse Mgr; Steven Lockhart, PLAT LA, Blue Rhino Delivery Driver; John Loomis, PLAT FL, Blue Rhino Delivery Driver; Juan Lopez, R4, Supervisor; Rodolfo Lopez, R4, Operator; Jose Lopez, PLAT LA, Production; Larry Lopez, PLAT LA, Production; Barbara Lounsbury, BRC, Sr. Collection Spec; Darius Lowe, BRC, Customer Care Spec.; AngieLower, BRC, Data Analysis Mgr; Jose Lucas, R4, Operator; Roberto Luciano, R4, Operator; Derrick Luderus, CARIBOU, Production; Javier Macbeath, PLAT SD, Blue Rhino Delivery Driver; Ronnie Macy, R4, Maint.Tech; Robin Manley, BRC, VP, Human Resources; LaTryce Martin, BRC, Customer Care Spec.; Jose Martinez, PLAT MIAMI, Blue Rhino Delivery Driver; Wanda Martinez, PLAT MIAMI, Office Administrator; Maria Mason, BRC, Customer Care Spec.; Denny Matthews, PLAT NC, Forklift Operator; James Mayhew, PLAT VA, Forklift Operator; Les Mayhew, BRC, Dir-Credit/Collectio; Steven McAbee, PLAT GA, Yard; Ronnie McAllister, CARIBOU, Production; Daryl McClendon, BRC, Director of External Affairs; Adrianne McCollum, BRC, Independent Accounts Mgr; Bobby McCoy, PLAT SC, Yard; Leslie McCraw, BRC, Mktg Materials Analyst; Thom McKearney, BRC, Inv Control Mgr.;

Doug McLaughlin, BRC, Director Strategic Accounts; Brandon McQuilkin, BRC, Sr. Network Engineer; Mac McQuilkin, BRC, President Direct Imports; Antonio Medrano, R4, Operator; Jennifer Mehaffey, BRC, EDI/EFT Project Mgr; Nicole Melander, UNIFLAME, Receptionist; Octavio Mendoza, PLAT LA, Production; Kimberly Menton, BRC, ; Wesley Miller, BRC SLC, Blue Rhino Delivery Driver; Tracy Miller, BRC, Customer Care Spec.; Clifford Minuth, PLAT CHIC, Assistant Manager; Eduardo Mireles, R4, Operator; Charles Mitch, PLAT MN, Production; Jason Mitchell, PLAT LA, Blue Rhino Delivery Driver; Walter Mitchell, RAVEN, Development Manager; Eric Montalvo, BRC, Warehouse; Eddie Montano, JAYHAWK, Production; Austin Monu, BRC, Accounting Intern; Daryl Moore, BRC, Collection Spec; Martin Morales, UNIFLAME, Warehouse; Sue Mortensen, UNIFLAME, Inv Control Supv; Chris Moxley, R4, Boonville Manager; Lura Moxley, PLAT NC, Office Administrator; Jeffrey Mumm, PLAT CHIC, Blue Rhino Delivery Driver; James Munkacsy, BRC, cust serv tech; Fernando Munoz, CARIBOU, Blue Rhino Delivery Driver; Dave Murray, BRC SLC, Production; Yancy Neiswanger, PLAT CHIC, Blue Rhino Delivery Driver; Angela Nelson, BRC, Collection Spec; Jorge Nieto, UNIFLAME, Warehouse; Michelle Noel, BRC, Dir, Sls-Home Depot; Escobar Nunez, PLAT LA, Production; Clemente Obispo, R4, Lift Truck Operator; Rodolfo Obispo, R4, Operator; Martin Ollenberger, PLAT GA, Blue Rhino Delivery Driver; Aquilino Olvera, UNIFLAME, Warehouse Manager; Elpidio Olvera,

UNIFLAME, Warehouse; Juan Ortiz, PLAT LA, Supervisor; Chris Osborne, QUICKSHIP, System Analyst I; Susan Osborne, BRC, Manager-Chain Sales; Rudy Padilla, PLAT SD, General Manager; David Parker, R4, Plant Manager; Kathryn Parks, BRC, Collection Spec; Mark Pasche, BRC, Regional Acct Mgr; Patrick Peck, PLAT CHIC, Blue Rhino Delivery Driver; Ronald Pence, JAYHAWK, Blue Rhino Delivery Driver; Michael Peterson, BRC SLC, Production;

Stephen Pettry, PLAT VA, Blue Rhino Delivery Driver; Emiliano Pineda, R4, Operator; Mario Pineda, R4, Forklift Operator; Rigoberto Pineda, R4, Operator; Servando Pineda, R4, Forklift Operator; Lucio Pineda, PLAT GA, Operator; Daniel Pogue, BRC, Sales; Milton Portillo, PLAT LA, Blue Rhino Delivery Driver; Larry Powell, BRC, VP of Manufacturing BRCE; Daniel Pray, R4, Plant Manager; Donald Price, PLAT NC, Blue Rhino Delivery Driver; Billy Prim, BRC, Chairman/CEO; Samuel Procopio, RAVEN, Blue Rhino Delivery Driver; Jon Proesch, PLAT CHIC, General Manager; Felix Ramirez, R4, Operator; Victor Ramirez, PLAT CHIC, Production; Jorge Ramirez, UNIFLAME, Warehouse; Rosie Ramos, R4, Yard; Rosi Ramos, PLAT NC, Yard; Angelica Ramos-Milan, R4, Operator; Rose Reaves, BRC, A/P Coor; Micah Redman, BUFFALO, General Manager; Keith Reichard, BRC, Sys. Integration Mgr; Delora Reizner, UNIFLAME, AR Clerk; David Renegar, BRC, VP Finance/Controller; Sergio Reyes, UNIFLAME, Warehouse; Joshua Richardson, R4, Blue Rhino Delivery Driver; Michael Richardson, PLAT GA, Blue Rhino Delivery Driver; Thomas Rieke, BRC, Financial System Mgr; Luis Rivera, RAVEN, Production; Kimberly Roberts, BRC, Executive Asst.; Jill Robertson, BRC, Strategic Acct Mgr; Jillian Robins, BRC, Human Resources Manager; Clifford Robinson, PLAT NC, Blue Rhino Delivery Driver; Iris Rodriguez, UNIFLAME, Exec Sales Asst; Jorge Rodriguez, BRC, Warehouse; Mark Romanik, CARIBOU, General Manager; Bruce Rook, PLAT FL, Route Supervisor; Tony Royall, R4, Forklift Operator; Jesus Rubio, UNIFLAME, Warehouse; Lucas Ruble, CARIBOU, Production; Juan Saabedra-Renobato, R4, Operator; Jeffrey Sadler, PLAT LA, General Manager; Emelia Sanchez, BUFFALO, Production; Jose Santana, PLAT LA, Production; David Santiago, PLAT LA, Production;

Danielle Scarlett, R4, Operator; Harold Scarlett, R4, Prev Maint Spec; Philip Schmidt, BUFFALO, Production; Robert Schmidt, BUFFALO, Blue Rhino Delivery Driver; Charles Schoolcraft, PLAT VA, Blue Rhino Delivery Driver; John Schuchard, PLAT LA, General Manager; Cristyal Scott, BRC, Customer Care Spec.; TimScronce, BRC, President, BRCE; John Sellers, PLAT FL, Blue Rhino Delivery Driver; Scott Selzer, BRC, Production Specialist; Michael Sexton, JAYHAWK, Yard; Jerry Shadley, QUICKSHIP, COO; Pranav Sharma, BRC, Director of Operations; Henry Sharpe, BRC, Sr Dir Reg Sales; Matthew Shaw, PLAT NC, Blue Rhino Delivery Driver; Barbara Shelton, BRC, Customer Care Spec.; Brian Shore, R4, Maintenance Lead; Karen Shuford, BRC, Customer Care Superv; Justin Siemsen, JAYHAWK, Blue Rhino Delivery Driver; Keith Simons, PLAT MN, General Manager; Rashad Simpson, PLAT NC, Blue Rhino Delivery Driver; Lester Simpson, PLAT VA, Blue Rhino Delivery Driver; Susie Simpson, BRC, Mgr, Dist Supp Svcs; Steven Sizemore, R4, Forklift Operator; David Slone, BRC, VP Tech Operations; Tremayne Smith, PLAT CHIC, Production; Bryan Smith, PLAT SD, Blue Rhino Delivery Driver; Heather Smith, BRC, Sr Accountant; Judy Smith, BRC, Senior

Products & Services Buyer; Ron Smith, BRC, Director, Gas Appliances; Nathan Snavely, BUFFALO, Blue Rhino Delivery Driver; Mark Snow, R4, Engineering Mgr; Nick Snyder, BRC, Marketing and Graphics Specialist; Andrew Spriggins, PLAT SD, Blue Rhino Delivery Driver; Tania Stafford, BRC, Payroll Coordinator; E Staley, R4, Operator; Tim Stinson, BRC, Controller; Felipe Suarez-Tapia, PLAT GA, Yard; Joseph Sugar, RAVEN, Blue Rhino Delivery Driver; Jeffrey Summers, PLAT GA, Blue Rhino Delivery Driver; Robert Sutton, PLAT CHIC, Blue Rhino Delivery Driver; Crystal Taylor, BRC, Staff Accountant; Ignacio Telesforo, PLAT GA, Yard; Laura Terry, BUFFALO, DSD Scheduler; Dean Thompson, RAVEN, Blue Rhino Delivery Driver; Enrique Torres, R4, Operator;

Bob Travatello, BRC, VP, MIS/CIO; Peggy Trivette, R4, Assistant Manager; Paul Trujillo, BUFFALO, Blue Rhino Delivery Driver; Javier Uriostegui, PLAT LA, Production; Alejandro Valadez, R4, Operator; Jesus Valdez, R4, Operator; Mario Valencia, BUFFALO, Yard; James Van Vorous, BUFFALO, Maintenance Lead; Casey Vanderwerf, JAYHAWK, Production; Daniel Varela, PLAT SD, Patio Heater Tech; Bernardo Varela, UNIFLAME, Warehouse; Martin Vargas, PLAT NC, Forklift Operator; Janet Varner, BRC, AR Supervisor; John Vega, CARIBOU, Blue Rhino Delivery Driver; Ann Vela-Rakoncay, UNIFLAME, Director of Specialty Sales; Valente Velazquez, R4, Operator; Shana Venable, QUICKSHIP, Staff Accountant; Michael Vestal, R4, Operator; Angela Vivas, BRC, Billing Assistant; Maria Vrito-Diaz, R4, Operator; Ronald Waksmunski, RAVEN, Blue Rhino Delivery Driver; Andy Walters, BRC, Accounting manager; Reginald Ward, RAVEN, Blue Rhino Delivery Driver; Jeff Ward, BRC, VP, Sales and Marketing; Kevin Warren, BRC, Systems Administrator; Roger Waters, PLAT NC, Blue Rhino Delivery Driver; Steven Watkins, PLAT GA, Yard; Joshua Webber, BRC SLC, Production; Chad Weldon, PLAT MN, Blue Rhino Delivery Driver; Jay Werner, JAYHAWK, General Manager; Stephen Werner, JAYHAWK, Yard; Randy West, JAYHAWK, Blue Rhino Delivery Driver; Erika West, BRC, Collection Spec; Brian Wheeler, CARIBOU, Blue Rhino Delivery Driver; Bradley Whitcomb, CARIBOU, Production; Donald White, R4, Operator; Michael White, PLAT CHIC, Production; Edward Williams, PLAT FL, Blue Rhino Delivery Driver; David Wingler, BRC, Customer Care Spec.; Robert Wolf, PLAT GA, Blue Rhino Delivery Driver; Ruby Wong, BRC, AP Manager; Michael Woodward, RAVEN, Blue Rhino Delivery Driver; Paula Young, BRC, Staff Accountant; Jeff Yourston, CARIBOU, Blue Rhino Delivery Driver; Tamria Zertuche, BRC, Director-Information Systems; Mark Zieske, PLAT CHIC, Production; Mark Zimora, BRC, Director of Corp. Development.